T0351924

THE FABLE OF THE KEIRETSU

The Fable of the Keiretsu

Urban Legends of the Japanese Economy

YOSHIRO MIWA *&* J. MARK RAMSEYER

The University of Chicago Press CHICAGO AND LONDON

YOSHIRO MIWA is professor of economics at the University of Tokyo. His books include *Firms and Industrial Organization in Japan* and *State Competence and Economic Growth in Japan.*

J. MARK RAMSEYER is the Mitsubishi Professor of Japanese Legal Studies at Harvard Law School. His books include *Japanese Law: An Economic Approach* (with Minoru Nakazato) and *Measuring Judicial Independence: The Political Economy of Judging in Japan* (with Eric Rasmussen), both published by the University of Chicago Press.

The University of Chicago Press, Chicago 60637
The University of Chicago Press, Ltd., London
© 2006 by The University of Chicago
All rights reserved. Published 2006
Printed in the United States of America

15 14 13 12 11 10 09 08 07 06   1 2 3 4 5

ISBN: 0-226-53270-4 (cloth)

Library of Congress Cataloging-in-Publication Data

Miwa, Yoshiro, 1948–
    The fable of the keiretsu : urban legends of the Japanese economy / Yoshiro Miwa and J. Mark Ramseyer.
        p. cm.
    Includes bibliographical references and index.
    ISBN 0-226-53270-4 (cloth : alk. paper)
        1. Conglomerate corporations—Japan. 2. Corporations—Finance.
        3. Japan—Economic policy—1989– 4. Japan—Economic conditions—1989–
        I. Ramseyer, J. Mark, 1954– II. Title.

    HD2756.2J3M588   2006
    338.8′70952—dc22

                                                        2005030814

Contents

Preface

Funny place, the modern university. Our colleagues devote the most meticulous attention to the smallest aspects of a problem—but take fundamental premises on faith, even blind faith. Sociologists spent much of the last century dissecting the effect of the Calvinist ethic on capitalist development—but missed the fact that Weber based his thesis on a typographical error (Hamilton 1996, chap. 3). Historians endlessly imitate the polysyllabic turgidity of Foucault's study of the prison—but miss the fact that he made up nearly the entire story (1996, chap. 6). And apropos of our book here, economists manipulate ten-thousand-point data sets of Japanese financial data to study the group bias to trade and investment—but miss the fact that a Marxist think tank invented their "group affiliation" variable out of whole cloth. It reminds us a bit of the poor souls finishing their political science dissertations in 1989 on the durability of Eric Honecker's government.

Devoted to the details, oblivious to the vacuum at the core. All too often, such is the state of the Western academy on the topic of the Japanese economy. In this book, we describe that state of affairs. Toward that end, we explain the logic by which the Japanese economy works. We do not write just for economists. Instead, we try to keep the intuition clear and to write for all readers with an interest in Japan, and for all those with an interest in comparative economic performance more generally. We presuppose no economic training. Rather than detail in this book the statistical work on which we base our analysis, we point specialists to the articles in which we report that analysis.

We try to do more though. We try to explain how modern scholars have come to share the myths about Japan that they do. Think intellectual history, or a cultural study of the modern university. In this book, we try to explain how our colleagues in Japanese and American universities came to invent, embroider, and propagate those tales of Japan they hold so dear.

We hope you enjoy the book. Buy it, borrow it, or (as the decidedly noncapitalist Abbie Hoffman once urged) steal it. Obtain it however you will; we hope you read it and enjoy it.

Tokyo and Cambridge
Spring 2005

Acknowledgments

We write this book for the nonspecialist reader. We presume no knowledge of Japan and no expertise in either economics or law. For that reason, although we base the book on scholarship we have published in specialized academic journals, we have written large portions of it afresh (and where we do use that material, we do so with the kind permission of the publishers). We cite more technical work as appropriate and draw more generally on the following material for each chapter. All the work has been authored jointly by the two of us.

CHAPTER 2

"The Fable of the Keiretsu," *Journal of Economics and Management Strategy* 11 (2002): 169. Copyright 2002, by Blackwell Publishing Ltd.; used with permission.

"*Keiretsu no kenkyu* no keiretsu no kenkyu" [Research on the keiretsu in *Research on the keiretsu*], *Keizaigaku ronshu* 67, no. 2 (2001): 36; *Keizaigaku ronshu* 67, no. 3 (2001): 68.

Nihon keizai ron no gokai: "Keiretsu" no jubaku kara no kaiho [Misunderstandings in the theory of the Japanese economy: Liberation from the spell of the "keiretsu"] (Tokyo: Toyo keizai shimpo sha, 2001).

"Rethinking Relationship-Specific Investments: Subcontracting in the Japanese Automobile Industry," *University of Michigan Law Review* 98 (2000): 2636. Copyright 2000, by the Michigan Law Review Association; used with permission.

CHAPTER 3

"Banks and Economic Growth: Implications from Japanese History," *Journal of Law and Economics* 45 (2002): 127. Copyright 2002, by the University of Chicago Press; used with permission.

"Seisaku kin'yu to keizai hatten: Senzenki Nihon kogyo ginko no keesu" [Policy finance and economic growth: The case of the pre-war Industrial Bank of Japan], *Keizaigaku ronshu* 66, no. 3 (2000): 2.

"The Fable of the Keiretsu" and "Rethinking Relationship-Specific Investments," both as noted for chapter 2.

CHAPTER 4

"Conflicts of Interest in Japanese Insolvencies: The Problem of Bank Rescues," *Theoretical Inquiries in Law* 6 (2004): 301. Copyright 2004, by Cegla Center for Interdisciplinary Research of the Law; used with permission.

"Does Relationship-Banking Matter: The Myth of the Japanese Main Bank," *Journal of Empirical Legal Studies* 2 (2005): 261. Copyright 2005, by Blackwell Publishing Ltd.; used with permission.

"The Myth of the Main Bank: Japan and Comparative Corporate Governance," *Law and Social Inquiry* 27 (2002): 401. Copyright 2002, by the American Bar Foundation; used with permission.

"Seisaku kin'yu to keizai hatten," as noted for chapter 3.

CHAPTER 5

"Does Ownership Matter? Evidence from the Zaibatsu Dissolution Program," *Journal of Economics and Management Strategy* 12 (2003): 67. Copyright 2003, by Blackwell Publishing Ltd.; used with permission.

"Financial Malaise and the Myth of the Misgoverned Bank," in *Global Markets, Domestic Institutions: Corporate Law and Governance in a New Era of Cross-Border Deals*, ed. Curtis J. Milhaupt (New York: Columbia University Press, 2003). Copyright 2003, by Columbia University Press; used with permission.

"Who Appoints Them, What Do They Do? Evidence on Outside Directors from Japan," *Journal of Economics and Management Strategy* 14 (2005): 299. Copyright 2005, by Blackwell Publishing Ltd.; used with permission.

CHAPTER 6

"Capitalist Politicians, Socialist Bureaucrats? Legends of Government Planning from Japan," *Antitrust Bulletin* 48 (2003): 595. Copyright 2003, by Federal Legal Publications; used with permission.

"Directed Credit? The Loan Market in High-Growth Japan," *Journal of Economics and Management Strategy* 13 (2004): 171. Copyright 2004, by Blackwell Publishing Ltd.; used with permission.

"Nihon no keizai seisaku to seisaku kenkyu" [Japanese economic policy and policy research], *Keizai kenkyu* 52 (2001): 193.

Sangyo seisaku ron no gokai: Kodo seicho no shinjutsu [Misunderstandings about industrial policy: The truth about high growth] (Tokyo: Toyo keizai shimpo sha, 2002).

In developing our ideas through these books and articles, we received invaluable advice from many friends and colleagues. We thanked them by name in these pieces and repeat those thanks more generally here. We unabashedly borrow the title of this book from two works we admire greatly, Casadesus-Masanell and Spulber's "The Fable of Fisher Body" (2000) and Spulber's *Famous Fables of Economics: Myths of Market Failure* (2002). We gratefully acknowledge the generous financial assistance of the University of Tokyo Center for International Research on the Japanese Economy, the University of Tokyo Business Law Center, the John M. Olin Center for Law, Economics, and Business at the Harvard Law School, and the East Asian Legal Studies Program at the Harvard Law School.

CHAPTER ONE

Introduction

Patronize any boathouse for the light and narrow racing rowboats called sculls and sweeps, and sooner or later a rower will tell you about the Japanese Eight. Most rowers set the story at the 1964 Tokyo Olympics—Japan's debut among the wealthy industrialized countries. The 130-mph bullet train had just tied Tokyo to Osaka in three hours and ten minutes flat. The government had recruited modernist darling Kenzo Tange to design the spectacular new sports complexes. Japan's membership in the Organization for Economic Cooperation and Development would soon follow, along with superhighways, more and faster bullet trains, and all the other indices of national wealth.

National pride was at stake. So determined to win for their country were the Japanese crew, the rowers continue, that two of the eight rowed themselves to death on the boat. Two more made it out of the boat but dropped dead on the dock. The other four died in hospitals over the several next months.

*   *   *

Patronize any social science or business panel on Japan and sooner or later the experts will tell you whether (and usually how) Japan is about to change fundamentally. Patronize any good book store and sooner or later you will find books such as *Japan's Democracy: How Much Change?* or *Economic Reform: Can the Japanese Change?* or *Japan's Economic Structure: Should It Change?* or the 1998 Brookings study *Is Japan Really Changing Its Ways?*

Search for comparable panels or books on the United States, Canada, or Germany and you come up dry. Brookings does not sponsor conferences on whether the United States is changing its ways. The University of Chicago Press likely will not publish a volume titled *Is Canada Really Changing Its Ways?* Indeed, we doubt it would even take one on *Economic Reform: Can the Germans Change?* You come up dry for a good reason: we know all too well that there is no "essential" U.S., Canadian, or German nature to change.

Switch to Japan, however, and authors, publishers, and readers happily soldier on—blithely writing, publishing, and buying books about whether Japan is changing. To be sure, these books do not give the same answer. Rather, they are "unanimous" (as one nineteenth-century Irish jury foreman famously put it) "in being unable to agree" (Minda 1999, 27). But they do ask the same question.

It is worth asking why we place Japan in this niche. The reason we can plausibly tell and re-tell the tale of the Japanese Eight is straightforward enough: kamikaze pilots. Until the Palestinians and Iraqis adopted the habit, we had precious little experience with suicide missions. No one tells tales of Harvard crew teams rowing themselves to death, even against Yale. They row hard, they win or lose, they throw up, and they go drink beer. Tennyson's light brigade did not ride into the valley of death out of fanatical loyalty. They rode because an officer had "blunder'd."

Like Fitzgerald's rich, however, "the Japanese" are different from you and me—or so we are told. Pity the poor economists (two of them Japanese nationals) who had the bad judgment to forget that fact in a recent book on Japanese labor markets. According to the decidedly mainstream *Journal of Economic Literature*, in "neglecting cultural determinants of Japanese internal labor markets" they committed "serious error." After all, "the philosophical foundation of Japanese culture is entirely anti-individualistic," continued the reviewer. The "collectivist ethics of Confucianism"—one can hear the wind sweeping over the oars as the Suicidal Eight surge forward—"naturally sustain giving and accepting orders rather than responding to incentives" (McLaughlin 2002, 944).

* * *

"Accepting orders" rather than "responding to incentives"? By now we all know that alligators never infested New York sewers, no department store ever soaked a patron $150 for a chocolate-chip cookie recipe, no poodle found itself fried in a microwave, and Eskimos do indeed have an all-purpose word for snow. We think we know urban legends when we hear them.

Yet urban legend comprises most of what we collectively think we know about the Japanese economy, and those urban legends are what this book concerns. The principal points are easy enough to relate:

- The keiretsu do not exist (chapters 2 and 3). They never did. An entrepreneurial "research institute" in the 1950s created the rosters to sell to Marxist economists looking for the "monopoly capital" that their theory told them would dominate their "bourgeois capitalist" world. Western scholars, hoping for examples of culture-specific forms of economic organization, then paired accounts of a couple dozen company presidents meeting for lunch with rosters of hundreds of firms whose presidents were never invited—and repatriated the stories to the United States.

- The zaibatsu of pre–World War II did not succeed because they bought politicians, exploited the poor, or manipulated dysfunctional capital markets (chapter 3). They succeeded for all the usual varied reasons a few firms succeed in any modern economy. They acquired the (pejorative) *zaibatsu* label because they happened to be thriving when muckraking journalists in the 1920s and 1930s came looking for someone to blame for the depression.

- Japanese firms have no "main bank system" and never did (chapter 4). Economists popularized the idea as an anecdote on which to peg their mathematical models, and non-economists use it (like the keiretsu) as yet another putatively culture-bound economic phenomenon.

- Japanese firms are neither short of outside directors nor badly governed (chapter 5). The charges represent yet another variant on populist journalism. Like firms in other competitive capitalist countries, Japanese firms survive only if they adopt governance mechanisms appropriate to the markets within which they must compete.

- The Japanese government never seriously guided or intervened in the Japanese economy (chapter 6). When the economy boomed, politicians and bureaucrats took the credit. They had created the success through their own farsighted leadership, they claimed. Marxist scholars dominated Japanese social science departments, and they were not about to suggest that market competition might have accounted for the success. Happy as they were to find an example of successful government intervention, neither were most Western scholars of Japan.

As all this should make clear, the tales in the West about the Japanese economy are not exaggerated. Nor are they biased or misleading. They are simply wrong, fictitious accounts with no basis (not little basis, but *no* basis) in anything on the ground. For the academy, the tales are nothing less than a profound embarrassment. But they serve also as a reminder—of how badly wrong things can go when academics write about an economy without studying economics, of how disastrously things can end when they subordinate their research to political agenda, and of how embarrassing matters can become when they focus on the detail and miss the vacuum at the center of their research.

We realize that readers intent on the current Japanese economy will grow impatient with our discussion of the 1960s and 1970s. If you are one of these, we beg you not to abandon the book mid-ship. We do indeed turn to the 1990s recession, but one cannot understand the 1990s without knowing what came before. To explain what came before, we leave the 1990s recession for chapter 7. By then, you should have the tools and instincts with which to analyze what went wrong during the decade. By then, however, we think you will also have much more: the tools and instincts with which to make sense on your own of what you hear about Japan over the years to come.

We ask you to remember that the Japanese economy is an economy first and Japanese second. Whether in Tokyo or in Peoria, all else equal, most people will prefer more money to less, and in transactions involving large amounts they will calculate their interests carefully. Given the same price, they will prefer higher-quality goods to lower; given the same quality, they will prefer cheaper goods to costlier; and given two investment opportunities presenting the same risk, they will park their money at the investment paying more. Because people do all this, firms necessarily compete with each other to raise the funds they use, to buy the supplies they need, and to sell the goods and services they produce. In the competitive markets that ensue, the firms that survive will—inevitably—tend to be those that maximize profits. Microeconomics simply traces the many logical consequences of this process.

People and firms buy, sell, and invest within institutional structures, of course, and those structures can vary from country to country. In this book, we try to couple standard microeconomics with a close look at the institutional constraints in place in Japan. Too often in writing about the Japanese economy, non-economists in the West have dismissed the logic of economics as so much culture-bound bias. Given that they "described" without understanding what they saw, they missed "reality" by a mile. Economists then premised their analyses of the Japanese economy on the institutional descriptions that these non-economists provided. Given that the economists "analyzed" nonsensical descriptions, they did no better.

* * *

Both of us remember Tange's Olympic buildings when they were new. We remember the first bullet trains. We remember the superhighways. And having watched the 1964 Olympics on television, we even remember Abebe Bikila winning the marathon. But neither of us remembers anything about eight rowers dying.

Fortunately, the Groton Academy crew coach decided to check. After a dinner lecture to the crewing alumni of a major Tokyo university, he popped the question. "There is a story," he began, "that in the Tokyo Olympics a

Japanese eight rowed [at a] very high [strokes/minute count]...and after the race, many of the men died. Do any of you know about this story?" He recalls the silence that followed (Anderson 2001, 4):

Finally, Mr. Okamura said, "We know of no such story." He looked around the group for confirmation. "The German eight rowed very high. Do you mean the German eight?"

"No, the story that everyone tells is of a Japanese eight. Most of the crew died because they had rowed so high." Long pause. "I've never believed it," I added.

"This is not a true story." He looked at me with steely eyes. "What do you think it means?"

"I'm not sure," I stammered. I'm your friend, I wanted to say. I'm not making this up.

"Maybe kamikaze idea? We Japanese would row to kill ourself?"

"Maybe that's it. So this story is not true? Now I can tell everyone in America."

"Do you remember the man who asked you the [technical] question about [boat geometry]?" my friend Mr. Ito asked. "That man rowed in the Olympic 8." He paused and looked around the group. "He was alive, *neh*?"

CHAPTER TWO

The Fable of the Keiretsu

"Quietly, secretly, without warning, *keiretsu* have infiltrated our daily lives and engulfed everything we know," a 1990s vintage business guide ominously assures us (Miyashita and Russell 1994, 7). "We are surrounded by the *keiretsu*," indeed we "deal with them every day—every time we turn on the TV, pick up a paper, eat at a fast-food chain, or go to work." Others claim the keiretsu used to dominate but do so no longer. The 1950s and 1960s was "the keiretsu era," write economists Takeo Hoshi and Anil Kashyap (2001, 91). When the government deregulated the financial services industry in the 1980s, that "system" then "unravel[ed]" (128).

If you know one Japanese business word, you know *keiretsu*, those massive corporate groups such as the Mitsubishi and the Sumitomo.[1] The term seems to capture the heart of Japanese business. The keiretsu exclude American firms. They embody the essence of the anti-individualist Confucian ethic. They epitomize the "socially embedded" character of markets. Or they prove the culturally contingent nature of the *Wall Street Journal*'s op-ed page.

And yet, one might wonder. Out of the blue, in the late 1980s, the Japanese Fair Trade Commission (FTC) called up Toyota Motors (Miwa and Ramseyer 2001a, 87). "Your firm's affiliated with the Mitsui group, isn't it," declared the FTC investigator. What fraction of your trades are with other group members?"

"To be honest, it was embarrassing," recalled the executive who handled the inquiry. "If you check, apparently quite a few books put us in the Mitsui group. The biggest reason seems to be that we're in the presidents' club. But it's not as if our keiretsu affiliation was something I kept in mind every day, and it's not as if we tracked the figures I needed to calculate the fraction the FTC wanted. We were really stuck."

"And when it comes to the Mitsui group, which of our business partners are in it anyway?"

The one Japanese word every sophisticated American executive knows, the Toyota executive could not understand. Why? What are the keiretsu anyway? How did they come to take center stage in our imagined Japan? And what—if anything—might they have to do with the actual business world? In this chapter we consider the keiretsu stories we tell ourselves and what the group rosters represent. We then ask whether many—or even any—of the stories we tell ourselves fit the data from Japan. Some observers locate a second set of keiretsu in the ties between automobile (and sometimes electronics) assemblers and their suppliers. Occasionally, they extend those supplier keiretsu to firms in several other industries. We conclude this chapter by examining these "vertical" keiretsu.

In chapter 3 we return to the tales of the keiretsu to ask how they came to be, why they capture our collective imagination, and what they tell us about ourselves. For the tales tell us nothing about Japan. There are no keiretsu and never have been any. They are not less important than we have thought, less clear than we have asserted, or currently in decline. Instead, they do not exist and never have. At root, the keiretsu instead represent a fable—a tale that, by capturing our mythical vision of the Japanese economy, tells us instead about ourselves and the world we wish we inhabited.

WHAT WE HEAR

What Are They?
By most accounts, there are (or were) six of them: the Mitsui, the Mitsubishi, the Sumitomo, the Fuji, the Daiichi Kangyo, and the Sanwa. At least until the mid-1990s, they dominated the Japanese economy. Within each group, a massive money center bank dominated the other members. (In the language of the literature, the money center bank was a "city bank" that played "main bank" to the others; see chapter 4.) To them, as *Business Week* explained, the bank "provide[d] low-cost, patient capital" (Kelly and Port 1992). Around it, dozens of industrial and service firms borrowed, built, and traded among themselves.

"Dozens" of firms—that figure is according to the more careful of writers. Like your grandfather's prize trout, however, the tale improves with the telling. The *Harvard Business Review* put keiretsu membership at 12,000 firms and claimed that in Japan "virtually all business activity is part of one or another *keiretsu* or cartel" (Cutts 1992, 49). One Japanese studies scholar put the number of the Mitsubishi firms alone at 15,540 (not 15,538, not 15,541) and the number of "people who are, in some way, directly associated with the Mitsubishi Keiretsu" at 31 million (Kensy 2001, 252). Given that only 130 million people live in Japan, he concluded—reasonably enough, given his Mitsubishi estimate—that "almost the entire Japanese population is directly or indirectly linked to the Keiretsu."

Whether several dozen or tens of thousands, the keiretsu firms in these accounts together scheme, invest, trade, and cooperate toward their collective self-preservation. From their money center bank, they obtain a variety of services. Most basically, they borrow most of their loans from that bank. Because they seldom raise money through stocks, they effectively obtain the bulk of their funds from the money center bank. From it they also receive strategic business advice and help in times of trouble, effectively obtaining insurance against financial distress. And from it as well they buy the myriad other financial services that modern firms need.

According to these standard accounts the keiretsu firms collectively adopt several other strategies besides. Together, for example, they insulate themselves from stock market pressure by each buying stock in the other group members. No one firm individually owns enough of another to control it, but collectively they hold controlling interests—by one estimate, over 60 percent at the Mitsubishi and Sumitomo groups (Richter 2000, 22). In the process, they eliminate the pressure to maximize short-term profits, shield the firm from hostile takeovers, ensure that foreigners will never gain control, and guarantee that they each follow group norms.

As much as possible, keiretsu firms route business through each other and keep their trades and finance within the group. By doing so, they assure each other preferential terms. For just that reason, claimed many Americans, they block foreign competitors. And for just that reason the Japanese FTC once investigated them for antitrust violations—hence the call to Toyota.

The keiretsu firms set group strategy and coordinate their activities, claim most writers, at monthly councils of their presidents. The "Mitsubishi, Mitsui and Sumitomo are tightly interwoven, well-organized firms," one business executive assures us (Richter 2000, 24). The presidents of the Mitsubishi firms meet on a Friday, for example, and call themselves the Voldemortianly unnamed Friday Council. The Mitsui presidents meet on the second Thursday of each month and call themselves the Second Thursday Club.

At these meetings, continue the commentators, the executives review each other's performance, discuss their competitive environment, and plan collective strategy. "The question is not 'Do they talk business?'" insisted one account. It is "What kind of business?" After all, if executives "whose firms control a very, very conservatively estimated $2 trillion in sales each year, went to such trouble to meet regularly and did not talk about business, something would be very odd" (Miyashita and Russell 1994, 64).

Good or Bad?

If most observers agree about what the keiretsu are, they disagree fundamentally about whether the keiretsu do good or do ill. To some, the keiretsu make Japanese firms more efficient. By moving finance in-house and eliminating the impact of the stock market, they reduce the pressure to maximize short-term returns. As one Amazon.com best-seller put it, "the Japanese group orientation is extremely long-term in orientation—but very well informed.... The groups can afford to invest heavily to finance corporate turnarounds, because their considerable knowledge reduces the risk of failure" (Womack 1992, 198).

Apparently they cooperate both on strategy and on finance. According to *Business Week*, by "collaborating on research and production, *keiretsu* members regularly deliver new products ahead of lone-wolf rivals" (Kelly and Port 1992). "There's a pressing need for U.S. manufacturers to develop something similar to *keiretsu*.... The horizontal groups provide security and stability to promote the risk-taking and long-term investment often shunned by U.S. companies." And according to the ever-quotable Clyde Prestowitz (1988, 43), Japanese firms were able to thrive in the semiconductor field because each firm "could count on support from other group companies, whose total resources might exceed $300 billion."

To others, the keiretsu simply cheat. No less an economist than Nobel laureate Paul Samuelson described them as "large oligopolies" (2000, 186). The Japanese FTC too thought they might be exclusionary, as did the U.S. Trade Representative's office.

Good or bad, however, by most accounts the keiretsu are on their way out. Indeed, according to most they are not just declining but unraveling entirely. Unable to make money in the current depression, firms are selling their stock in each other to generate paper profits. As they do, they lose their common ownership. Symptomatic of their decline, declare observers, is that in 2002 the two institutions most pivotal within two of the most dominant keiretsu, the Sumitomo and Mitsui banks, merged. The Fuji and Daiichi Kangyo banks merged as well.

Across the Disciplines

Writers in the popular press are not the only ones fascinated with the keiretsu. For thirty-odd years, earnest social scientists studied them too, from disciplines as varied as economics, business, political science, and sociology. A quarter century ago, Harvard and University of Tokyo economists Richard Caves and Masu Uekusa (1976b, 63) called the keiretsu "a major and conspicuous force in the Japanese economy." A more recent economics team claimed they "coordinate[] the activities of member firms and ... finance[]

much of their investment activity" (Hoshi, Kashyap, and Scharfstein 1991, 34).

Business school professors have been just as obsessed, albeit differently obsessed. More than their colleagues in economics, many will happily attribute the keiretsu to Japanese "culture." According to the *Harvard Business Review*, the keiretsu are simply "evidence of Japan's basic nature." They differ from U.S. organizational forms because, it continues, "Japanese capitalism differs greatly" from that in the West (Cutts 1992, 48).

East is east and west is west, but if you thought Kipling passé, a business team from Berkeley eagerly raced even farther down the culturalist path. Keiretsu firms were "bound to one another in a web of obligation," it explained. "Opting in or out of *keiretsu* commitments to troubled corporate kindred on the basis of unilateral calculations of advantage" just is "not the Japanese way of business." Firms "that try it risk a stern lesson in the importance of team play" (Lincoln, Gerlach, and Ahmadjian 1998, 318).

Johns Hopkins political scientist Kent Calder (1993, 142) argued that the keiretsu "have been a key element in Japan's rapid industrial development and transformation since the early 1950s." "In sectors as diverse as petrochemicals, telematics, atomic power, real estate development, and Middle East oil exploration," the keiretsu "have taken the strategic initiative for Japan." And sociologist Ronald Dore (1987, 178) characterized them as "networks of relational contracting" that were "a bit like an extended family grouping, where business is kept as much as possible within the family, and a certain degree of give and take is expected to modify the adversarial pursuit of market advantage."

It is "all in the family," apparently. But do the keiretsu really do all this? Do they do any of this? Do they even exist? Or are these tales just so many urban legends, yet more variations on alligators in sewers, Eskimo snow words, and suicidal crew teams? Might these too be tales we repeat because they so perfectly illustrate points we so fervently want to be true?

WHO'S IN, WHO'S OUT?

Before we can determine what the keiretsu do, we face the problem that bedeviled our Toyota informant: which firms are members and which independent? As the range from dozens of firms and to 12,000 suggests, this question is not as easy to answer as one might have thought. Outsiders (e.g., Miyashita and Russell 1994, 10) may occasionally assure us that Toyota is "officially a member of the Mitsui Group," but the executives in Toyota did not know that—nor have we seen any "official" list.

In fact, there is no membership list for a simple reason: there are no keiretsu. Our point is not that some firms are only borderline members, that membership changes, much less that in Japan everything is fluid—one pair of scholars (economists, no less) ducked the crucial inquiry with the classic culturalist throwaway: "the word *keiretsu* is deeply flavored with the characteristic Japanese taste for ambiguity" (Morck and Nakamura 2003, 83). Nor is our point that the keiretsu are shrinking in importance. Rather, our point is that there is no membership list because there are not now and never have been keiretsu groupings. The phrase echoes Joe McCarthy, of course, and rightly so. Accusations of keiretsu membership are as easy to make and hard to disprove as are those about communist sympathies.

The Lunch Clubs

To be sure, there are the lunch club lists: the lunch invitations to those cryptically ambiguous "presidential councils." Here, at least, the membership is clear enough. A man is either invited or not invited. Come noon on the second Thursday of each month, keiretsu or no keiretsu, he must decide where he will eat his lunch.

Yet while the invitation lists are clear, keiretsu observers seldom use them. For if they did, no one would care about the keiretsu. Moving the keiretsu from an academic sideshow to the central legend in Japanese business instead involved a crucial slight-of-hand: coupling the accounts of regular presidential meetings with lists of hundreds (or thousands) of firms whose presidents are never invited. Even Tokyo, after all, does not have a dining hall big enough to feed 15,540 presidents every fourth Friday.

The men involved apparently started their lunch clubs in the early to mid-1960s. Mostly these men headed what had been zaibatsu firms before the war and had spent their earliest working days in those zaibatsu firms. We discuss these family-owned conglomerates in chapter 3 but note here that in the late 1940s Gen. Douglas MacArthur's staff ordered the owners to sell their shares.

By forcing the families to sell their stock, MacArthur's staff transformed what had been closely affiliated firms into independently owned and operated institutions. Although the staff also banned the firms from using their old names, that obviously jeopardized customer and supplier loyalty. As a result, although the firms abandoned their old owners, as soon as MacArthur left in 1952 they retrieved their trade names and trademarks.

The presidents of the former Mitsui, Mitsubishi, and Sumitomo firms were the first to start "doing lunch." Their Fuji, Sanwa, and Daiichi counterparts began a few years later. Importantly, these men did not necessarily run major firms, notwithstanding claims by Westerners that "each of these...firms is one of the top companies in their sector" (Kensy 2001, 244; writing of the Mitsubishi).

Instead, what the lunch club members had in common was that they each ran a firm that used to be in the zaibatsu. In truth, that was all they had in common. Many of the firms were minor affairs. As of 1967 (the earliest date for which we have invitation lists), the lunch clubs included firms such as the Hokkaido Colliery and Steamship Company (1965 market capitalization of ¥6.9 billion; at the then current exchange rate of ¥360/US$, about $19 million). They similarly included the Toshoku trading firm (¥3.0 billion), Mitsubishi Steel (¥2.8 billion), Mitsubishi-Edogawa Chemicals (¥3.1 billion), Sumitomo Coal (¥3.2 billion), Mitsubishi Mining (¥3.5 billion), and Mitsubishi Plastics (¥3.7 billion).

These lunch clubs could not have dominated the Japanese economy if they had tried. Not only did they include firms that had gone nowhere, they missed the hottest new arrivals. Mostly they included firms in industries that had thrived before the war—industries such as finance, mining, fertilizer, ocean shipping, warehousing, and cement. They missed the firms that became central to growth postwar. As of 1967, they were missing Toyota (1965 market capitalization of ¥135 billion), Toshiba (¥91 billion), Takeda Pharmaceuticals (¥61 billion), Kinki Nihon Railway (¥43 billion), Honda (¥42 billion), Bridgestone Tire (¥42 billion), Kajima Construction (¥37 billion), not to mention Matsushita Electric (Panasonic), Sharp, Sony, Kyocera, Suzuki, Canon, and Nikon. The clubs did not even include the Mazda firm whose "rescue" in the 1970s from its rotary engine fiasco (ostensibly) by the Sumitomo Bank would become the paradigmatic tale of keiretsu virtue (see chapter 4).

Even collectively, the lunch groups made but a modest affair. Compare, for example, the total number of employees (1973 data) of all lunch club firms with those of selected international firms:

Mitsui	259,084	IBM	268,130
Mitsubishi	269,147	Siemens	302,000
Sumitomo	159,395	ITT	433,000
Sanwa	414,731	Philips	386,500
Fuji	345,549	GM	804,571
Daiichi Kangyo	546,312	Ford	458,463

If one added all employees at the Mitsubishi lunch club firms, together they rivaled IBM. For all we know, IBM ran monthly lunches for its senior executives too—but we have yet to see an article (much less hundreds of books) detailing them. None of the groups even remotely approached the size of GM. When keiretsu spokesmen protest their irrelevance, Americans typically accuse them of disingenuous modesty, but not all modesty is disingenuous. As Churchill said of Clement Atlee, he was "a modest man who has a good deal to be modest about."

So what did the keiretsu presidents do at lunch? Call them "presidential councils" and one imagines fat, well-tailored men sipping cognac while pooling trade secrets, plotting to knife their foreign rivals, scheming over business strategy, and cutting billion-dollar deals. The "inner sanctum" of the keiretsu, one guide called them (Miyashita and Russell 1994, 10). The "supreme decision making organ," wrote another (Kensy 2001, 244). In fact, the word (*kai*) observers translate as "council" they could just as validly translate as "meeting," "group," "club"—indeed, Japanese children even use the word for their birthday parties.

So why *do* the presidents get together for lunch? Well—why *not* get together for lunch? Even CEOs have to eat. Before the war, they worked in family-owned, collectively operated corporate empires. As they worked their way up the ranks, they learned to know many of their peers at the other family firms. Some were probably friends. By the late 1950s, these men had reached the top of their firms. Once there, they discovered a cross-cultural universal that college teachers and middle managers rarely notice: life is lonely at the top. By eating lunch from time to time with other ex-zaibatsu men, they not only met with old friends. They also met with people who did not always answer yes.

For all the cheap innuendos about the meetings, we know of no one who has produced a lunch club decision that mattered. From time to time the clubs (particularly the Mitsubishi) have passed on whether to license the old zaibatsu trademark. In the late 1960s, they apparently planned group exhibitions for the 1970 Osaka World's Fair. At one point, by keiretsu lore the Sumitomo club tried to stop Sumitomo Metals and Sumitomo Chemicals from expanding their aluminum refining facilities. The Mitsubishi club tried to stop Mitsubishi Chemicals and Mitsubishi Petrochemicals from expanding ethylene production. Both times, the firms ignored the group and proceeded as planned.

Many of the lunch club firms had similar names. Before the war, they had sometimes used common names, and brand loyalty is a precious thing. As noted earlier, as soon as MacArthur disappeared, several of the Mitsubishi, Mitsui, and Sumitomo firms retrieved their old brand names. By 1967, of the 27 firms that attended the Mitsubishi club, 19 of them had put the word *Mitsubishi* back in their name. Of the 27 firms in the Mitsui lunch club, 14 had returned *Mitsui* to their names. Of the 16 firms in the Sumitomo group (by the 1972 roster), 14 had a Sumitomo name. The firms in the other three groups had a different lineage and less brand loyalty to preserve. The Fuji group traced its ancestry to the Yasuda zaibatsu, but the Yasuda had run a primarily financial empire, and only three Fuji lunch club firms used Yasuda in their names. The Sanwa and Daiichi Kangyo groups had weaker pre-war antecedents and included no firms with common names.

Lunch club membership did change. None of the groups has changed much since the mid-1980s. But where the Sanwa group had had 23 members in 1967, it added 17 over the succeeding decade and another 6 during the next. Even the putatively stable Mitsui added 5 firms and dropped 8 from 1967 to 1976—this on an original membership of only 27.

Practice apparently varies from club to club, but at several the CEOs currently do not attend lunch. Although most Japanese firms have one senior executive who focuses on the firm's internal affairs, many have another who serves as its liaison to the outside. At many firms, this senior liaison now comes to lunch. That need not mean the lunches do not matter. It does, however, suggest that those who claim they do matter need to explain why they matter more than the many other functions these men regularly attend— whether Rotary Club dinners, trade association meetings, or chambers of commerce parties.

Among these groups, observers usually declare the Mitsubishi the most disciplined. After all, writes one observer (Kensy 2001, 245), "it is a well-known fact that Mitsubishi has the best organized, comprehensive decision-making structure of all the Keiretsu." Yet even the Mitsubishi presidents meet only once a month for ninety minutes. They hold no other meetings. Because many members make business appointments for the early afternoon, they enforce the ninety-minute limit ruthlessly. They eat a quick lunch. As befits men raised in Spartan 1950s and 1960s Japan, they favor the decidedly non–haute cuisine curry-on-rice. They then discuss any philanthropic requests and trademark disputes, and hear a sixty-minute talk from an outside speaker.

Of the eleven lectures to the Mitsubishi presidents in 2000, only two even arguably related to business: May's lecture, "The Japanese Economy in the Age of Globalization," and the December presentation on e-commerce. The rest of the talks were "Tales of London" by the British ambassador to Japan (February); "Thirty Years of the Mitsubishi Foundation" (January); "Cloning" by a Ministry of Agriculture and Fisheries official (March); "China, Taiwan, Hong Kong, and Japan" by a university professor (November); long-term care for the elderly, by a medical school professor; a report on the Russian election from a Japanese diplomat (July); "Issues in Japanese Education" by a former president of the University of Tokyo (September); a report from the head of an East Asian classics library (April); and a lecture from a language professor titled "Angkor Wat and the Japanese" (October).

Research on the Keiretsu

Although rhetorically crucial, the lunch clubs are economically trivial, and to disguise that triviality most writers couple the accounts of the meetings with much longer lists of firms. For that list, they most commonly turn to the rosters published by the obscure Keizai chosa kai or Economic Research Institute (ERI) as the annual *Research on the Keiretsu* (*ROK*).

The *ROK* did not obtain its lists from the firms themselves. Instead, it made them up. In virtually all cases, it merely grouped firms by the principal source of their loans. In turn, it obtained that loan data from the disclosure statements required by Japanese securities law. Because the law requires only major firms to file the statements, the *ROK* limited itself to firms listed on section 1 (the largest firms) of the Tokyo Stock Exchange (TSE). In 1965, that section included 625 nonfinancial firms.[2]

Definitions

Unfortunately, even the *ROK* did not offer *a* definition of the keiretsu. Instead, during the 1960s it simultaneously used at least four. Through each, it produced substantially different rosters. For all, however, it relied almost exclusively on a firm's loans.

That the *ROK* relied on loans poses at least two implications that matter here. First, in all of the many studies relying directly or indirectly on these *ROK* rosters, keiretsu membership in itself says nothing about anything else. Absent more, it says *nothing* about the cross-shareholdings, personnel exchanges, long-term commercial ties, or any of the other characteristics routinely attributed to the keiretsu. Instead, it merely reflects the amount a firm borrowed from several designated financial institutions.

Second, although keiretsu firms borrowed money within the group, that fact says nothing about the significance of the keiretsu. Instead, it simply reflects the definition. *Of course* the firms borrowed heavily from the grouped financial institutions. With but a few exceptions, the *ROK* would not have listed them in the keiretsu otherwise.

To calculate the debt on which it based its rosters, the *ROK* first grouped the biggest financial firms. To allocate those firms, it asked whether they had been part of a zaibatsu before the Allied occupation. Never mind that by 1965 those financial firms had been independently owned and operated for nearly twenty years. The *ROK* asked who owned them in 1945. It then assigned firms to a group according to the total amounts they borrowed from these financial firms.

Take an example. To create the Mitsui keiretsu, the *ROK* added the amounts a firm borrowed from four firms that had been part of the Mitsui zaibatsu before the war: the Mitsui Bank, the Mitsui Trust Bank, the Taisho

Marine and Fire Insurance Company, and the Mitsui Life Insurance Company. To identify the Mitsubishi keiretsu, it added the amounts a firm borrowed from the Mitsubishi Bank, the Mitsubishi Trust Bank, the Tokyo Marine and Fire Insurance Company, and the Meiji Life Insurance Company. It then listed a firm on a given keiretsu roster if the firm borrowed more from one set of grouped financial institutions than it borrowed from any other set or bank. In all this, it systematically ignored all loans from financial institutions with significant government ties such as the Japan Development Bank.

Depending on the use to which it planned to put a roster, the *ROK* in the mid-1960s grouped firms by one of four definitions. If this seems tedious, bear with us. It *is* tedious, but in academic research as in most of life, the devil is in the details. For its table on general bank-firm affiliation, the *ROK* used the simplest definition:

Definition 1. Firms for which keiretsu financial institutions are collectively the largest source of borrowed funds.

To the Mitsui keiretsu the *ROK* assigned 82 firms. Of those 82, a total of 66 firms had borrowed the most from the grouped Mitsui lenders for three years in a row and 16 others for one or two years.

For its study of cross-shareholding arrangements, the *ROK* used a narrower definition:

Definition 2. Firms meeting one of three criteria:
(a) The firm had keiretsu financial institutions as its largest lending source for three years in a row *and* had at least 20 percent of its stock held by other members of the keiretsu;
(b) The firm obtained at least 40 percent of its debt from keiretsu financial institutions, and that amount "significantly" exceeded the amount it borrowed from the next largest lender; *or*
(c) The firm was in the keiretsu "by tradition."

To the Mitsui, it assigned 48 firms.

For its table on the ratio of keiretsu lending to gross assets, the *ROK* used a third definition:

Definition 3. All firms falling within definition 2, *plus* all others for which keiretsu financial institutions were the largest lender for three years in a row, but excluding firms owned at least 30 percent by firms in other keiretsu.

Using this approach, it compiled for the Mitsui keiretsu 71 firms.

Three definitions may seem enough but not for the *ROK*. Instead, to assign firms to different industries it used yet another list, this time without explaining what it was. There, it listed 53 nonfinancial Mitsui firms. Fourteen firms were on the definition 4 roster but not on the 48-member definition 2 roster, and 9 firms were on the latter but not the former ($53 - 14 + 9 = 48$). Unfortunately, because we ourselves depend on the *ROK* for data, we too will sometimes switch from one definition to another.

Just as many writers describe the presidential lunch clubs but then use a list dominated by presidents no one ever invited, so academics (e.g., Hoshi, Kashyap, and Scharfstein 1990a, 1990b, 1991) sometimes recite the *ROK*'s apparently nuanced definition 2 but then use the longer loan-based list of definition 1 or 3. To follow the usual practice, we rely on the roster of definition 1 or 3 when we can. Unfortunately, because the *ROK* collects shareholding data only for the definition 2 groups, we use that roster in discussing cross-shareholding.

The groups of definition 2 firms are almost entirely a subset of the exclusively loan-based definition 1 groups. Of the 48 firms in the definition 2–based Mitsui keiretsu, only 3 were not also in the definition 1 keiretsu. Apparently, they enter by the "tradition" catchall of clause (*c*). Toyota, for example, had almost no debt and would not have fit within any keiretsu under definition 1 or 3.

The group formed by definition 3 is even closer to the exclusively loan-based first. Again, take the Mitsui. Obviously, the definition 3 group includes the 48 firms in the second group. Of those 48, 40 had used Mitsui financial institutions as their largest lender for three years straight. Since 66 firms had used Mitsui institutions as their largest lender for three years, that leaves 26 that were not in the second group. All remaining 23 firms in the third group ($71 - 48 = 23$) came from this group of 26.

The Mitsubishi list similarly reflects the way the *ROK* relied overwhelmingly on loan patterns. As noted earlier, by definition 1 the *ROK* generated a group of 79 Mitsubishi firms. Of these, 67 had used the Mitsubishi financial institutions as their largest lender for three years. The definition 2 group included 46 firms, all of which came from the definition 1 group and 45 of which had used Mitsubishi institutions as their principal loan source for three years. The group formed by definition 3 also included 67 firms: all 46 firms in the second group, plus 21 of the 22 firms ($67 - 45 = 22$) that had borrowed the most from Mitsubishi institutions for three years but were not in the second group.

Dodwell Marketing Consultants
Among business executives and scholars who do not read Japanese, Dodwell Marketing Consultants has posed the stiffest competition to the *ROK*. Every

few years since the early 1970s it has published its own keiretsu roster, *Industrial Groupings in Japan.*

Dodwell does not clearly explain how it chooses its groups. Seemingly, it starts with the luncheon invitation lists. To those lists, it adds firms in which lunch group invitees appear prominently among the ten largest shareholders. Like a Michelin guide to industrial organization, it then assigns group members one to four stars based on the size of those shareholdings. Where *ROK* collected information on eight groups (Mitsui, Mitsubishi, Sumitomo, Fuji, Sanwa, Daiichi, Tokai, and Daiwa), Dodwell lists the first six of those plus Nippon Steel, Hitachi, Nissan, Toyota, Matsushita, Toshiba, and Tokyu. The latter groups are manufacturer-centered (so-called vertical) groups. As such, they raise different issues, which we address later in the chapter.

The Rosters Compared

If the different keiretsu definitions—arbitrary as they seem—captured otherwise real but unobservable group characteristics, the *ROK* and Dodwell should produce similar rosters. They do not. Just as the various *ROK* definitions produced Mitsui keiretsu ranging from 48 firms to 82, the *ROK* (definition 3) and Dodwell produce Mitsui keiretsu in which fewer than half of the members overlap (table 2.1). The fraction of *ROK* members appearing on Dodwell's roster (TSE section 1 firms only) runs from 48 to 65 percent; the fraction of Dodwell members appearing in the *ROK* runs from 49 to 55.

The lunch clubs are much smaller than either the *ROK* or Dodwell groups. Where the Mitsui keiretsu had about 80 members by either the

Table 2.1. *ROK*, Dodwell's, and lunch club rosters

	Mitsui	Mitsubishi	Sumitomo	Fuji	Sanwa	DKB
	A. ROK and Dodwell's (1975)					
Firms in *ROK* (def. 3)	85	107	100	82	60	59
Firms in Dodwell's	83	127	102	93	75	62
Firms in both	41	68	55	51	39	33
ROK firms in Dodwell's (%)	48.2	63.6	55.0	62.2	65.0	55.9
Dodwell firms in *ROK* (%)	49.4	53.5	53.9	54.8	52.0	53.2
	B. Lunch clubs (1975–76)					
Lunch club members	24	27	16	29	37	30

Sources: ROK 1975; Dodwell Marketing Consultants 1975; Toyo keizai shimpo sha, *Kigyo keiretsu soran*, various years.

Notes: TSE section 1 firms only were counted. We use 1975 as that was the earliest date for which we were able to locate Dodwell's data.

Dodwell or *ROK* counts (albeit fewer than half in common), only 24 were in the lunch club. Of those 24, by definition all were on Dodwell's roster (as the four-star members), and all of the nonfinancials were in the *ROK* group.

WHAT DO THEY DO?

Trades

If the keiretsu mattered so much, one might have thought the members would trade with each other. Observers certainly do claim they trade. Within the keiretsu, writes one from a business school (Gerlach 1992, 4), firms transact under "diffuse sets of obligations that overlap over time" and use "equity investment and personnel interlocks . . . to consolidate financial, commercial, and other business ties." The result: "an extremely strong pattern of preferential trading" (xvii).

So observers claim. But what do the firms do? We know of no source that documents the intragroup trades within the keiretsu. As the Toyota account shows, even putative group members do not track intergroup trades. To our knowledge, the best study of intragroup trades remains the very survey the FTC compiled through the inquiries that so bedeviled our Toyota informant (Kosei torihiki iinkai 1994a, 139). By that account, manufacturing firms in 1992 in the six lunch clubs *sold* a mean 12.58 percent of their output within the group. They made most of these intragroup sales to the trading company, which then resold the goods elsewhere. Excluding the sales to the trading company, they sold only 2.38 percent of their output within the group. The amounts ranged from 5.57 percent (1.49 percent, excluding the trading company) for the Sanwa group to 31.67 percent (0.61 percent, excluding the trading company) for the Sumitomo.

These same manufacturing firms *acquired* a mean 6.71 percent of their supplies within the group. Again, much of this volume they bought through the trading company, which in turn had acquired them elsewhere. Excluding the purchases from the trading company, the firms acquired only 2.24 percent of their supplies within the group. The amounts ranged from 3.67 percent (1.23 percent, excluding the trading company) for the Fuji to 15.87 percent (5.40 percent, excluding the trading company) for the Mitsubishi.

Apparently within each group a few firms accounted for much of the intragroup trade. In 1988 Mitsubishi Heavy Industry produced 7.4 percent of the products that the Mitsubishi trading firm sold, and Mitsubishi Auto products produced another 5.3 percent. Mitsubishi Metals, Mitsubishi Electric, Mitsubishi Petroleum, Mitsubishi Chemicals, and Mitsubishi Paper together produced barely 1 percent of the trading firm's sales, and all other lunch club members together produced only 4–5 percent.

Cross-Shareholding

The Accounts

By most accounts, the keiretsu firms control each other by holding each other's shares. Some observers even purport to define the keiretsu by these shareholdings arrangements: for example, "a group of companies linked by stable intercorporate shareholdings is called a keiretsu" (Morck and Nakamura 1999a, 320). Others characterize the "elaborate cross-holdings of debt and equity" as one of the "main features" of the keiretsu (Bergloef and Perotti 1994, 260).

Two prominent law professors explain how it works. "Each member of a keiretsu," write Jonathan Macey and Geoffrey Miller (1995, 83), "owns about 2 percent of every other firm in the group." Because the ties are so extensive, collectively "between 30 percent and 90 percent of the stock in each firm will be owned by other keiretsu members." *Ninety* percent? They almost posit an empire with no shareholder equity at all.

Taking these purported "facts" as given, however, scholars have made a cottage industry out of explaining the role the posited cross-shareholdings play. Some see in the shareholdings an attempt to protect member firms from hostile takeovers (Morck and Nakamura 1999a, 2003). Lock up enough stock in friendly hands, they explain, and no T. Boone Pickens will ever launch a tender offer.

Other scholars see them as "hostage" mechanisms that trading partners (note the assumption about intragroup trades) can use to ensure that they each keep their word (Gilson and Roe 1993). Neither firm will cheat on its deals, they reason, if its partner can retaliate by dumping its stock. Still others see their role as more mysteriously symbolic (Lincoln, Gerlach, and Takahashi 1992, 564): "interlocking shareholding binds Japanese firms into cohesive, horizontal communities."

Alas, all this has more than a bit of the medieval unicorn debate to it. Working so hard to explain the cross-shareholdings, few scholars have bothered to check the facts. Had they tried, they would have noticed that the nonfinancial firms rarely invest in each other at all. Even more rarely do pairs of such firms invest in each other. Notwithstanding the sometimes brilliant academic theorizing about *why* the firms invest in each other, the actual firms do not invest.

Nonfinancial Firms

Most of the nonfinancial firms invest nothing in each other. Although the law generally allowed them to buy each other's stock, they rarely did. As of 1965 the 46 Mitsubishi nonfinancial firms (*ROK* definition 2) could each have invested in 45 other firms—for a total of 2,070 investment opportunities.

Of these, the firms made investments in 219, or 10.6 percent. They made at least 1 percent investments in 61, or 3.0 percent. In only 11 cases (0.5 percent) did any nonfinancial firm hold more than 5 percent of the stock of another. The Daiichi firms made 1 percent investments in 4.8 percent of the potential cases, Sumitomo firms in 3.7 percent, Mitsui firms in 2.6 percent, Sanwa firms in 2.1 percent, and Fuji firms in 1.8 percent.

Nor did the nonfinancial firms *collectively* own much stock of each other. In the Mitsubishi keiretsu, the nonfinancial firms together held 4.9 percent of all outstanding shares of the group. In the Sumitomo, they held 6.1 percent of the shares of member firms, in the Daiichi 4.8 percent, in the Mitsui 3.5 percent, in the Sanwa 2.1 percent, and in the Fuji 2.0 percent.

Financial Firms
Although the financial firms do hold stock in members allocated to the keiretsu by the *ROK* rosters, the point misleads. Where U.S. law banned banks from holding corporate stock during this period, Japanese law allowed it—and Japanese banks responded by diversifying broadly. Although they owned stock in keiretsu firms, they owned stock in nonkeiretsu firms as well. Crucially, however, the *ROK* did not count that stock. Instead, it created the impression of intragroup investment by counting only group-member stock.

The stock in the nonfinancial keiretsu members (*ROK* definition 2) held by all other members (including the financials) ranged from 7.6 percent at the Sanwa to 17.6 percent at the Sumitomo—a far cry from the 90 percent some U.S. academics trumpet. By law the financials could have held up to 10 percent of any other firm's stock, and had they wanted to control the firms they would have done so. They did not. Although the Mitsubishi Bank invested in 41 of the 46 nonfinancial group members, it held more than 5 percent of the stock of only 8 and more than 8 percent of the stock of only 2. The trust bank held more than 8 percent of only 3, the life insurer more than 8 percent of only 3, and the casualty insurer more than 8 percent of none.

Instead, the financials invested in other group members as part of a broadly diversified portfolio. Much the same could be said of the trading firms. Among the nonfinancial firms in the Mitsubishi group, the trading company held the most group shares. Of the 28 nonfinancials in which it held at least some stock, it held 0.5 percent in 24. Like the banks, however, it invested broadly. Here too, of course, the *ROK* did not bother to count the stock the trading company bought in nongroup firms. Yet in a 1969 securities disclosure statement, the firm gave some information about those other shareholdings. There, it listed 37 Japanese "related firms" in which it had equity investments. That related stock it carried on its books for ¥2.68 billion. Its entire portfolio of Japanese securities it carried for ¥33.17 billion.

Cross-Shareholdings

If intragroup shareholdings were rare, true *cross*-shareholding arrangements were rarer still. Equity investments seem consistently highest at the Sumitomo group (*ROK* definition 2), and in 1965 there were eleven pairs of cross-shareholdings involving at least 1 percent there. Yet among the Mitsui and Sanwa firms there were only six such pairs, among the Mitsubishi four pairs, among the Fuji three pairs, and among the Daiichi firms two.

Lunch Clubs

Although the lunch club members were more likely to buy stock in each other than the *ROK* group members were, the amounts remained small. Even within the Mitsui and Mitsubishi (1965), the nonfinancial firms bought stakes larger than 1 percent less than a tenth of the time. Again, the equity investments were highest at the Sumitomo, where the nonfinancial lunch club members collectively held 9.1 percent of the member firms' stock. Among the Mitsubishi, though, they held 4.3 percent, and among the Mitsui 3 percent.[3]

Once again, *cross*-shareholding arrangements were rare. Among all non-financial Sumitomo lunch club members, eleven pairs of firms held at least 1 percent in each other. Among the Mitsubishi only one pair did, and among the Mitsui, none. Nor did the keiretsu financial institutions often hold large stakes in the lunch club member firms. In 1965, the Sumitomo Bank held more than 5 percent of six firms, the Mitsui Bank more than 5 percent of four firms, and the Mitsubishi Bank more than 5 percent of only one.

MAIN BANKS

Writers routinely assert that keiretsu firms use the group's money center bank as their main bank. (We explore the practical insignificance of main bank relations and the logical incoherence of main bank theory in chapter 4.) Each keiretsu, explained economist Iwao Nakatani (1984, 231), "has a major commercial bank . . . as the major lender to the member firms." Because they assume that the group's money center bank plays this role, some observers even define the keiretsu rosters as a "classification of listed Japanese firms into main-bank groupings" (Sheard 1989, 401).

Again, however, scholars seem to be quarreling over the function unicorns serve. In fact, many firms listed as part of keiretsu groups do *not* use the group's money center bank as their main bank (following convention, we define a firm's main bank as the bank from which it borrows the most). To see why this could result despite the *ROK*'s use of loans to create the rosters, recall its allocation rule: ask whether the *sum* of the amounts a firm borrowed from a given pool of financial institutions exceeded the amounts it borrowed from other pools. Now take the Tobu Railroad. In 1975 it had a total financial-institution debt of ¥192,942 million. Its largest loans (in million yen) were as follows:

Mitsui Trust Bank	24,059
Mitsubishi Trust Bank	21,844
Yasuda Trust Bank	20,975
Japan Development Bank	16,789
Fuji Bank	15,404

The *ROK* placed Tobu in the Fuji group. Since the predecessors to the Yasuda Trust and Fuji banks had both been in the Yasuda zaibatsu before the war, the *ROK* treated them as Fuji financial institutions. Because Tobu borrowed from those two banks *together* more than it borrowed elsewhere, the *ROK* called it a Fuji group member. Yet the Fuji Bank was but its fifth-largest lender. For its main bank Tobu apparently used Mitsui Trust.

Similarly, the *ROK* placed the Chori firm in the Mitsui group because it borrowed ¥4,434 million from the Mitsui Bank and ¥9,013 million from the Mitsui Trust Bank. Yet Chori borrowed ¥11,121 million from the Fuji Bank, ¥10,440 million from the Daiichi Kangyo Bank, and ¥9,809 million from the Sanwa Bank. It placed Nippon TV in the Mitsubishi group because it borrowed ¥936 million from the Mitsubishi Bank and ¥892 million from the Mitsubishi Trust Bank. Yet Nippon TV borrowed ¥987 million from the Fuji Bank. And it placed Daido Wool in the Sumitomo group because it borrowed ¥970 million from the Sumitomo and ¥501 million from the Sumitomo Trust Bank. Yet Daido borrowed ¥1,220 million from the Daiichi Kangyo Bank and another ¥970 million from the Fuji Bank.

On the other hand, in the late 1970s fertilizer maker Nihon kasei borrowed more from the Daiichi Kangyo than from Mitsubishi Bank, Mitsubishi Trust Bank, and Meiji Life combined. Yet Mitsubishi kasei owned 37 percent of its stock, and Mitsubishi Trading owned another 16 percent. Between them, the latter two firms named Nihon kasei's president, board chairman, and several directors. As the principal source of its loans, however, it still used the Daiichi Kangyo.

Mitsubishi kasei also owned 26 percent of Nitto Tire, and Mitsubishi Trading owned 18 percent. As its principal creditor, Nitto did use the Mitsubishi Trust Bank. When it encountered financial distress, however, Nitto did not rely on any of these firms. Instead, it turned to its third largest shareholder, Toyo Rubber, which sent one of its executives as Nitto president. Toyo, in turn, borrowed the most from the Long-Term Credit Bank and attended the Sanwa lunch club.

More generally, in 1975, of the firms in each of the keiretsu (*ROK* definition 3), only the following percentage used that keiretsu's money center bank as the principal source of their loans (Miwa and Ramseyer 2002b, 198, table 9):

Mitsui	40.1
Mitsubishi	42.7
Sumitomo	47.6
Fuji	56.4
Sanwa	61.5
Daiichi Kangyo	86.0

OTHER KEIRETSU ATTRIBUTES

Still, all this will leave some readers unconvinced. In the past two decades, scholars have used keiretsu affiliation as a variable in a wide range of empirical studies. In peer-reviewed journals they then report the significant results they obtain. If a variable yields significant results, surely it captures some real aspect of the Japanese economy?

Not so. Unfortunately, the work illustrates one of the by-products of editors who insist on statistical significance: authors build their articles around the 1 in 20 results that come in as significant at the 5 percent level. We ourselves replicate many of these studies, and our peers replicate others. We omit the detail here, but this body of work goes to the following issues.

Access to Credit

The best-known keiretsu studies explore the ability of troubled firms to borrow (Hoshi, Kashyap, and Scharfstein 1990a, 1990b, 1991). On the one hand, some troubled firms lose money because they cannot compete. Every day they stay in business, they drain resources. The sooner creditors shut them down, the richer society will be.

Other troubled firms are fundamentally healthy concerns that find themselves temporarily short of cash: economically healthy but financially constrained. If creditors shut down these essentially sound firms too, society loses their going concern value. If these firms could but obtain the cash they need to weather the hard times, they could once again thrive.

By this logic, bankruptcy law should distinguish the fundamentally uncompetitive from the financially constrained, and close the former and protect the latter. But why, one might ask, should the law do that? Will not creditors do it on their own, bankruptcy law or no? If fundamentally competitive, a firm will eventually rebound and pay its obligations as they come due. Why would creditors shut it down (and collect only a few cents on the dollar) when they could recover so much more by renegotiating the debt and waiting?

To this question, bankruptcy scholars give several replies. First, creditors often lack the information they need to distinguish the uncompetitive from the financially constrained. Although the financially constrained firms will try hard to prove their economic health, so will the fundamentally uncompetitive. Absent inside information, creditors may not know which is which.

Second, financially constrained firms often owe money to many creditors. Had they borrowed only from one source, they might indeed renegotiate their debt. Owing money to several, however, they must induce their creditors to cooperate among themselves. Any time negotiations move from the bilateral to the multilateral, the complexities expand exponentially. The more complex the negotiations, the higher the odds the creditors will not reach even those deals that would make them all better off.

Third, creditors will not want a reputation for renegotiating with troubled debtors. After a firm hits financial distress, a bank might indeed find it profitable to cut it some slack. Unfortunately, how it deals with one firm after the fact will affect what happens to its other loans in the future. Once the bank acquires a reputation for saving distressed firms, it faces two classic problems. First, its existing borrowers will have an incentive to switch to higher-risk projects (a phenomenon scholars call *moral hazard*). Second, it will attract a higher percentage of those potential borrowers who know they cannot perform as well as outsiders expect (*adverse selection*). Faced with these twin problems, a bank may rationally refuse to renegotiate even with the financially constrained but fundamentally healthy borrower.

What lawyers and legal scholars often miss, of course, is that bankruptcy law itself causes moral hazard and adverse selection. By restricting the tactics a creditor can use when a firm defaults, bankruptcy law changes the arrangements creditors and borrowers make at the outset. If the law prevents creditors from using the harshest tools against defaulting debtors, it (*a*) gives all borrowers an incentive to undertake riskier projects (moral hazard) and (*b*) makes debt finance relatively more attractive for the riskier firms (adverse selection). Aware of this risk, investors will lend less money. By restricting the options available upon default, bankruptcy law reduces the credit available at the outset.

To some, the keiretsu promised an escape from this quandary—for initial empirical work (Hoshi, Kashyap, and Scharfstein 1990a, 1990b, 1991) suggested that banks helped financially constrained keiretsu firms. Within the keiretsu, scholars reasoned, firms knew each other well, and creditors could more accurately distinguish the uncompetitive from the financially constrained. Within the keiretsu, creditors could better coordinate their responses and less often fall victim to self-defeating collective-action problems. And within the keiretsu, cross-shareholding ties, the prospect of future dealings, and general reputational concerns combined to mitigate moral hazard and adverse selection. For firms in financial distress, all this translated into easier access to credit if they were part of a keiretsu (by *ROK* rosters) than if independent.

What this account promised in logic it missed in fact. Perhaps lunch club firms know each other well—or perhaps not. Our Toyota informant did not know that his president attended, much less who else did. And the vast majority of firms on the *ROK* rosters are not even invited to the lunches anyway. Perhaps closely affiliated financial institutions work together well—or again perhaps not. Firms assigned to the keiretsu by these lists only haphazardly use the group's money center bank as their principal bank, and the financial institutions assigned to the keiretsu do not work together at all. As we show elsewhere, they simply do not coordinate their funding decisions (Miwa and Ramseyer 2002b, 180, table 2).

Upon closer examination, the claimed empirical evidence of keiretsu aid to distressed members unravels anyway. Econometrician Fumio Hayashi (2000) explored the Hoshi-Kashyap-Scharfstein data more closely and found that the results hinged on four outlying firm-years. Drop those four firm-years and the statistical significance disappeared. Another team of economists (Hall and Weinstein 2000) asked whether banks responded differently to keiretsu and nonkeiretsu firms, and found not. "Main banks" no more readily lent to financially distressed keiretsu firms than to nonkeiretsu firms.

Profitability

With observers painting keiretsu success in such glowing terms, one might have thought keiretsu firms would earn higher profits than independents. Think again. Most scholars who check find that keiretsu firms do not earn more than independents. Some even claim keiretsu firms earn less. Early on, for example, Harvard economist Richard Caves and University of Tokyo economist Masu Uekusa (Caves and Uekusa 1976b, 76; Uekusa 1974a, 1974b) claimed that keiretsu firms earned lower profits than did independents. To gauge relative profitability, however, they simply chose sixteen nonrandomly selected independents. Since then, though, several scholars have made similar claims with better data.[4]

To explain this lack of keiretsu profitability, scholars alternatively posit the following: that the firms dissipate their earnings; that they use their financial cushion to reduce risk; or that the keiretsu main bank extracts earnings through higher charges. Alas, these claims make no sense. Keiretsu firms are not monopolists that could plausibly dissipate earnings and stay in business. They have no more reason than other firms to want to overpay their employees and no more reason to be able to do so. They have no more reason to want to or to be able to minimize risk. And they have no more reason to want to overpay for banking services, and given that keiretsu firms borrow from many banks, neither do keiretsu banks have any way to force them to pay higher charges.

In any case, this lower-earnings result among keiretsu firms is fundamentally unstable as well. One study (Morck, Nakamura, and Shivdasani 2000) regressed stock market performance (Tobin's Q) and accounting profitability on keiretsu affiliation (by the *ROK* rosters) and found no significant effect. With an analogous exercise, we obtain similar results: at root, keiretsu profitability is both time and definition dependent. Although firms in five of the six *ROK* keiretsu earned lower profits than did independents during 1968–75, only two of the six did so in 1976–82. Even within 1968–75, at none of the lunch clubs did members earn lower profits than independents, and the Sumitomo firms actually earned *higher* profits (Miwa and Ramseyer 2002b, 210, table 14).

Interest Rates

Do keiretsu firms pay higher interest rates? As this discussion suggests, several scholars have claimed they do (Caves and Uekusa 1976a, 1976b; Weinstein and Yafeh 1998). The keiretsu banks charge the higher interest, they explain, by using their stronger bargaining power.

What bargaining power? Firms assigned to the keiretsu groups by the rosters borrow widely. During the 1960s and 1970s, they relied on their lead bank for only 10–15 percent of their loans. That would hardly have enabled the bank to "hold up" a borrower for higher charges. Neither would the bank's low shareholding levels have given it any "bargaining power."

When we regress interest rates on keiretsu affiliation, we again find what logic implies: keiretsu firms do *not* pay interest at higher rates. Whether we use the *ROK* or the lunch club rosters, the results are uniformly insignificant (Miwa and Ramseyer 2002b, 206, table 12).

Volatility

What of volatility? If keiretsu firms either (1) have better access to funds during financial distress or (2) pool their returns to lower risk, might they earn less volatile profits than their independent peers (e.g., Nakatani 1984; Khanna and Yafeh 2000)? Begin again, however, with the logic. How could keiretsu firms reduce volatility? Equity interests do not allow the firms to pool earnings: the shareholdings are too trivial. Neither do the trade relations allow it: the ties are just as trivial. Debt could conceivably work, but no one has shown that keiretsu interest charges move countercyclically.

In any event, the lower-volatility thesis implies that independent firms would pay a premium on their bond issues relative to keiretsu firms—and this does not happen (Hall and Weinstein 2000). When one economist regressed stock price volatility on keiretsu affiliation, he obtained no significant results either (Beason 1998). In our own work, we regress the volatility of a firm's profitability on keiretsu affiliation and again find no evidence that keiretsu firms earn less volatile profits than do independent firms. If anything, they experience *higher* volatility (Miwa and Ramseyer 2002b, 203, table 11).

The Lawrence Hypothesis
During the trade wars of the early 1990s, Kennedy School scholar Robert Lawrence (1991, 1993) claimed that the keiretsu excluded foreign competitors. The bigger the keiretsu share in an industry, argued Lawrence, the lower the level of import penetration. The debate was a nonstarter. When University of Michigan economist Gary Saxonhouse (1991, 1993) corrected Lawrence's equations, the effect of keiretsu affiliation on trade disappeared. More basically, reasoned Saxonhouse, if U.S. firms could not sell in industries dominated by keiretsu firms, that fact showed stiff competition rather than collusion. Indeed, when two other scholars explored Saxonhouse's hypothesis, they found exactly that result: if anything, keiretsu firms had profit/cost margins lower than those of independents (Weinstein and Yafeh 1995).

THE VERTICAL KEIRETSU
Even if they attach the same keiretsu nameplate to the two purported phenomena, keiretsu buffs distinguish between horizontal and vertical keiretsu. The former, they explain, are the groups like the Mitsubishi and Mitsui that encircle major banks. The latter encircle large manufacturers. Typically, the buffs focus on the automobile manufacturers, but they sometimes add firms in industries such as electronics as well.

The Theory behind the Story
Keiretsu buffs do not just use the horizontal and vertical keiretsu to sort different "facts." They use them to motivate different theories. Just as they sometimes invoke the horizontal groups to address insolvency issues, they use the verticals to illustrate themes in industrial organization and contract theory. More specifically (we discuss the issue further in chapter 3), they argue that Japanese manufacturers and suppliers use the vertical keiretsu to resolve problems raised by large "relationship-specific" investments.

Scholars use the term *relationship-specific investments* to refer to those investments that have value only within an ongoing relationship. Because of that relational specificity, the parties have an incentive to maintain the relationship long term. Simultaneously, however, they expose themselves to the risk that their partner will "hold them up." Suppose, for example, that to make a Camry headlight a supplier needs a customized machine. If the supplier buys the machine, it can earn a return on that investment as long as it makes Camry headlights. However, because the supplier will find itself saddled with worthless equipment if Toyota takes its business elsewhere, Toyota, by *threatening* to move its business, can hold up the supplier for a price cut.

For two decades, scholars in industrial organization puzzled over the issues raised by this relational specificity. To some, the vertical keiretsu seemed the perfect illustration. According to the late Kyoto University economist Banri Asanuma (e.g., Asanuma 1989), the relations between Japanese automobile assemblers (such as Toyota) and their suppliers (such as the air conditioner firm Denso) were long standing, and long standing precisely because the two firms invested so heavily in relationship-specific investments. According to Asanuma, the firms in the automobile industry trade in "customized parts," and to produce those parts the firms need both relationship-specific equipment and relationship-specific skills. To make air conditioners for Toyota, Denso technicians will both buy special equipment and study Toyota cars. The machines they buy and the skills they learn will help Denso design and make air conditioners for Toyota. They will not help Denso design and make air conditioners for Nissan.

Asanuma had long admired the work of Berkeley economist Oliver Williamson. Williamson, in turn, had won considerable acclaim for the way he integrated relational specificity into his more general accounts of business transactions. Asanuma had translated Williamson's early book into Japanese, and when Williamson visited Japan Asanuma had organized a tour of a Toyota plant for him. Williamson responded by using Japanese automobile manufacturing to illustrate some of the different ways firms can resolve issues raised by relationship-specific investments.

For many observers, these relationship-specific investments were key to (what they then saw as) the Japanese juggernaut. According to the *Harvard Business Review*, again, they were crucial to the success of the Japanese car makers (Dyer 1994). The investments led, the magazine reasoned, to "lower costs, higher quality, and greater profits." In the process, they gave Japanese manufacturers "substantial competitive advantages." Relationship-specific investments led to production efficiencies, in short, and the vertical keiretsu enabled Japanese manufacturers to make those crucial investments.

Two prominent corporate law scholars (Gilson and Roe 1993, 884) detailed how the vertical keiretsu facilitated the relational efficiency. The key, they reasoned, lay in (what they wrongly assumed to be) the high keiretsu cross-shareholdings. Japanese production, they explained, involves high levels of specific human expertise and physical investments. Elsewhere, firms so worry about being held up that they either avoid the investments or make costly governance changes. In Japan, the keiretsu prevented those holdups by collectively holding controlling equity stakes in the partners.

The Detail

Alas, modern scholars understand economic theory better than they do automobile production. Although firms involved in production do invest large amounts in physical assets and technical skills, they make few investments that are specific to a manufacturer. When they do, they can (and often do) straightforwardly mitigate the problems involved by contract. They hardly need frameworks as elaborate as keiretsu and controlling equity stakes.

Supplier Associations

Most Japanese automobile assemblers maintain associations of their first-tier suppliers. To keiretsu aficionados, these associations constitute the clearest evidence of the vertical keiretsu. And in truth, the associations do meet from time to time and—unlike the lunch clubs—do swap business information (see JAPIA 1998). As of 1998, Toyota had 189 suppliers in its network, Nissan had 234, and Mitsubishi 377.

Yet these associations belie the usual assumptions about the keiretsu. Most basically, they are anything but exclusive. Of the 189 Toyota and 234 Nissan association members, 68 are in both associations. Among the 1,098 firms in a Toyota, Nissan, Mitsubishi, Subaru, Mazda, Daihatsu, Hino, Isuzu, Yamaha, Suzuki, or Honda network, the average firm is a member of 1.91. Although 738 firms limit themselves to one association, 135 are in two, 135 are in three to five, 62 are in six to eight, and 28 are in nine or more.

Nor are the assemblers the only firms to maintain these associations. Many suppliers maintain their own associations of subsuppliers: Denso (air conditioning and electronic equipment; 40,000 employees and sales of ¥1.3 trillion) has an association of 67 suppliers; Koito (lighting equipment; 4,600 employees and ¥148 billion in sales) has an association of 68 suppliers; Akebono Brake (2,900 employees and ¥108 billion in sales) has an association of 79 suppliers; and Kayaba (oil pressure equipment; 4,200 employees and ¥177 billion in sales) has an association of 270 suppliers.[5]

More generally, of the 373 firms on which the broader industry trade association provides data, 188 (50 percent) maintained their own supplier associations. Do we then add 188 keiretsu corporate groups to our tally? Among the firms with 500 or fewer employees, 39 percent (62 firms) had such associations; among those with 501–1,000 employees, 53 percent (46) did; among those with 1,001–5,000 employees, 67 percent (72) did; and among those with 5,001 or more employees, 40 percent (8) did.

Honda

The Firm

For a better sense of the production process, consider the conditions at several Honda suppliers.[6] Founded a half century ago, Honda conquered the motorcycle world in the 1960s. It remains near the apex of that industry and now stands as Japan's third largest automobile producer besides. Where Toyota sold 3.2 million cars in 1998 and Nissan 1.6 million, Honda sold 1.2 million. Where Toyota had 1998 sales of ¥7.8 trillion and Nissan ¥3.5 trillion, Honda had sales of ¥3.1 trillion. Where Toyota had a workforce of 70,000 and Nissan 40,000, Honda had a workforce of 29,000.

Honda buys its parts from about 280 firms. It deals with perhaps 80 of these long term but owns stock in only a third of the 80. It pays about 80 percent of its sales revenues to these suppliers for parts. Many of the suppliers are substantial firms in their own right: Keihin (carburetors, fuel injection systems; 4,000 employees and sales of ¥144 billion), for example, or Nippon seiki (gauges; 1,700 employees and sales of ¥87 billion sales), and Yutaka giken (exhaust systems; 1,100 employees and sales of ¥72 billion).

Honda buys shock absorbers from three firms but relies most heavily on A^1. With sales of ¥103 billion and 2,800 employees, A^1 is one of Honda's largest subcontractors. In turn, A^1 buys from over two hundred suppliers. Many of A^1's suppliers (the steel producers, for instance, or rubber) are large and do not rely heavily on A^1 sales. Others (like the stamping and machining firms that make peripheral products) are much smaller.

Generally, A^1 buys peripherals from 8 stamping and 13 machining companies. Of the former, 3 firms sell less than 20 percent of their output to A^1, 2 sell 40–60 percent, and 3 sell over 60 percent. Of 11 machining firms (we lack data on 2), 3 sell under 10 percent of their output to A^1, 2 sell 10–30 percent, 3 sell 50–60 percent, and 3 sell over 70 percent.

Among these second-tier subcontractors, B^1 runs stamping operations and B^2 machining operations. In turn, B^1 buys from 62 suppliers and B^2 from 15. Among these third-tier subcontractors, C^1 does spot-welding jobs and C^2 stamping work for B^1. Consider first these third-tier firms, then those of the second tier, and finally those of the first.

Third-Tier Subcontractors

Formed in 1968 as a welding firm, C^1 initially consisted of the president, his wife, and two part-time employees. Together, they produced television parts. They started selling to B^1 in 1985, and by 1989 they had annual sales of ¥78 million, eleven workers, and seventeen welding machines. By the early 1990s the firm was selling half its output to B^1. For its other sales, it made electrical equipment, water heaters, and automobile accessories such as audio and lighter parts.

On the 27th or 28th of each month, B^1 sent C^1 the next month's order plan. Twice a day, it dispatched a truck with the materials for C^1 to weld. Simultaneously, it picked up any finished work.

For all practical purposes, only the president at C^1 had any engineering expertise. Of the eleven workers, three were members of his family. The other eight all had less than ten years' experience. When B^1 ordered a new product, the president himself decided how to make it: what voltage to set for the weld, for instance, how much time to use, or what pressure to apply.

C^2 began in 1973 with five workers. For several years, it did stamping work for air conditioners and vending machines. As demand fell the president asked B^1 for work. When B^1 agreed, C^2 bought the new equipment it needed; within a year it had fifteen employees and sent 70 percent of its work to B^1.

Of the fifteen people at C^2, three were part of the president's family, five were full-time employees, and seven worked part time. Few of the jobs involved any expertise. Instead, they were simple enough that employees could perform them with little experience. B^1 paid C^2 on a piece-rate basis and charged it for the supplies and stamping dies it needed.

C^2 subcontracted jobs that accounted for about 10–20 percent of its sales to four other firms. These fourth-tier subcontractors too were mostly family operations. Typically, they had only one or two nonfamily employees.

Second-Tier Subcontractors

A former employee of Nakajima Aircraft opened B^1 for business in 1947. Through the firm he initially produced agricultural machines, and in 1954 he started stamping work. In 1962 he incorporated the firm and two years later began selling door-handle parts.

In 1971, B^1 began stamp work for A^1. By 1984, it had eighty-five employees (including seven part time) and ¥2.13 billion in sales. As of the early 1990s, it paid its own suppliers amounts equal to 40 percent of its revenues. It sold two-fifths of its output to A^1 and two-fifths to another firm that incorporated the work into Honda-bound brake assemblies. It owned its own stamp presses.

When faced with a new job, A^1 and B^1 first negotiated the expected quantity and price, and set a depreciation charge for the stamp dies. The 20th of every month, A^1 projected its demand for the next ninety days. It kept the right, however, to change orders on five days' notice.

As of 1987, B² had fifty-five employees and ¥667 million in sales. It had begun in 1964 with machining work for a textile machine producer. Because the president knew the president of a first-tier automobile supplier, it began machining car parts the next year.

In 1970, with fifteen to sixteen employees, B² started selling directly to a different first-tier supplier, A¹. Its initial first-tier supplier did not object. By 1987, it sold half its output to A¹.

As of early 1990s, B² specialized in precision machining. Of its 55 employees, 37 were "regular" employees (27 male and 10 female; 27 full time and 10 part time). Of the 27 full-time regular employees, 20 had less than ten years' experience.

As part-time employees, B² mostly hired housewives from nearby farms. These women performed the same labor-intensive manufacturing work as their full-time counterparts. Yet this was not the "exploitation" of women and part-timers that American academics like to trumpet. Instead, B² wanted the women to work full time, but they insisted on part-time status so that they could stay home during peak agricultural work seasons.

In 1987, B² hired a retired A¹ director as a technical adviser. This man coached the firm twice a week on equipment investment, negotiations with A¹, and assorted other managerial issues. B² owned its own equipment. It bought from its own suppliers products and services worth a quarter of its total sales.

First-Tier Suppliers
Founded in 1938, A¹ began as an aircraft parts maker. In 1953, it started making motorcycle shock absorbers for the young Honda firm. When Honda moved into automobiles, A¹ followed. In 1970, it needed money, and Honda responded by buying an equity stake (by the early 1990s, about a one-third interest). It has since listed its stock on the TSE. Its president and about half its directors come from Honda.

A¹ now makes shock absorbers and several other air pressure– and oil pressure–related goods. As of 1998, 61 percent of its sales went into cars or trucks, 33 percent into motorcycles, and 8 percent into boats. By buyer, 72 percent of its sales went to Honda, 8 percent to Suzuki, and smaller amounts to such firms as Kawasaki, Yamaha, Fuji Heavy Industries (Subarus), Mazda, and Mitsubishi Auto. Purchases from its own suppliers accounted for about 63 percent of its sales.

A¹ regularly designs products in collaboration with Honda and sends its technicians to Honda as guest engineers. In developing new products, A¹ and Honda generally ignore the lower-tier suppliers. As the discussion suggests, most of those lower-tier suppliers lack much engineering expertise anyway.

Honda designs its models on a four-year product cycle and makes minor annual changes. Many of A¹'s products are subject to those annual changes.

Relationship-Specific Investments

The Smaller Firms
These descriptions suggest two obvious points about the investment patterns at the smaller suppliers. First, the firms invest very little in relationship-specific employee expertise. We know they invest little in relationship-specific expertise because they invest so little in expertise at all. At many of these firms, only one or two employees know any engineering. The other employees are so new that if they did have any expertise it would be general (e.g., knowledge about how to run a stamp press generally) rather than specific to the firm or its clients (e.g., knowledge about how to stamp specifically Toyota-bound parts).

Second, small as they are, the firms can and do sell to several manufacturers. Indeed, they sell to manufacturers in several distinct industries. Depending on their niche, they stamp, they machine, they assemble, they weld. If the price is right, they will stamp, machine, assemble, and weld Honda-bound parts. If the price is not, they will do the same for aircraft, air conditioners, boats, textile equipment, television sets, and vending machines.

Industrywide data confirm these impressions, although loosely to be sure. First, employees do not stay long at the smaller firms. Consider data from the government's annual census of wages (Rodo sho 1998). Among the smallest firms (those in the two-digit transportation equipment sector with 10–99 employees), nearly 40 percent of the workers have been at the firm for less than four years. Another 20-odd percent have worked there five to ten years. Even among the firms with 100–999 employees, half have less than ten years' tenure.

Second, the smallest firms lack substantial capital equipment of any sort, much less relationship-specific equipment. There, per employee capital investment runs a mere ¥4 million—at ¥120/US$, about $33,000. Even among plants with two hundred or more employees, the figure approaches only ¥7.8 million or about $65,000.

The Larger Firms
If any suppliers in the industry do make large relational investments, they must be the bigger first-tier suppliers. Yet we should wonder. First, the biggest firms are least likely to be members of any meaningful keiretsu. Take the 248 automobile industry firms on the TSE. On average, they maintain memberships in 3.2 supplier associations. The firms for which we have data on

sales to automobile assemblers (again, about 250 firms) on average sell only half their output to their lead customer.

Second, the parts that assemblers need to buy from their suppliers do not much vary. Whether for Toyota, Nissan, or Honda, the suppliers make windshields, shock absorbers, headlights, seats, piston rings, and cigarette lighters. The parts may come in different sizes and different shapes, but a supplier that makes a windshield for Honda can probably make one for a comparably priced car at Toyota.

Third, those investments that are indeed specific are probably specific to a model rather than to a given assembler. Suppose a supplier needs to invest in idiosyncratic equipment or training to make Camry-bound tail lights. If those investments would not transfer to Accord-bound tail lights, they probably would not transfer to Corolla-bound ones either.

This last point poses two further implications. First, if an investment is specific to a model, it will not earn its owner long-term returns. Most Japanese assemblers keep a model only four years. As a result, if a supplier invests in model-specific equipment, it will generally need to amortize its costs over four years. Second, because firms can usually anticipate what will happen over four years, they can readily protect any model-specific investments by contract. In the Japanese automobile industry, they do exactly that. Most suppliers already sign contracts with assemblers that last the term of the model. If the contract does not eliminate opportunistic conduct, the prospect of market competition at the end of the four years usually will.

From time to time, theorists add discussions of site-specific investments— railroads that lay track to a coal mine, for example. The discussions have little to do with automobile production in Japan. After all, Japan is small. The entire country covers roughly the size of California, and Toyoda City is a scant two hundred miles from Tokyo. If Japan is small, so are most automobile components. They may not be microchips, but most car parts are relatively easy to ship. Given the elaborate networks of railroads and superhighways in Japan, most suppliers everywhere should be able cost-effectively to deliver components to most assemblers anywhere.

Other Issues

Cross-Shareholdings

As with the horizontal keiretsu, firms in the vertical groups hold fewer shares in each other than observers typically claim. We have equity ownership data on 462 suppliers (162 listed firms and 300 unlisted). In 57 percent of the suppliers (262 firms) the lead automobile assembler buyer owns no equity. In an additional 15 percent (68 firms), it owns under 10 percent. In only a quarter of the suppliers does it have at least a 10 percent interest, and in only 5 percent does it own a majority interest.

Exclusivity

As suggested earlier, automobile suppliers maintain less exclusive relationships than most observers suggest. We have sales data on 249 suppliers (firms with mean employees of 1,260). In only 127 of the firms (51 percent) did the lead assembler buyer buy 50 percent or more of the supplier's output. In only 74 (30 percent) did it buy 70 percent or more.

To be sure, the smaller firms tend to diversify less than the larger. Bear in mind, however, that these smaller firms produce a relatively minor fraction of the industry output: firms with less than ¥10 billion in sales constituted the smallest 40 percent of the firms but produced less than 7 percent of the industry total. And even these smaller firms still diversify: only a quarter of these smaller firms sold all their output to one firm, and over half sold to three or more.

Relational Stability

The suppliers also maintain less stable relations than often claimed. Second- and third-tier firms are particularly prone to shift their business partners. Frequently they are family firms. Like family firms everywhere, they come and go as the talents and interests of family members ebb and flow in generational cycles. Yet even first-tier contractors shift their ties. In 1998, Toyota had 189 suppliers in its supplier association. Of these, only 122 (65 percent) had been members in 1973. Of the 150 firms in the association in 1973, 28 (19 percent) had disappeared by 1998.

To the extent that the relations continue, they continue only because the firms involved do their jobs better than their potential rivals. The firms involved understand this. As one Toyota director explained, "our policy of maintaining double- and multiple-sources is not an opportunistic one. It follows from the notion that a reasonable level of competition is good. We're all human, after all. It's through competition that we'll get improvements in quality, in price, in managerial coordination" (Matsuo 1973, 138–39). Only by winning the perpetual tournament do the suppliers maintain—much less expand—their business with any given assembler.

Take one stamp press firm in the Toyota network. It sold a variety of stamped and plastic products to Toyota, and had for years. But it did not wait for Toyota to place orders. At its own cost, on its own initiative, and with no explicit or implicit commitment from Toyota, it regularly and aggressively explored new technologies. When it found something it thought Toyota might want, it proposed it. If Toyota liked the idea, it obtained a contract. If Toyota did not, it went back to the lab.

Board Seats

Assemblers maintain fewer representatives on supplier boards than observers typically assert. Only exceptionally do assemblers put their people on those boards. We have information on the board composition of 209 firms among Japanese automobile parts suppliers. In 132 of these firms (63 percent) the assemblers had no board representative. When an assembler did have a board member, it most commonly had only one (26 firms, or 12 percent). At only 27 of the suppliers (13 percent) did the principal buyer among the automobile assemblers have five to nine board members, and at only five (2 percent) did it have ten or more.

CONCLUSIONS

The keiretsu? What keiretsu? Observers typically couple descriptions of cryptically unnamed lunch meetings for a couple of dozen company presidents with data on nearly a hundred firms, grouped by loans. They then suggest that the idiosyncratically Japanese organizations shape and pervade (or shaped and pervaded) the Japanese economy. In fact, they do neither, for a simple reason: there are no keiretsu and never were. As central as they are to the academic imagination, in the Japanese economy itself they do not exist and never did.

What this leaves, of course, is the etymological question: What caused this profoundly embarrassing intellectual disaster? From where could so central, so widely shared, so pervasively repeated—yet so fundamentally vacuous—a myth have come? To this question, we turn in the following chapter.

CHAPTER THREE

And of the Zaibatsu

There are no keiretsu and never were. The central "fact" by which we understand the Japanese economy is not a fact at all. It is a story, no more and no less. It is not that we academics have exaggerated the significance of the keiretsu. It is not that their boundaries are more ambiguous than we have thought. It is not that they no longer have the importance they once did. It is that they do not exist and never did.

The stories we recount about the keiretsu tell us nothing about the Japanese economy, but they do tell us about ourselves. They reveal aspects of the world we wish we inhabited. They reveal the people with whom we battle within the universities. And they reveal the way we academics work.

Because we academics invented the keiretsu as the unrepentant children of the pre–World War II zaibatsu conglomerates, to understand why they took the shape they did we need first to understand those zaibatsu. Yes, Virginia, there were the zaibatsu, but they were not the groups academics claim. We thus begin by explaining what the zaibatsu actually were and how they acquired their intellectual prominence. We then trace the ties between the zaibatsu and the fable of the keiretsu, and discuss what the fable tells us about ourselves.

THE ZAIBATSU

The Story

Just as the fable of the keiretsu captures so much of what we collectively think we know about the post–World War II Japanese economy, the stories about the zaibatsu capture what we think we know about the pre-war economy. Four families (the Mitsui, the Iwasaki of the Mitsubishi empire, the Sumitomo, and the Yasuda), the story goes, wheeled, dealed, and bribed their way to government largesse. Through that largesse, they built powerful banks.

But the families did not stop with banks. Instead, scholars continue, the families used their banks to build massive industrial empires. In pre-war Japan, they explain, firms could not raise capital through the stock and bond markets because the markets did not work. Instead, an industrial firm that wanted to grow had to borrow from a bank. To find a major bank, however, such a firm could turn only to one of those families, and the families would lend only at disadvantageous rates. Essentially, the families used the banks to route national savings to their private firms at preferential rates. The zaibatsu empires ensued.

Such is the story in brief. From time to time, scholars add assorted groups like the Hitachi and Nissan, but the basic story they tell revolves around banks: zaibatsu firms could borrow; nonzaibatsu firms borrowed only at the sufferance of zaibatsu banks; and no firm anywhere raised substantial funds in any other way. Through their lock on finance, the zaibatsu families built themselves the powerful empires that dominated pre-war Japan.

The Standard Accounts

These accounts are easy enough to find. In his vintage economic history, William Lockwood (1954, 222) describes pre-war Japan as a place where "big banks and trust companies were securely locked into" zaibatsu conglomerates. These "financial institutions of Japan, concentrated as they were in the hands of the government and big business, were the major source of capital for modern industry." After all, "banking connections were especially important in a country where a wide public securities market was lacking."

Vintage the account may be, but it differs little from most current ones. Like Lockwood, many modern scholars begin by denying that pre-war Japanese securities markets amounted to much. Take Berkeley business school professor and keiretsu authority Michael Gerlach (1992, 116). Banks "provided, through loans, over half of Japanese companies' total external capital" during the pre-war period, claims he. Harvard business scholar Carl Kester (1991, 37) flatly declares that "late nineteenth- and early twentieth-century Japan had essentially no securities market."

After denying that securities markets worked, scholars turn to the za-ibatsu banks. In doing so, they turn to a legend with a pedigree reaching back to Edwin Reischauer, Harvard historian and easily the most popular U.S. ambassador to Japan ever (1978, 181). Each of the zaibatsu, writes Reischauer, was "centered around its own bank, which financed the other component parts." Harvard and University of Tokyo economists Richard Caves and Masu Uekusa (1976b, 60)—key scholars in the keiretsu myth— argue that for the zaibatsu the "banks and financial intermediaries were principal suppliers of capital to the operating companies." Business scholar Rodney Clark (1979, 42) explains the logic more fully: "Each *zaibatsu* had a bank, which acted as a money pump. Deposits from the public were channeled toward the other member companies of the group."

Through these internal financing practices, the zaibatsu extended their power. Lockwood (1954, 222) describes zaibatsu credit as a "most important... instrument of expansion." Zaibatsu banks "held the deposits of affiliated companies... and were at the same time their chief source of capital. They were also powerful instruments for extending control over competitors, customers, and suppliers." Eleanor Hadley (1970, 29; see also 2003, 7–75) (who had herself spent time working in the postwar Occupation) contends that "financing (pre-1945 style) was done mainly on an intracombine basis." She then uses the Mitsui to illustrate how this purportedly helped the zaibatsu dominate the economy. "Although [Mitsui] Banking certainly did not confine extension of credit to the combine alone," she asserts, "combine interests naturally came first. More than this, Banking gave combine firms preferential interest terms and was slow to extend credit to outsiders who challenged or might challenge an important subsidiary in a particular field."

In her recent economic history of Japan, Penelope Francks (1999, 250–51) nicely summarizes it all:

> Companies within each *zaibatsu* group depended on finance from the group's bank.... [C]ontrol over sources of finance was in many ways the key to *zaibatsu* organisation and to the ability of group companies to expand in capital-intensive areas. The growth of share-ownership among the wider public was very limited and the role of the stock exchange as a source of business capital has remained relatively small until quite recent times.... [As a result, the] system made it extremely difficult for businesses outside *zaibatsu* control to obtain investment funds on anything like the same terms as those within and inhibited the spread of capital ownership outside the groups.

The Pre-War Japanese Economy

The logic is clear enough: pre-war firms relied crucially on bank loans; the zaibatsu controlled the key large banks; through those banks they funneled money to their favored firms; and through those preferential credit policies, they extended their grasp over the pre-war Japanese economy.

Unfortunately, the story is not true. Large firms simply did not rely on banks for their working capital. Instead, for the bulk of their funds they issued stock. Secondarily, they sold bonds and retained their earnings. Banks, by contrast, played only a minor role in financing substantial firms. Because accounting data for the economy as a whole do not exist, consider

Table 3.1. Cross-sectional capitalization measures: Mean capitalization of firms, 1897

	Food	Chemicals	Bricks	Cement	Metals	Machines
Paid-in capital (%)	64.6	71.1	71.8	53.1	72.5	66.3
Retained earnings (%)	15.6	5.3	14.9	18.4	7.3	7.3
Bonds (%)	3.4	0.0	0.0	10.3	0.0	0.0
Bank debt (%)	5.2	1.8	9.7	4.5	13.2	2.6
Other debt (%)	11.3	21.7	3.7	13.8	7.1	23.8
No. of firms	15	7	8	4	5	5
Mean assets ($\times 1{,}000$ yen)	196.7	206.5	57.9	340.4	253.5	596.3

Source: Imuta 1976, 138.

Note: Sample construction is described in the text.

several distinct perspectives: large-firm balance sheets across several industries; flow-of-funds data for big firms in several industries; the size of the securities markets; and finance data for all firms (whether large or small) in the textile, railroad, and electrical utility industries.

Balance Sheets

For funds, large firms relied overwhelmingly on stock issues. Consider Toshimitsu Imuta's (1976) study of 44 firms in six industries. Imuta first identified those 187 firms that published their balance sheets in the Osaka *Asahi* newspaper between January and June 1898. He then excluded textile (51 firms), railroad (27 firms), and trade firms (21 firms). Of the remaining 88 firms, he chose 44 that were in industries with data on multiple firms. Independent of Imuta, we report the financing patterns of textile and railroad firms as follows.

Table 3.1 summarizes the results: at the turn of the century, banks seldom mattered. Instead, the firms raised 53–73 percent of their funds through stock issues and another 5–18 percent through retained earnings. They raised 0–11 percent through bond issues and only 1–13 percent from banks. As we note later, cotton textile firms in 1898 raised 58 percent of their funds through stock issues, 10 percent through retained earnings, 5 percent through bond issues, and 11 percent through bank loans; railroad companies in 1898 raised 92 percent through stocks, 2 percent through retained earnings, 6 percent through bonds, and 1 percent through bank loans.

Independently, we collected balance sheet data on the largest Japanese firms in the 1920s and 1930s. This allowed us both to avoid the bias introduced by Imuta's decision to examine firms advertising their financials and to ask whether this reliance on equity continued into the twentieth century. We began by replicating Shoichi Asajima's (1995) study of corporate flow of funds. Asajima collected information on how large firms funded their

Table 3.2. Cross-sectional capitalization measures: Mean ratios of bank debt to assets and to total capital, 1919–1941 (percentage)

	1919		1926		1931		1936		1941	
	BD/A	BD/TC	BD/A	BD/TC	BD/A	BD/TC	BD/A	BD/TC	BD/A	BD/TC
Food and paper	6.18	8.51	7.50	12.70	12.63	51.90	4.78	8.23	5.64	8.38
Chemicals	4.75	7.06	4.70	6.97	6.99	16.89	2.12	4.12	14.29	25.22
Steel machinery	4.17	8.68	11.98	60.95	12.46	27.40	4.94	7.30	12.98	33.96
Mining	2.17	3.03	4.07	5.12	7.53	11.43	8.27	10.20	14.22	29.78
Sugar	0.19	0.30	1.75	4.93	8.12	27.54	7.98	20.64	1.64	3.73
No. of firms	57		61		52		67		104	

Sources: Osakaya shoten, various years.

Notes: BD/A, bank debt (*shakunyukin*)/assets (*so shisan*); BD/TC, bank debt/total capital. For total capital, we sum legal capital (calculated at par value), reserves, carryforwards, and current profits. These are the largest firms; the size cutoffs are given in the text.

projects during four periods, 1911–19, 1919–26, 1926–31, and 1931–36. He defined "large" as all firms appearing in a prominent corporate yearbook and identified as having capital of at least ¥1 million in 1911, ¥5 million in 1919, or ¥10 million in 1926, 1931, or 1936.

We assembled data on five of Asajima's industries (unfortunately, these do not track Imuta's industry categories): textiles, mining, food and paper, chemicals, steel machinery, and sugar. Like Asajima, we used 1919, 1926, 1931, and 1936. We then added those firms in 1941 with capital of ¥20 million or more.

In table 3.2 we report the mean ratio of bank debt to gross assets for these firms, catalogued by industry and by date. For most industries and years, the ratio ranges from 2 to 8 percent. Of the twenty-five cells in table 3.2, in only six is the ratio over 10 percent, and in none is it over 20 percent. We follow that ratio with the ratio of bank debt to total capital (legal capital plus reserves, carryforwards, and current profits). The number is larger, given that gross assets usually exceed total capital. Other than the few cells having firms with large losses and very small capital values, the ratios remain small.

Fundamentally, pre-war Japanese bankers saw themselves as specializing in short-term loans and transactional services. They did not see their banks as investing in firms long term. As the war intensified, the government increasingly pushed them to make those long-term loans to war-related firms, but it was a push they resisted when they could. When Sumitomo CEO Masatsune Ogura became Minister of Finance in 1941, he promptly assembled the leading bankers to discuss what would become the new corporate finance program. As he outlined it, the government would now require

Table 3.3. Source of additional funds, 1911–1936

	1911–19	1919–26	1926–31	1931–36
Equity (%)	34.4	48.8	39.4	53.6
Earnings (%)	33.4	4.8	−2.0	28.6
Bonds issues (%)	4.5	26.4	44.1	9.1
Bank loans (%)	4.6	6.4	14.6	−1.7
Trade credit (%)	6.3	11.4	−3.6	−2.6
Other loans (%)	16.9	2.2	7.5	13.3
Total net increase (in million yen)	2,292	4,394	2,601	2,676
No. of firms	123	111	134	155

Source: Calculated from data found in Asajima 1995, 235–38.

Notes: The first six lines give the percentage of the net increase in funding over the period accounted for by a given source. The seventh line gives the total net increase in funding for the firms, in million yen.

banks to supply funds long term to the favored firms. Banks have "generally maintained lending practices directed toward commercial finance," he noted (Nihon ginko 1971, 31:480). "No longer." Henceforth, they would need to change "the methods they have traditionally used."

Flow of Funds

If corporate balance sheets show no evidence that big Japanese firms relied on bank debt, consider flow-of-funds measures—the question of where large firms turned for any new funds they needed. Toward that end, we use Asajima's study of the largest firms. Using the size cutoffs described earlier, Asajima obtained a cohort of 123 firms for 1911–19, 111 for 1919–26, 134 for 1926–31, and 155 for 1931–36.

As table 3.3 shows, the big firms seldom borrowed the extra money they needed from banks. Instead, they relied on equity. When they needed additional funds, for 35 to 55 percent of the amount they sold stock. For more modest amounts, they accumulated earnings and sold bonds. Even during the Japanese recession of the 1920s, they turned to banks for only 14.6 percent of any extra funds they needed.

Exchanges

The turn-of-the-century Tokyo and Osaka stock exchanges were thriving institutions. Just as the industrialists were importing and adapting engineering technology, investors were doing the same in finance. The Tokyo Stock Exchange (TSE), founded in 1878, by 1900 listed the bonds of 7 firms and the shares of 113. Ten years later it listed 43 bonds and 142 stocks. By 1920, those numbers had climbed to 157 bonds and 569 stocks, and by 1925 to

492 bonds and 665 stocks. The Osaka Stock Exchange (OSE), similarly founded in 1878, by 1900 listed the bonds of 1 firm and the shares of 50. By 1920, it listed 8 bonds and 206 stocks, and by 1925 an unspecified number of bonds and the shares of 191 firms (Tokyo kabushiki 1928, table 1; Osaka kabushiki 1928, suppl., 35–186).

Individuals invested in these shares, and not just (or even primarily) individuals from the zaibatsu families. Kaichi Shimura studied investors with at least a thousand shares of stock in the 511 firms covered by a 1919 national investor registry. Through this, he created a database of 8,506 investors in 379 companies—firms responsible for 62 percent of the legal capital of all extant corporations.

Among these investors, banks held only 3.2 percent of the stock. By contrast, individuals held 76.2 percent, and nonbank firms held the rest. Zaibatsu families held only 2 percent of the stock. Of all firms nationally, from 1930 to 1940 banks held only 3.2–4.6 percent of the stock, and the large city banks (primarily zaibatsu banks) held only 1.3–2.4 percent (Shimura 1969, 386–90; Nihon ginko 1960).

These shareholders traded actively. During 1890, investors on the TSE contracted to sell 1.6 million shares. During 1900, they contracted for 3.7 million shares, in 1910 for 11.0 million, in 1920 for 37.5 million, and in 1925 for 59.8 million. On the OSE during 1890, investors contracted to sell 982,000 shares. During 1900, they contracted for 5.2 million shares, by 1920 for 22.3 million, and in 1925 for 13.0 million (Tokyo kabushiki 1928, table 3; Osaka kabushiki 1928, table 1).

Collectively, investors on the two exchanges traded stocks worth ¥512 million in 1900, ¥2.09 billion in 1910, ¥8.13 billion in 1920, and ¥4.13 billion in 1925. As a percentage of GDP, these figures amounted to 21.2 percent, 53.3 percent, 51.1 percent, and 25.4 percent, respectively. These numbers place the exchanges within the range of *modern* advanced economies: 1990 turnover/GDP ratios of 31.5 percent for the United States, 28.6 percent for the United Kingdom, 22.1 percent for Germany, and 12.4 percent for Canada (World Bank 2000, table 5.2).

Textiles
Both to give context to this data and to examine financing patterns at firms too small to appear in these samples, consider more comprehensive data on three important industries: cotton textiles, railroads, and electrical utilities. In the early 1900s, the Japanese cotton-spinning industry grew spectacularly fast. From ¥60 million in 1894 (in constant 1934–36 prices), production climbed to ¥167 million in 1904, ¥447 million in 1914, ¥657 million in 1924, and ¥1,104 million in 1934. By the 1920s the Japanese firms were using more raw cotton than their British competitors. Domestically, they

dominated the economy. During the 1930s, the cotton-spinning firms produced a quarter of all domestic manufactured goods and employed 40 percent of all factory workers (Fujino, Fujino, and Ono 1979, 246; Miwa and
Ramseyer 2000, 178).

The men who started these firms sold stock to a broad array of investors.
Although the investors often came from a few towns or cities (a point
that obviously facilitated trust), rarely did a single shareholder or group
of shareholders dominate the firm. Kazuo Yamaguchi (1968) studied the
60-odd spinning firms operating in 1898. On average, the firms had 331
shareholders. The largest investor held about 8 percent of the stock, the
largest 5 together held 24 percent, and the largest 10 held 33 percent. Only
11 percent of the firms (7 firms) had fewer than 100 shareholders, while
52 percent (32 firms) had 300 shareholders or more. In no firm did the
largest shareholder hold 50 percent or more of the stock, and in only 3
firms did a single shareholder hold 20 percent of the stock or more.

In general, spinning firms in 1898 raised 58 percent of their funds through
stock issues, another 10 through earnings, and 5 through bonds. Only 11
percent of their funds did they borrow from banks. Although the largest
half of the firms raised the least from the banks (9–10 percent for the 27
firms with 10,000 or more spindles), even the smaller firms raised less than
20 percent from banks.

Railroads

By 1869, U.S. entrepreneurs were running trains across the North American
continent. They also brought tales of these machines to Japan. Hearing their
accounts, the new Japanese government responded eagerly. After some initial
missteps it ran tracks from Tokyo to Yokohama (eighteen miles). By 1874
it had finished the line from Osaka to Kobe, and the Tokyo–Yokohama
line carried 1.6 million passengers a year (Ramseyer and Rosenbluth 1995,
chap. 9).

In 1883, private entrepreneurs began running trains too. As they did,
the focus in the industry increasingly shifted from the national railway to
the private. In 1890, the national government owned 550 miles of track,
while private firms owned 1,165 miles. By 1900, the government owned
1,059 miles and private firms 2,966, and by 1905 the government owned
1,531 miles to the private firms' 3,251. In 1906, by fiat the government
nationalized 2,823 miles of private track. By then, the various railroads
constituted some 14 percent of all domestic investment (Minami 1965, 6).

From the outset, the railroads (they were much larger than the spinning
firms) relied on stock issues. Within a year of starting operations, the first
private railroad listed its stock on the Tokyo Stock Exchange. In 1886 another firm listed its stock; in 1887, 2 more; in 1888, 3 more; and in 1889

another 3. During the 1890s, 23 additional railroad firms listed their stock, and through 1905 another 14. On the Osaka Stock Exchange, 8 railroads listed their stocks during the 1880s, and another 26 during the 1890s (Tokyo kabushiki 1928; Imuta 1976, 18).

Even more than the cotton-spinning companies, the railroads sold their stock to a wide swath of investors. During the 1890s the mean number of shareholders per railroad ranged from 600 to 1,100. Toshimitsu Imuta (1976) studied shareholder lists at three of the railroads and found that from these stockholders the railroads raised virtually 85–100 percent of their funds. What else they needed they obtained by selling bonds. From banks, they raised only 0–3 percent.

Electrical Utilities

Like textiles and railroads, electrical power was a growth business in pre-war Japan. The first commercial electrical power plant began operations in Great Britain in 1882. The first in Japan began in 1887, and from there the industry boomed. From 1 percent of gross national investment at the turn of the century, the industry grew to 9 percent of GNI within two decades. From 1910 to 1920, consumption of electrical power in Japan rose from 523 kilowatt-hours to 3,795. By 1930 it stood at 12,618 (Minami 1965, 6, table 14; Kikkawa 1995, 28).

Although per capita consumption of electrical power lagged that of the United States, among manufacturing firms the pace of electrification tracked the U.S. pace. From 1910 to 1920, the percentage (by horsepower) of electrically powered machines in Japan rose from 20 percent to 61 percent, and over the next decade to 81 percent. In the United States, the percentage of electrically powered machines rose from 25.4 percent (1909) to 55.0 percent (1919) to 82 percent (1929).[1]

During most of this period, the Japanese electrical utility industry remained both competitive and unregulated. So competitive was it that of the 39 firms listed in a prominent stock directory for 1911 and 1918, barely 15 were still in business in 1924. Only during the 1930s did the situation change: in 1932 the firms formed a cartel to stop price competition, and in 1939 the government began regulating them (Kikkawa 1995, 8, tables 1.11 and 1.16; Minami 1965, 4).

Like the spinning and railroad firms, the electrical utilities (closer in size to the spinning than the railroad firms) relied on stock and bond issues for their funds. From 1910 to 1935 the fraction of funds from stocks fell from 83 to 57 percent, while the fraction from bonds climbed from 4 to 32 percent. Bank debt, however, hovered in the 7–13 percent range. When firms needed extra money, they relied heavily on stock and bond issues. Generally, they obtained 60–80 percent of any additional funds from stock (although lower during 1925–30), and another 10–40 percent from bonds. From banks, they obtained less than a fifth.

Electrical utilities issued stock broadly. To explore shareholdings among the smaller firms as well as the larger, Takeo Kikkawa catalogued all 53 firms with relevant data for 1903. Only 5 of the firms had fewer than 30 shareholders, while 23 had 100 or more. Of the 130 firms with available data in 1911, only 22 had fewer than 30 shareholders and over half had 100 or more (Kikkawa 1995, table 1.6).

Zaibatsu Banks

Scholars in Japanese studies routinely argue that the zaibatsu families used their control over banks to manipulate capital market imperfections to their private advantage. Typically, they proceed in three steps. First, they argue that some firms had easier access to credit than others and that this access gave them a competitive advantage in the product market. Second, they claim that the large zaibatsu groups had the market power to manipulate the allocation of credit. Third, they assert that the zaibatsu used that power in the credit market to gain control over various product markets.

Debt and Firm Success

Again, the claims are not true: the most successful firms did not rely on bank debt, and the zaibatsu banks did not route funds to their group manufacturing firms. In more detailed work (Miwa and Ramseyer 2002a, 152, table 12), we assembled financial data on large firms in six key industries: steel machinery, chemicals, textiles, food and paper, mining, and sugar. Holding constant a variety of explanatory variables, we first asked whether a firm's leverage (both total leverage and bank debt/gross assets) is associated either with the performance of the firm's stock (measured by stock market capitalization/accounting equity) or with the firm's growth.

In none of our statistical tests is stock performance positively associated either with total leverage or with bank debt. Instead, in several tests it is associated negatively—the more a firm borrowed (either total debt or bank debt), the lower the market evaluation of its stock. Investors did not find debt advantageous. If anything, they valued most highly those firms that did not borrow.

In general, successful firms will both enjoy higher share prices and grow more rapidly than their competitors. As a result, if leverage and bank debt do not increase share prices, they should not increase growth rates either. They do not. Again holding constant a variety of other explanatory variables, we find that higher leverage and bank debt levels are not associated with faster growth rates. Simply put, the more highly leveraged firms and firms with higher levels of bank debt did not grow more rapidly than others.

Zaibatsu Affiliation and Success

But what of zaibatsu affiliation? Table for now the prime question—whether the groups gave their manufacturing firms a competitive edge by offering them preferential access to funds. Start instead with the preliminary inquiry—were the zaibatsu firms in fact more successful than their competitors?

Again using our data on pre-war firms, we ask whether—all else held equal—zaibatsu affiliation is associated with higher levels of market capitalization/equity. Unlike keiretsu affiliation, the zaibatsu rosters are relatively straightforward—the group firms are the firms with the highest direct or indirect family stock ownership. Holding constant the usual variables, we find that zaibatsu firms were indeed more successful: at various times before the war, but particularly in the late 1930s, several of the zaibatsu (Mitsui, Mitsubishi, Sumitomo, and other groups like Nissan) did indeed have higher stock prices or growth rates (Miwa and Ramseyer 2002a, 151–52, tables 11 and 12). Simply put, zaibatsu firms did outperform their rivals.

Zaibatsu Affiliation and Debt

Did the zaibatsu firms succeed because their affiliated banks routed them funds preferentially? No. Most obviously, as we noted earlier, the firms that borrowed heavily did not do well. The zaibatsu firms could not have succeeded because they borrowed, because the firms that succeeded were not the borrowing kind.

Second, zaibatsu firms did not borrow heavily anyway. Using our data set and holding constant a variety of financial variables, we ask whether zaibatsu firms borrowed more heavily than other firms. They did not. Instead, they borrowed less (Miwa and Ramseyer 2002a, 154, table 13).

Third, some of the most successful pre-war enterprises were enterprises without any affiliated banks at all. Take the Suzuki trading empire. A turn-of-the-century upstart, the Suzuki group grew with phenomenal speed. By 1917 its trading firm had sales of ¥1.5 billion to the Mitsui trading firm's ¥1.1–1.2 billion. By the mid-1920s, the group revolved around two trading firms that directly controlled 35 other firms and more indirectly another 30. All told, it controlled paid-in capital of ¥239 million compared to the Sumitomo zaibatsu's ¥188 million (Hashimoto 1992, 92–93; Takeda 1992, 274; 1995, 179–80; Takahashi 1930, 36). And all this it did without a bank.

Or take the Nissan group, generally called one of the "new zaibatsu." From modest turn-of-the-century mining roots, it too expanded quickly. By the mid-1930s it controlled paid-in capital of ¥470 million to the Sumitomo's ¥380 million. Again, it did this without a bank (Udagawa 1979, 204–6).

Last, directly contrary to the received wisdom, the zaibatsu banks tried to *limit* their loans to group firms. For example, from the central Mitsui firms, the Mitsui Bank took more than it lent. During 1923–34 (in semi-annual accounting periods), from its five key firms (the holding company and the trading, mining, trust, and life insurance companies) it obtained 5–16 percent of its entire deposit base. It then lent these firms substantially less. From 1923 to 1934, in only one six-month period (the second half of 1923) did it lend these firms more than they deposited. Even if we include the 17 next-tier Mitsui firms, the bank lent this group of 22 in 1939 (the only year on which we have data) only slightly more (112 percent) than the amount they collectively deposited (Mitsui ginko 1957, 387, 423; Asai 1977, 258).

Because the Mitsui Bank found it so hard to locate good borrowers, by policy it restricted the deposits it took. Rightly seen as safe, it faced during the 1920s a large influx of deposits from other banks. Had it wanted to route funds to affiliated firms, it would have welcomed the money. Instead, it actively discouraged it, first by cutting the interest it paid other banks and later by simply restricting new deposits (Asai 1977, 278–79).

Already in 1902 the Sumitomo Bank stipulated by contract that it would pay the Sumitomo holding company no higher an interest rate on its deposits than it paid anyone else and demanded that the company provide security for all loans above ¥300,000 . More informally, it declared that it would never lend the holding company more than 10 percent of its deposit base. Even during the boom years of World War I, it lent the company no more than 7 percent of its loans. From 1932 to 1939, it lent the holding company and its fourteen central affiliated firms only 1–9 percent of all loans, or 0.8–6 percent of all deposits (Sumitomo ginko 1979, 242–45, 357, 362; Sawai (1992, table 4.16).

Nor did the Mitsubishi bank lend its affiliated firms a large fraction of its loans. From 1926 to 1937, the holding company and eight central affiliated Mitsubishi firms borrowed (from all sources) a combined ¥19–76 million. For any given year, these amounts were equivalent only to 5–12 percent of all loans made by the Mitsubishi financial firms, or to 8–22 percent of all loans made by the Mitsubishi Bank (Asajima 1987, 152–53; Sawai 1992, table 4.16). According to internal company documents, the Mitsubishi life insurance company (Meiji seimei) loaned no funds at all to Mitsubishi-affiliated firms (Asajima 1987, 154).

We lack comparable data on the Yasuda zaibatsu, but the point is irrelevant. The Yasuda financial firms could not have routed substantial funds to affiliated industrial firms—for the group lacked the industrial firms to which to route. The group began and ended as primarily a financial group.

Zaibatsu Etymology

The Tie to SCAP Policy

Academics did not invent these tales of the zaibatsu. Instead, American academics borrowed them from the people in the Occupation (known as office of the Supreme Commander for the Allied Powers, or SCAP) assigned to destroy the zaibatsu families. A key figure among the academics in SCAP was Corwin Edwards, Northwestern University professor and former New Deal bureaucrat. As head of the zaibatsu committee (the Mission on Japanese Combines), Edwards wrote the report that would justify confiscating zaibatsu family wealth. He released the report in 1946 (Edwards 1946), and SCAP began dispossessing the families the next year.

Edwards understood his job: it was not to decide what to do about the zaibatsu but to justify destroying them. As his report forthrightly began (Edwards 1946, iii; ital. added), his "*assignment* was to *recommend* ... the basic objective of destroying the power of the great Japanese combines and managerial families which are collectively known as the zaibatsu."

As rigged as the assignment may have been, it was not one Edwards likely would have dreaded. As befitting a former New Dealer, he attacked large firms in his academic own writing for what he saw as their anticompetitive impact (1956). The zaibatsu he skewered with relish. The families had created, he asserted, an economy that "tends to hold down wages, to block the development of labor unions, [and] to destroy the basis for democratic independence in politics." They were, he concluded, "among the groups principally responsible for the war."

For an essay by an economist, the report was remarkably devoid of economic logic. For a report from a mission nominally charged with collecting data, it was equally devoid of new information. But if neither theoretically coherent nor empirically serious, it nonetheless set out what would become the orthodoxy for decades (Edwards 1946, 36): "bank credit has been the principal source of capital for Japanese industry. The older zaibatsu—the Mitsui, Mitsubishi, Sumitomo and Yasuda—have relied heavily for their growth upon their affiliated banks and insurance companies."

The argument was not one Edwards invented. Occupation bureaucrat—and occasional Soviet agent—T. A. Bisson had already begun writing about Japan before joining SCAP.[2] After the Occupation, he would explain that "under the old regime" in Japan, "privileged groups had exercised despotic power in every phase of economic life. Whether one looked at agriculture, labor, industry, banking, or trade, the picture was the same" (Bisson 1954, 3, 6). Given this semifeudal history, Japan could not have had—and had not had—a working economy. Instead, it "had almost no laissez-faire experience or tradition." The blame for Japanese economic problems lay in the zaibatsu, he explained, and the key to zaibatsu domination lay in their control over banks (Bisson 1945, vii):

> At the center of each of the economic empires controlled by Mitsui, Mitsubishi, Sumitomo, and Yasuda ... is a great bank with deposits running into billions of yen. From these four banks, with their associated or subsidiary trust, insurance and holding companies, radiates the corporate network which owns the factories, the mines, the shipping firms, and the commercial enterprises of Japan. Eight *Zaibatsu* concerns, together with the Emperor ... and some 3,500 big landlords, have held the country and its people as their economic fief.

Restating the Question

On its principal points, Edwards' report (along with the work of people like Bisson and Hadley) tracks the 1930s Japanese reformist literature. Against the zaibatsu these journalists and essayists had made much the same charges as Edwards. In doing so, like Edwards, like Bisson, like Hadley, and like most academics since, they had focused on the question of why the zaibatsu firms had succeeded. The zaibatsu had succeeded, they had claimed, by manipulating the government and the credit market. They had succeeded, in short, by cheating.

In asking why the zaibatsu had succeeded, however, Edwards and the reformers focused on the wrong issue. Fundamentally, the very question of why zaibatsu firms succeeded misstates the inquiry—and illustrates the familiar problem of hindsight bias. These firms did not succeed because they were zaibatsu firms. They were zaibatsu firms because they succeeded, and they succeeded for all the various reasons some firms succeed in competitive markets while others fail. More precisely, the reformists named these firms zaibatsu in the late 1920s because they happened to be making money for their owners at the time.

Put differently, the zaibatsu firms differed from other firms only after the fact. In the mid-nineteenth century many rich families resembled the Mitsui and Sumitomo. In the transition to the new Meiji government, most lost their fortunes. If they survived the transition, most lost their fortunes during the next two decades.

Scholars sometimes claim that the zaibatsu succeeded because of government patronage, but even this did not distinguish them at the outset. True, in the 1870s the Mitsui house provided the new national and prefectural governments with various exchequer and tax-collecting services, but so did the Ono and Shimada houses. In the 1920s the Mitsui and Mitsubishi bought politicians, but so did the Suzuki trading firm.

Even as late as the turn of the century, many firms resembled closely the ones that would become the zaibatsu. The Suzuki firm, for example, was rapidly amassing both financial wealth and political connections. The Konoike house had branched out of its sake-brewing and money-changing experience into shipping and financial services. By the early twentieth century, it boasted one of the most powerful banks in the country.

Hind-Sight Bias and Journalists

What distinguished the Mitsui, Mitsubishi, Sumitomo, and Yasuda from all these other groups was observable only after the fact: in the 1920s and 1930s they were doing well where the others were not. The Ono and Shimada did not survive the 1870s. The Suzuki did not survive the 1920s. The Konoike survived (merging its bank into what would become the Sanwa Bank), but with no panache. In the Japanese economy from 1870 to 1930, as in all competitive economies, many firms failed while some survived and a few thrived. What distinguished the Mitsui, Mitsubishi, Sumitomo, and Yasuda (as well as firms like Nissan) was that they were making their investors rich in the late 1920s, when muckraking journalists came looking for them.

The idea's etymology appears in the term itself. *Zaibatsu* is not a classical Japanese word. It is a word journalists invented as a variation on other pejorative epithets they were already using. In the late nineteenth century, military and political leaders sometimes showed regional loyalties. When they did, journalists and commentators called the resulting groups *hanbatsu*, "domainal factions." When military officers tried to manipulate the government, they decried the *gunbatsu* or "military factions." And when wealthy industrialists seemed to buy political influence, they coined a term for them too. *Zaibatsu*—or "wealth factions"—was the result.

At root, academics take (and SCAP officers took) the concept of zaibatsu too seriously. As used by its contemporaries, the idiomatic translation of *zaibatsu* was nothing so serious as "conglomerate," "corporate group," or even "financial clique." It was "robber baron." Although the term occasionally appears in the 1910s, it does not become widespread until populist journalists adopted it in the 1930s (Takeda 1995, 4). These writers had no analytic category in mind. Instead, they simply wanted a catchy pejorative term.

Catchy it was. But as it caught on, business leaders increasingly found their flexibility restricted by public and government pressure. Whether on the left or on the right but particularly on the right, zealots railed against what they saw as zaibatsu greed. The Blood Pledge Corps acted first, and in 1932 shot and killed both an ex-finance minister and the Mitsui CEO. Police found another Mitsui and three Mitsubishi executives on its hit list. Two months later, renegade military officers killed the prime minister and tried to bomb the Mitsubishi Bank. The zaibatsu leaders resisted the fascists at their peril, and by then they knew it.

Given this etymology, to ask why the zaibatsu succeeded is to invent a problem where none exists. In the second half of the nineteenth century, some would-be industrialists had wealth, some had drive, some had talent, and some had luck. The few with a combination of several of these qualities made money; many others lost it. Those who made it diversified their wealth into several industries and protected their investments by currying favor with politicians. When they did, journalists and commentators called them the *zaibatsu*.

THE INVENTION OF THE KEIRETSU

Absent a modern keiretsu to focus the mind, the zaibatsu would not attract the notice that they do. Absent their putative postwar offspring, they would find themselves a historical footnote, and to the American mind a foreign historical footnote at that. Let the keiretsu capture the essence of modern Japanese business, however, and the zaibatsu move to the fore. They become the more coherent and cohesive antecedents to modern Japan. Once the motley creation of muckraking journalists, they emerge transformed into the font of Japanese business organization. In truth, the zaibatsu do at least lie at the heart of the etymology of the keiretsu. After all, the fable of the former did beget the fable of the latter. The tale of how it did so begins in the 1940s and parallels the intellectual history of western Europe.

From the chaos of war in August 1945, the right emerged discredited and in disarray. The left seemed poised to dominate Japan. By 1947, a so-cialist became prime minister. Although his cabinet collapsed within a year, through the 1950s the left retained at least a plausible hope of recaptur-ing the government. Although it would not form a cabinet again until the 1990s, as in western Europe it dominated intellectual debate. The princi-pal newspapers followed the socialist line, the labor federation followed the socialist line, and communists and socialists vied for the urban vote. Few self-styled intellectuals admitted voting for the ruling conservative party, and by one standard joke even government bureaucrats talked socialist but voted conservative in secret.

Within university social science departments, Marxists ruled. The ex-tent of their domination varied, but at economics faculties they excluded market-oriented scholars when they could. At virtually all economics de-partments, they at least framed the debates. They framed a bizarre series of debates indeed. Take a few articles from a standard index of journal arti-cles in economics for first half of 1967: "Lenin's Concept of Imperialism," "Dehumanization in Marx's Concept of Class," "The Method of Monopoly Capitalism," "New Currents in the World of Soviet Economics," "A Study of 'The Capital Accumulation Process' in Part I Section 7 of *Das Kapital*," and "Lenin's Critique of Rosa Luxembourg's 'Theory of Capital Accumulation.'"

To the contemporary economic scene, Marxists brought a theoretically driven need to find within the "contradictions" of "bourgeois capitalism" the "domination" by "monopoly capital." In the 1930s they had identified that "monopoly capital" with the zaibatsu. By 1960 they were stuck. Although caught in the world of "bourgeois capitalism," they faced ruthlessly competitive markets. Their "monopoly capital," it seems, was no where to be found.

Enter the Economic Research Institute (ERI). To a shrewd entrepreneur, a Marxist market niche is as good as any other niche. If the Marxists could not find their "monopoly capital," well, the ERI would invent it for them. It would name the monopoly capital *keiretsu*, publish an annual membership roster called the *ROK*, and sell university libraries a pricey subscription.

To the Marxist-inclined, the ERI had a plausible story to tell. The war had largely bankrupted the zaibatsu, but the Americans, just to make sure, had confiscated (actually, bought on credit and then massively inflated the currency) the families' stock. They then banned the old trade names besides. The companies themselves they left mostly intact.

Once the Americans left in 1952, the government lifted the ban on the old names. Given the enormous reputational capital the firms had earlier invested in those names, they almost immediately retrieved them. Yet Marxist theory does not deal with reputational capital. It does deal with "monopoly capital." When the formerly zaibatsu firms retrieved their old names, the action signaled to a good leftist nothing so much as a resurgence of the monopoly capital that had so cruelly (they asserted) dominated Japan before.

From among these independently owned and operated former zaibatsu firms, the ERI picked the banks and insurance companies. In them and their borrowers it then located the firms that would dominate its bourgeois capitalist world. The keiretsu, it proclaimed in 1960 (*ROK* 1960, 3–4), were nothing other than "monopolistic organizations of giant firms... that constitute trusts and industrial-capital combines." They "have a bank at their apex, and pursue their domination of capital through loans and their consolidation of that domination through equity."

In short order, the keiretsu had been born.

THE DEMAND FOR THE KEIRETSU IN AMERICAN UNIVERSITIES

If Japanese Marxists supplied the fable of the keiretsu, Americans greedily consumed it. In the late 1980s, American business executives consumed it for the tactical advantage it gave them in trade talks. To win concessions

from their Japanese counterparts, their trade negotiators needed all the putative barriers they could find. For them, the keiretsu promised another trade
barrier with which to castigate the Japanese bureaucrats and then an item
to swap for concessions on other issues.

Academics greedily consumed the fable too. In the main, they were
not economists, for only a handful of Western economists could read the
Japanese accounts of the fable. If serious economists were a minority in
1960s Japan, Western economists with serious Japanese-language ability
were rarer still.

Given the shortage of Japanese-literate Western economists, Western
readers learned most of what they knew about Japanese business from academics in other disciplines. Most commonly, they read accounts by historians, sociologists, and political scientists. On the keiretsu they read these
scholars as well, and these scholars in turn followed the Japanese-language
literature. That, of course, was the ERI-based Marxist literature.

Parenthetically, note the obvious explanation for why Americans see U.S.
businesses as so different from Japanese businesses. When they read about
U.S. firms, only occasionally do Americans turn to sociologists. Usually
they read accounts by professional economists based on econometric studies. When they read about Japanese firms, though, they only rarely turn to
economists. Instead, they read elaborations on Japanese Marxist scholarship
by American historians, sociologists, and political scientists. *Of course* the
two groups of firms seem radically different. What else would one expect?

But return to keiretsu, for this disciplinary disjunction explains much
of the Western demand for the fable. In the late 1950s and early 1960s,
economists like Ronald Coase and Gary Becker began applying economic
theory (positing that people try rationally to maximize their utility) and
method (mathematical modeling and statistical analysis) to phenomena outside the traditional bounds of the discipline. As they did, scholars in the
adjacent disciplines started to see the attraction of the theory and method.
By the 1980s, younger scholars in those disciplines increasingly turned to
economics.

As non-economists adopted economic theory and method, their colleagues recoiled. At least at the business and law schools, scholars had
no theory of their own to abandon, and without an indigenous scholarly
tradition the advantages to economics were more obvious. Even so, the
resulting battles still pushed law school politics into the *New York Times*
more than once. In fields such as sociology and political science, scholars
could turn to economic theory only by jettisoning long and hoary disciplinary traditions. With the reified "communities" of sociological theory or
the "neo-corporatist" tradition in political science, the radically individualist economic theory simply did not fit. Necessarily, a young sociologist

or political scientist incorporated economic theory only by admitting the essential bankruptcy of his field.

Faced with this challenge from economics, committed sociologists and political scientists did not just roll over and die. Instead, they attacked. Given the universalism inherent in economic theory (the theory is not about cultural differences but about the essentially identical dynamic by which people everywhere respond to the world they experience), they attacked economics by looking for prominent counterexamples. Ideally they wanted examples of worlds that economic models did not fit.

For scholars on this anti-economic crusade, Japan provided the perfect example. By virtually all accounts in English, the Japanese economy ran by a radically different dynamic. Never mind the obvious reason (noted earlier) for this difference. If the Japanese economy seemed not to fit the individualism at the core of modern economics, so much the better.

Hence the demand for the keiretsu. As told by most sociologists and political scientists, the fable is a story about firms that run by a group rather than an individualist dynamic. It is a story about markets that do not clear. It is a story about businesses that do not compete as economic theory classically posits. In many accounts, it is even a story about people who do not maximize. Told appropriately, it is a story that proves economics wrong.

THE DEMAND FOR THE FABLE IN AMERICAN ECONOMICS DEPARTMENTS

Despite these fundamentally (and rabidly) anti-economic ends to which so many scholars put the fable of the keiretsu, a few economists welcomed this state of affairs—this odd division of labor, in which they relied on sophisticated financial studies for their accounts of Western markets but repeated bizarre tales told by sociologists, based on accounts by Marxists, for their descriptions of Japanese markets. We speculate here (and know we generate more than the usual hostility for doing so), but we suspect that at least some theorists welcomed the fable for the wealth of anecdotes it gave them on which to hang their theoretical models. The largest rewards in the discipline go to theoretical innovation, and theorists do find it hard to innovate about markets that clear at competitive prices.

Tell any tale about Japan and scholars will find a story practically begging for new theory. To the fable of the keiretsu, they responded enthusiastically. Year in and year out, they offered a shifting catalog of models making economic sense of the fable: some used the keiretsu to show the costs (Morck and Nakamura 1999a) or benefits (Hoshi, Kashyap, and Scharfstein 1991) of close bank–firm relationships; some used it to stress the place of social norms in economic interactions (Milhaupt 2001); some used it to illustrate the threat that "tunneling" and "private benefits of control" posed to capital markets (Morck and Nakamura 2003). No match made in heaven, F. M. Scherer once observed, produces more bliss than an economist who meets new facts to apply his model to.

If theorists welcomed the fable for the odd anecdotes it supplied, empiricists occasionally welcomed it for the sophisticated exercises it let them undertake. Because the groups supposedly derived from the late-nineteenth century zaibatsu affiliations, scholars could plausibly present the keiretsu rosters as "exogenous" to most any modern issue they might investigate (making it a nice "independent variable"). Because no one had any clear notion of what the groups do, they could plausibly use them to motivate most any (well, not quite—but a wide variety anyway) modern inquiry as well. And after all (cynicism knows no bounds), if they randomly assembled any twenty sets of variables, they should generate in at least one of them results significant at the 5 percent level.

Relation-Specific Investments

Of all the theoretical models scholars have hung on the keiretsu, few have been as central to economics as the work on relationship-specific investments (RSIs) detailed in the latter half of chapter 2. The work goes to the heart of market contracting, for at root the theory challenges our routine assumption that straightforward contracting produces something close to socially optimal arrangements.

The Theory

According to RSI theorists, the scope and size of RSIs directly affect the governance arrangements that firms choose. Whether business partners negotiate long-term contracts, spot contracts, equity investments, franchise arrangements, or even mergers—whether they negotiate any of these depends vitally on the RSIs at stake.

Crucially, investments specific to a relationship generate a return that the partners to the relationship can threaten to appropriate. In turn, as Scott Masten, James Meehan, Jr., and Edward Snyder (1991, 6) put it, that appropriability will increase the "resources expended attempting to negotiate a favorable distribution of the gains from trade." In the words of the scholars who pioneered the idea—Benjamin Klein, Robert Crawford, and Armen Alchian (1978, 298)—"after a specific investment is made and such [appropriable returns] are created, the possibility of opportunistic behavior is very real." To avoid the resulting problems, firms adopt governance arrangements (like mergers) that they would otherwise avoid. RSIs can potentially transform a competitive market exchange into a bilateral monopoly, in other words, and that transformation will call forth arrangements that otherwise would be superfluous at best (Williamson 1979, 241–42).

Appealing as the theory is, to date it has been a theory without data. As hard as scholars have looked for evidence to support the theory, largely they have come up dry. To be sure, they find some evidence of the posited connection between RSIs and governance in idiosyncratic industries such as aerospace or defense (Crocker and Reynolds 1993; Masten 1984). They find some evidence in site-specific investments when a firm like a public utility builds a generating plant next to a coal mine (e.g., Joskow 1985, 1987, 1988). In more ordinary industries and ordinary circumstances, they find virtually none.

Japan

In this empirical vacuum, the Japanese keiretsu have stood as a glaring exception—an important example of RSI-driven extracontractual governance arrangements (like cross-shareholding) in an "ordinary" industry (like automobile manufacturing). Does not Toyota buy its parts from hundreds of small firms? Are these firms not located near Toyota? Do they not sell the bulk of their output to Toyota? And does not Toyota own significant shares of their stock?

The answer to all these questions is yes, sort of—as chapter 2 should have made clear. Toyota does buy parts from many firms, and they in turn do buy from many others. But most of these firms invest no substantial funds in any equipment specific to making parts for Toyota. The firms do locate near Toyota, but Japan is small and these firms make parts they can easily and cheaply ship elsewhere. At the smaller firms, even the factory itself they could cheaply ship, as it comprises no more than a few pieces of industrial equipment in a large shed. The firms do sell most of their output to Toyota—now. But many began by selling products elsewhere and could readily switch to selling elsewhere again. And Toyota did buy some stock in some suppliers, but not in all, not in the smaller firms, and—according to the company histories—usually only in response to a cash crunch at the supplier.

Some commentators (Gilson and Roe 1993) have gone so far as to extend aspects of RSI theory to the larger "horizontal" keiretsu. Yet if the theory does not fit the vertical keiretsu, even less does it fit the horizontal. Fundamentally, the industrial firms in the horizontal keiretsu neither deal with each other nor own any substantial stakes in each other.

At root, RSI theory does not fit Japan. Most likely, it does not fit many major capital transactions anywhere. Where courts work well, parties to a deal can rely on contract. Where parties are long-lived, they can rely on reputational sanctions. And in countries like the United States and Japan, parties can—and do—rely on both. And when they can rely on both, they simply do not need the more complex governance arrangements that RSI theory posits.

CONCLUSIONS

Contrary to the financial press, the postwar keiretsu are not losing economic power, for they had no power to lose. Never cohesive, they are not unraveling. Never significant, they are not in demise. Not so, the pre-war zaibatsu. They did exist, they were cohesive, they could act collectively, and they did make money. ·

The zaibatsu did not make the money they did because they manipulated either the government or the capital markets. Although they did try to buy politicians, so did many other firms. For that matter, so do many U.S. and Japanese firms today. They could not have made money by using their market power over capital, for they had no market power to use. The capital markets were simply too competitive.

Instead, the zaibatsu succeeded for all the usual reasons that some firms succeed in competitive markets while others fail and most merely survive. They did not succeed because of some attribute they had as zaibatsu. Rather, they became known as the zaibatsu because they happened to be making money when muckraking journalists and essayists started searching for villains.

By contrast, from the start the keiretsu existed only because we collectively willed them to exist. From the start they were creatures of the academic and journalistic imagination. As committed Marxists, Japanese journalists and economists in the 1960s faced a quandary. According to their theory, "monopoly capital" should have been "dominating" the "bourgeois capitalist" world in which they found themselves. Yet look around—that monopoly capital was nowhere to be found.

For them, the ERI created the keiretsu. As we explain in chapter 2, it grouped the biggest financial institutions by their pre-war affiliation and summed the loans they made to listed firms. If the total at any firm exceeded the amount it borrowed from the next largest source, the ERI called it a keiretsu member and defined it into one of its monopoly capital empires. To university libraries it then sold the annual rosters at what, by the early 2000s, had become $400 a pop.

The Marxists are mostly gone now, but the mischief they do lives after them. Specialists on Japan use the fable of the keiretsu as evidence of culture-specific group behavior, the "socially embedded" nature of commercial transactions, and the inapplicability of economic theory to vast portions of the world. Theorists in economics use it for evidence of the effect of relationship banking on information asymmetries, of the importance of social norms in economics, of "tunneling" in capital markets, and of the importance of RSIs on governance structures.

The result has been a motley econometric corpus. Predictably (again as we showed in chapter 2), some of the significant results depend on misspecified equations, some on outlying data points, some on one roster rather than another, some on one period rather than another. When we try to replicate the results, we largely obtain insignificant results. By standard economic theory, that is exactly the right result: if a variable captures nothing of substance, statistical analysis should yield insignificant results. And insignificant results are what the data yield.

There is a lesson here, and it goes to the importance of knowing one's sources. A glance at how the ERI collected the keiretsu rosters and any economist would have known there was no "there" there. Yet the fable of the keiretsu persists, of course. Like the best urban legends, it persists because we wish it to persist. No one knows better how to wish than young university professors—and my, how they do wish (Kensy 2001, 254):

> The Keiretsu, *per se*, is only discernible via its diverse subgroups and sub-subgroups, each of which uses minor structural correlations to convey sense and meaning to outsiders. This deconcentrated market force is created and co-ordinated by means of a kind of autopoeticism, self-referentially and without direct causal relationship to a universal, hierarchic, superior "concern." Its coordination and combination is effected more by means of informal, local, and contingently-changing partial forces and the latent strength (characterized by the vagueness tolerated by dissent) provided by superior symbols, values, and visions.

Right. It was, as W. S. Gilbert would have put it, the very model of a modern major metaphor.

CHAPTER FOUR

The Myth of the Main Bank

Somewhere along the frozen Himalayas, Frank Capra crashed the British expatriates in their twin-prop plane. They crawled from the fuselage. Stumbling through the blizzard, they crossed the lost horizon and discovered a land where no one died. Stripped of lust and greed, everyone lived forever.

"The Japanese system's fabulous," a Chinese scholar in the early 1990s assured Miwa. "You've got a system where no firm ever fails. Instead, whenever one gets into trouble, its main bank—you know, that bank at the center of its keiretsu—steps in. It then restructures the firm, and takes it back to economic health."

The Chinese scholar did not learn this in Beijing. He learned it as a graduate student along the banks of the Charles River. The immortality that the southern Californians of the 1930s saw along the snowy border of south China, the Cantabridgeans of the 1990s apparently saw in 1990s Japan. And New Yorkers too. "When all else fails, the *keiretsu* saves the day," *Business Week* assured its readers in the early 1990s (Treece and Miller 1992). GM faced hard times, and its reporters wondered how such a firm would have fared in Japan. "If GM were indeed GM K.K., 'it wouldn't have reached this stage, because of the *keiretsu*,'" they quoted a Stanford scholar to conclude. "'Banks are so involved in management that they can see far ahead of the situation' and take action early on."

No one says that—or anything like it—about Japanese banks today, of course. But institutions that seem barren in the early twenty-first century could pass as bliss in 1990. Of course as time passed, several of Capra's passengers increasingly thought eternal life less than eternal bliss too. Yet if Americans have changed how they gauge the Japanese banking relationship, they have not changed how they describe it. Instead, they continue to place the putative "main bank system" front and center. And if those banks do not currently save Japanese firms, they conclude that the main banks *no longer* save them. Banks *used to* save firms, they explain, but "the system" has unraveled.

The story starts with a bank. Every large Japanese firm has a long-term relationship with a leading bank, begin American (and U.S.-educated Chinese) observers. Call it the firm's "main bank," that bank maintains (or at least maintained, until the depression of the 1990s) a set of implicit contracts with the firm. Under that implicit deal, it agrees to monitor the firm. It promises not just to monitor for itself but to monitor on behalf of other creditors. It agrees to intervene in governance when appropriate. As necessary, it agrees to loan extra funds, to subordinate its claims to those of other creditors, and to send in experts to save the day (think high-IQ SWAT teams of men in black—bankers who parachute in to rescue car companies and detergent makers).

As one pair of scholars (Miyashita and Russell 1994, 43) captured it:

> A main bank in Japan does much more than simply make loans. It is also the central clearinghouse for information about group companies and the coordinator for group activities. It monitors the performance of its group, holds equity in most of the major companies, and provides management assistance when it deems necessary. In the worst case, if one of the group firms is in serious trouble, the main bank is expected to step in with both financial assistance and a whole new management team selected from among the bank's executives.

"Suspension of disbelief," they call it in the humanities. At least until the curtain falls, Capra can make us believe in eternal life. Tolkien makes us believe in short, furry humanoids and Rowling in quidditch games and triple-headed guard dogs.

And so the "experts" on Japan. One might have thought bankers would avoid troubled borrowers when they could. Not so, the experts reply. One might have thought troubled borrowers would fool their banks when they could, that banks would try to fool each other, that banks that discovered troubled clients would ditch the clients and leave their rivals holding the bag. Why else, after all, demand security interests for loans or negotiate elaborate priority for claims in bankruptcy?

Never mind "why else," the experts tell us. The main bank knows its role. Should a firm have trouble paying its debt, the main bank ignores its own legal rights and reaches out to help. After all, explains sociologist Ronald Dore (1987, 94, 109), this is Confucian Japan. There, people "start[] from the premise of original virtue" and maintain a "'multi-umbrella system' of cooperative support and risk-sharing." There, business executives know their place. There, the main bank rescues because people expect it to rescue. It does not rescue to make money. Instead, as Dore (2000, 34) puts it, it shoulders the "highly loss-making" obligation "less for profit than from obligation."

Would that we could all live in such a world. But then, would that we could all live forever. Eventually, novels end and movies stop. Tibetan peasants die, hobbits vanish, and broomsticks—well, broomsticks sweep up dirt. If the tales of the main bank seem too good to be true, they are. Like the tale of the keiretsu, they are urban legends all. Professors and American reporters do not recite the stories because they are true, for they are not. They recite them because they so badly wish they were true.

Firms do not fail in contemporary Japan because the "system" that would have rescued them in the past has collapsed. They fail because no such "system" ever existed. Like bankers everywhere else, Japanese bankers avoided potentially troubled firms when they could. They pulled their loans when they could not. They never trusted their rivals to monitor on their behalf. They never drafted legal protections they intended to abandon.

And the high-IQ SWAT teams? Bankers did not restructure troubled manufacturing firms. After all, they were bankers. They would not have known how.

We begin by summarizing the accounts of Japanese "main banks" and the "implicit main bank contract." We then describe several examples of the way banks deal with troubled firms. We test main bank theory both against data from all firms listed on section 1 of the Tokyo Stock Exchange in the 1980s and early 1990s and against data on more severely troubled firms from the late 1970s and early 1980s. We conclude by speculating about the role bankers did play in the Japanese economy.

THE MYTH OF THE MAIN BANK

As just noted, according to modern observers most Japanese firms maintain a long-term relationship with one bank. That bank, called its main bank, monitors the firm. This main bank intervenes in the firm's governance through board appointments. It monitors not just on its own behalf but implicitly on behalf of the firm's other creditors. And should the firm fall into distress, the main bank implicitly agrees to subordinate its legal claims, to guarantee the firm's debt to other creditors, to lend whatever funds the firm needs, and to send in experts to remake the firm as necessary.

For scholars in the nascent field of "relationship banking," this arrangement makes Japan something of a godsend. The main bank system, writes Columbia economist Hugh Patrick (1994, 359), constitutes nothing less than "the epitome of relationship banking." Such "a long-term relationship between a firm and a particular bank from which the firm obtains its largest share of borrowings," contends Stanford economist Masahiko Aoki and his coauthors (Aoki, Patrick, and Sheard 1994, 3; Aoki and Dinc 2000, 19), captures the essence of "relational contracting between banks and firms."

Yet by basic logic, the terms of the arrangement should trouble. A bank that commits itself to rescuing defaulting borrowers would attract the highest-risk firms. As a result, banks would seem to do best if they refused ever to become a main bank. A bank that sends good money after bad usually loses both. As a result, banks that did agree to rescue troubled firms would seem to face incentives to renege after the fact. A bank can often avoid disaster by pulling its loans at the first sign of trouble. As a result, banks would seldom want to promise to monitor "on behalf" of their rival banks—and those rivals would not trust them if they did. Given all these problems, if firms and banks did negotiate these terms, one would think they at least would do what insurance companies do with their own obligations: draft fine-print contracts about each.

Yet banks and firms draft none. Indeed, according to main bank scholars, banks and firms do not just leave the "main bank contract" unwritten. They leave it unspoken to boot. In the language of the literature, they negotiate their terms "implicitly"—and to say that they negotiate them implicitly, of course, is to say that they negotiate them not at all.

Make no mistake: not only do banks and firms never negotiate legally enforceable main bank contracts, but they never even designate a main bank. Our "Japan experts" do not claim that banks and firms leave the details to these "main bank contracts" unspecified. Ambiguous contracts are still explicit, and Japanese courts regularly interpret and enforce them. Neither do they claim banks and firms leave these contracts unwritten. Oral contracts are explicit too, and Japanese courts regularly referee swearing contests over who said what to whom. Instead, our experts claim that firms and banks never mention the arrangements to each other, elaborately negotiate explicit contractual terms to the contrary, and then ignore the explicit terms and comply with the unnegotiated, unwritten, unspoken arrangements.

Faced with why Japanese firms would rely on unarticulated assumptions in such a high-stakes, conflict-ridden environment, Aoki (2000) claims that banks comply with the unspoken terms because government bureaucrats make them comply. The Ministry of Finance manipulates branch-bank license denials, he explains, to engineer a world in which banks implement his (Aoki's—we know of no bureaucrat who ever articulated such a policy) knife-edge optimal strategy: rescue firms if, but only if, they are financially distressed (temporarily short of cash) but economically healthy (still able to make good products cheap). Others (e.g., Rajan 1996, 1364) more cryptically assure us that in Japan "reputational concerns" make it all work. And prominent author and investment banker Paul Sheard (1994b, 17) simply dismisses the question as "somewhat of a puzzle."

THE TERMS OF THE MAIN BANK CONTRACT

If no one has seen a main bank contract, what might the (nonexistent) contract contain? The absence of any explicit deal makes any hypothesis about whether and when parties comply with it tantalizingly hard to test. (Are most hobbits left-handed or right-handed?) Nonetheless, subject to a variety of qualifications, most observers posit the following core terms:

Most big firms have a main bank. First, most major firms have a main bank. Scholars may quarrel about how many little firms maintain main bank relations, but none contests the notion that most big firms do. Although banks and firms never actually negotiate a "main bank contract" or designate a bank as a "main bank," everyone knows his place. Every big firm knows which bank among the many from which it borrows serves as its main bank; every bank knows for which firms among its thousands of borrowers it serves as main bank; and each bank and each firm maintain the same expectations about what each of them must do under the never-articulated terms of their unspoken deal.

The main bank lends money, holds shares, and collects information. Second, the main bank lends the firm the bulk of its debt and holds the largest amount of its stock. In the process, it becomes what Columbia legal scholar Curtis Milhaupt (2001, 2087) called the "central repository of information on the borrower." Indeed, writes Sheard (1989, 403), the "close information-sharing relationship that exists between the bank and the firm" constitutes the "cornerstone" of the main bank arrangement.

The main bank dominates governance. Third, using that information, the main bank dominates the firm. By putting its men on the firm's board, it plays a key role in shaping firm policy. Write Aoki, Patrick, and Sheard (1994, 15), "the main bank often has its managers sit as directors or auditors on the board of client firms." And the resulting "central role" of the main bank in the "corporate governance of large firms," proclaims Sheard (1994a, 210), "is beyond dispute." Indeed, continue Aoki, Patrick, and Sheard (1994, 4), main banks are key "to the way in which corporate oversight and governance [are] exercised in the Japanese capital market."

The main bank monitors for all creditors. Fourth, the main bank monitors on behalf of all creditors. Lest a firm's many creditors waste resources by each monitoring the firm, they implicitly delegate their monitoring among themselves. Although they lend broadly, they monitor only those firms for which they act as main bank. When they do, they monitor not just for themselves but as "delegated" monitor for all.

The main bank agrees to rescue distressed debtors. Last, the main bank implicitly agrees to save borrowers that fall into distress. Exactly what the rescue entails varies from scholar to scholar, yet most writers seem to believe that the main bank at least will subordinate its claims to other creditors, will guarantee the firm's debts, will send in personnel, and will lend its own money.

Given that the firms and banks leave this obligation unspoken and unwritten, the arrangement hinges on spontaneous cooperative behavior. One might have thought lawyers and economists (trained in nothing if not the science of cynicism) would avoid the story like the plague. Not so. Even the latter have told the tale for years. Already in the 1970s, a Brookings study (Wallich and Wallich 1976, 273) declared that "the main bank assumes a special responsibility with respect to the borrower. In an emergency other creditors therefore can expect their claims to effectively though not legally outrank those of the main bank."

In the thirty years since, the tale has thrived. According to Takeo Hoshi and Anil Kashyap (2001, 5) of keiretsu fame, when "firms [run] into financial difficulty," the main bank "step[s] up and organize[s] a workout." By Aoki's account, it launches "rescue operations [that] prevent the premature liquidation of temporarily depressed, but potentially productive, firms" (2000, 86).

One might have thought the economically inclined (trained too in the gains from diffuse market competition) would also shun the claim for the way it celebrates centralized control. In the end, after all, the claim both touts gains from centralized monitoring and posits elite bankers who transform manufacturing firms that manufacturers themselves could not run. But no. Nobel laureate Paul Samuelson (2000, 186) describes (with a straight face) the main banks as "stallions who preside over a harem of mates, . . . feed[ing] capital and advice to a collection of companies." Prominent economists Paul Milgrom and John Roberts (1994, 24) describe the main bank "as an ultimate risk-bearer in circumstances of financial distress." And erstwhile University of Chicago faculty members Jonathan Macey and Geoffrey Miller (1995, 85) celebrate the arrangement as one in which "firms sacrifice control and flexibility for the safety and security of a main bank relationship."

Instead, in the legal and economic literature the Japanese "main bank system" stands (or at least until the mid-1990s stood) as everyone's textbook bankruptcy regime. Should an economically viable firm face financial distress, the bank rescues the firm. Its pin-striped prodigies then rebuild the firm into the thriving institution it once had been. Just as the state in Eastern Europe would forestall wasteful failures by setting production schedules in advance, so Japanese banks prevent them by parachuting in the funds and experts as necessary.

SEVERAL EXAMPLES

At the firm level, the evidence at least shows that Japanese banks never tried to save all large troubled firms, even before the 1990s recession. And if they did not try to save the firms that did fall into distress, they of course could not credibly (albeit implicitly) have promised to save the rest either. To see the point, take several troubled firms in the 1970s. The Arab oil embargo in the early years of the decade had thrown many sectors of the economy into a tailspin, a quandary much like that in many sectors today. The affected firms faced travails many readers will likely find depressingly familiar. For us, however, that familiarity is the point: the very problems that plagued banks and troubled firms in the West plagued banks and firms in Japan, induced them to adopt much the same tactics, and caused much the same problems.

Mazda

For two decades, Mazda has served as the poster child of bank rescues in Japan. As the legend in the West recounts it (told best in Pascale and Rohlen 1983), the firm entered the 1970s with an iron-willed, engineering-obsessed, and somewhat pigheaded CEO from the original Matsuda family. Under his leadership, it invested heavily in rotary engines. Alas, when the OPEC-induced price hikes hit in the middle of the decade, consumers abandoned the technologically "cool" rotaries for the more fuel-efficient Toyotas, Nissans, and Hondas.

To turn Mazda around, the Sumitomo Bank stepped in as main bank. It sent personnel, loaned money, repositioned the product line, enforced austerity—and saved the firm. In improving the firm's cash flow during this "rescue stage," wrote Stanford scholars Richard Pascale and Thomas Rohlen (1983, 257), the Sumitomo Bank "played the pivotal role..., its bold action virtually guaranteeing the company's debts."

Yet the way Mazda reacted to the bank belies the notion that its officers implicitly agreed that the bank would rescue the firm. Had they cut such a deal in advance, the bank should not have faced the resistance it did after the fact. In fact, as Pascale and Rohlen (1983, 233, 236) acknowledge, the firm fought the bank at every turn—with its managers referring to the new arrivals as the "occupying army."

Under pressure in December 1974, Mazda accepted several outsiders to its thirty-member board. Yet the new men did not come just from the Sumitomo Bank but instead from the Sumitomo Trust Bank, two local banks, and the trading companies with which Mazda dealt as well. Although Mazda named a Sumitomo Bank representative as vice president in early 1976, it was late 1977 before the outsiders could oust the pigheaded Matsuda as CEO. When they did, they did not fire him or install a banker in his stead.

Instead, the firm named him chairman of the board and replaced him with its incumbent third in command, a long-term Mazda engineer. By 1978, Mazda still had only four bankers on its board.

To keep Mazda alive, several institutions helped. The Sumitomo Bank did lend money, but so did the Sumitomo Trust Bank. In November 1979 Ford took a 25 percent equity interest. The director from the Trust Bank supervised capital budgeting issues, one director from the Sumitomo Bank managed exports while another directed accounting and cost controls, the director from the C. Itoh trading firm coordinated sales, and the director from Sumitomo Trading took charge of managerial consolidation.

The legend in the West characterizes the Mazda "turnaround" as a story of main bank rescue, but one should wonder. The Sumitomo Bank never had the stake in Mazda that would induce a bank or firm to invest much in saving it. Although it had lent more to Mazda than anyone else, it had long kept its share of Mazda's debt modest: 13.6 percent in October 1974 and 14.5 percent in October 1977. By October 1977 it was *cutting* the amount it lent Mazda: from ¥53.6 billion in October 1976 to ¥46.1 billion in October 1977, and by October 1980 to ¥26.3 billion. As of 1974 (and still in 1977) it held less than 4 percent of the stock. Had it wanted to own more, at the time it legally could have held up to 10 percent. Instead, it kept its share below 4 percent, and even below that of the Nippon Life Insurance firm.

In truth, the Sumitomo Bank did *not* rescue Mazda. Instead, the institutions with the greatest stake in the firm *collectively* rescued it. None of them knew how to make cars, of course, but Mazda's problems did not lie in automotive engineering. Instead, they lay in financial management and marketing. Banks do know how to balance books, and trading companies know how to read consumer preferences and cultivate markets. What Mazda needed, these others could contribute. They did, and Mazda survived.

Eidai Industries

Mazda still makes cars, but troubled firms do not always recover. Sometimes banks and trading partners intervene and fail. Eidai Industries mass-produced prefabricated housing and by the 1970s listed its stock on section 1 of the Tokyo Stock Exchange. In the mid-1970s it found itself outcompeted. Outmaneuvered by its competitors, in December 1975 it posted a large loss.

Eidai's banks had known of its travails by late 1974. To resolve those problems, in the fall of 1975 the largest five creditors agreed collectively to lend it more and to excuse it from its ¥2 billion semiannual interest payment. True to their word, they lent large amounts. From 1971 to 1977 they boosted their loans to Eidai from ¥7.5 billion to ¥75.3 billion.

The banks took a variety of other steps besides. They enlisted the help of two trading firms that handled Eidai accounts. They encouraged Eidai to increase its sales force. They introduced clients to Eidai branches. They placed three bankers on Eidai's eleven-member board. They replaced the Eidai president, first with a former president of a Daiwa Bank–affiliated securities firm, then with the number-four man at Daiwa itself.

But monitoring a borrower effectively is hard. If its rivals outcompeted Eidai, Eidai outfoxed its banks. The second Daiwa-sent president had planned to rebuild Eidai within two years—but it was not to be. Despite having had three bankers on its board and a banker in its vice presidential post even before the crisis, despite eventually accepting its president and fourteen other senior executives from the Daiwa Bank—despite all this, Eidai's problems went deeper than any bank knew. By 1978, one year after the ambitious second Daiwa-sent president took office, the banks petitioned the court for its reorganization. "Banks know they're easy to fool," a senior Daiwa executive recalled (*Chuo koron*, Winter 1978, special issue, 334). "But they got fooled again anyway."

Sasebo Heavy Industries

When a rescue occurs and a firm does survive, sometimes it survives only by happenstance. During the 1960s and early 1970s, the Sasebo Heavy Industries (SHI) shipbuilding firm had thrived. What with the explosive economic growth and the increasing need for large tankers, demand had boomed. Come 1977, however, the Arab oil embargo and the massive revaluation of the yen (from ¥290.3/US$ in January 1977 to ¥195.4/US$ in December 1978) had turned the boom into a bust. With total industry shipbuilding capacity of 19 million tons, Japanese firms in 1977 had orders of only 5 million tons. At least the largest shipbuilding firms had diversified their product line. Medium-sized SHI had not. By the fall of 1978, it had no orders at all.

Like most large Japanese firms, SHI had borrowed broadly. From over a dozen banks, it had borrowed (as of March 1977) more than ¥79.7 billion. Among the commercial banks, it had borrowed the most from the Daiichi Kangyo Bank (DKB)—¥3.3 billion. It had four major shareholders: the Kurushima dry-docks firm (25.0 percent), the Nippon Kokan (NKK) steel firm (24.2 percent), Nippon Steel (14.1 percent), and the Nissho Iwai trading firm (10.1 percent). Kurushima had bought its interest because its CEO Toshio Tsubouchi wanted to integrate SHI's large dock facility into Kurushima. When he had earlier tried to become president, however, NKK had blocked his move and instead engineered the appointment of its own representative.

To deal with the nonexistent demand, in early 1978 SHI asked for early retirements. By April 1, six hundred employees had volunteered, but to finance their retirement package the firm needed ¥8.2 billion. It would also have to finance other changes, of course, and all told could expect to need about ¥20 billion. When it approached its banks, they balked.

Rather than volunteer more money, the banks told SHI to file for bankruptcy. At least on much of their debt, they held security interests. If the firm filed for bankruptcy immediately, they could expect some repayment. If they now loaned funds unsecured (and the firm apparently had no more assets to post), rather than repayment they could expect a steady stream of requests for yet more funds. The additional funds they loaned would effectively become hostage and lock them into future demands indefinitely.

The banks offered to lend the money only if SHI's lead shareholders guaranteed the debt, but the shareholders would not guarantee. NKK controlled SHI, and Tsubouchi—bitter still about the way NKK had blocked him from becoming president—was not about to guarantee any loans suggested by its handpicked managerial team. Absent a coguarantee from Kurushima, neither would NKK guarantee a loan. And if Tsubouchi and NKK would not guarantee, Nippon Steel and Nissho Iwai would not do so either.

In short, neither the firm's creditors nor its shareholders would invest anything more in the firm. Ordinarily, such a firm would promptly fail. It did not, but only because SHI dominated the city of Sasebo and Prime Minister Takeo Fukuda owed the city a massive political debt. When the government's nuclear-powered ship *Mutsu* had developed a radioactive leak in 1974, all other ports had refused to take it. With a ship leaking nuclear fuel sitting off the Japanese coast and nowhere to send it, Fukuda faced a political disaster. He averted it, but only when Sasebo agreed to take the ship.

For that favor Fukuda now intervened personally. He struggled mightily to accomplish anything at all. Repeatedly he urged the banks to fund SHI. Repeatedly they refused. They would not loan the money unsecured and unguaranteed, they declared, and the firm could not secure and the shareholders would not guarantee.

Tsubouchi eventually did gain control, and SHI did survive, but it survived largely without banks and only on a reduced scale. From ¥79.7 billion in March 1977, by 1979 its debt had fallen to ¥51.1 billion, by 1981 to ¥38.7 billion, and by 1983 to ¥10.2 billion. From a total of 6,968 employees in 1977, by 1979 its workforce fell to 4,223, by 1981 to 3,422, and by 1983 to 2,760.

Other Cases

Other distressed firms—even big firms—expeditiously go out of business. In the early 1970s, with its forty-year history, the venerable Hanasaki firm was one of the largest Japanese manufacturers of women's clothing. When it tried to expand in 1976, it found itself with enormous unsold inventory: ¥1.6–1.7 billion on annual sales of ¥18.5 billion.

"We begged it several times to come up with a consolidated rationalization plan, and a plan to rebuild," recalled one Sumitomo Bank representative ("Apareru sangyo" 1978, 81). "But it wouldn't comply." So when in October it saw Hanasaki's winter clothes moving slowly, the bank offset Hanasaki liabilities of ¥200 million against Hanasaki's deposits. Early the next year it announced that "there are limits to a bank's assistance" and declared an end to all further loans. Hanasaki promptly went out of business.

Sometimes a rescue succeeds, but only after creditors manipulate the bankruptcy process to oust the incumbents. The Hayashi firm had been one of the largest wool spinning firms in Japan. When business fell in 1977, the founder-president resigned. Because his family had earlier pledged their stock in Hayashi Spinning to the Tokai Bank in exchange for its aid, they now sued to retrieve that stock.

Soon rumors began to circulate that the family would liquidate the firm at the February shareholders' meeting. Apparently they planned to use their equity stake to demand concessions from their creditors. Afraid of losing control, the Tokai Bank promptly filed for reorganization under the bankruptcy laws. Through the bankruptcy proceeding, it cut the incumbent shareholders' interests to less than 10 percent of the firm's stock. It then reorganized and revamped the firm. The factories continued to operate with the labor force uncut—but now under bank control.

Sometimes if banks try to intervene, the firms reject the banks and restructure on their own. Electrical parts maker Mitsumi had fallen on hard times in 1970 after issuing bearer securities in Germany the previous year. In 1971 the Mitsui Bank (despite the similar names, the bank and the firm are otherwise unrelated) sent in one of its men as Mitsumi vice president and another as director—this in addition to the Mitsui banker already on the ten-member board. As of early 1970, the Mitsui Bank as Mitsumi's fourth-largest creditor had lent Mitsumi ¥340 million. By 1972 it was its largest creditor and had ¥635 million outstanding.

Within a year the Mitsui officers had largely disappeared. The vice president had become an ordinary director, and the other directors had vanished. Apparently the incumbent managers—still under the control of an autocratic CEO—had fought the bankers and pushed them out. Where Mitsumi had had 3,528 employees in January 1971, three years later it was down to 2,002 employees. It survived, but for several years only on a much reduced scale.

TESTING THE TALE: ECONOMYWIDE DATA

Such are the accounts of some firms that faced hard times, and the tale of the main bank does not fit them. Does the tale fit broader industrywide patterns any better? To test whether it does, we need first to identify a firm's "main bank." Unfortunately, because no firm ever cuts a main bank contract (even orally), we have no clear way to do so. Left to our devices, we follow the perhaps dominant custom in the literature and define a firm's main bank as the bank that lends it the largest share of its debt. Note that this prevents us from testing the proposition that all firms have a main bank (by this definition, every firm in Peoria has a "main bank"). We also follow custom in focusing on TSE-listed firms.

As we understand it, the main bank story raises the following testable implications:

Main bank governance. If (as the conventional wisdom posits) banks dominate governance by placing their men on borrowers' boards, then most firms should include several bankers among their directors. And if banks focus their intervention on their most troubled borrowers, then the worst-performing firms should have more banker-directors than the rest.

Delegated monitoring. According to the conventional wisdom, banks implicitly delegate their monitoring to a borrower's main bank. If so, then virtually all bankers on corporate boards should come from a firm's main bank.

Main bank rescues. Main bank theorists also claim that main banks implicitly agree to rescue a borrower if it falls into distress. If so, then firms flirting with insolvency (1) should not be switching their main bank affiliation and (2) should be borrowing disproportionately large amounts from their main bank.

Governance by Main Banks

According to most accounts, banks dominate the firms for which they act as main bank by naming their officers to the boards. In fact, they almost never do so. To explore the issue, we examine board composition at all nonbank firms on section 1 of the Tokyo Stock Exchange (the largest 1,000-odd firms) in 1980, 1985, 1990, and 1995. During those years, 92–96 percent of the firms had *no* directors with appointments at the firm's main bank (see table 4.1; we discuss board composition more fully in chapter 5).

Bankers could not dominate Japanese firms for a simple reason: there are not enough. In 1985, for instance, the average firm had only 1.3 bankers on its 27-member board. What is more, very few of these men were still with a bank. Instead, most were *retired* bankers: the mean firm had 1.1 men who had once held a bank post, but only 0.2 who still did.

If a bank wanted to use a board slot to monitor a firm, it would not name someone it had retired—someone who had quit the bank, could not return to

Table 4.1. Bankers and retired bankers on corporate boards

	Main bank				Any bank			
	1980	1985	1990	1995	1980	1985	1990	1995
Mean number of directors per bank holding								
Conc. bank appts.	.078	.059	.052	.048	.254	.216	.211	.210
Past bank appts.	.562	.619	.598	.599	1.021	1.060	1.060	1.087
Percentage of firms with no directors holding								
Conc. bank appts.	.927	.949	.956	.954	.820	.846	.854	.851
Past bank appts.	.617	.591	.618	.623	.459	.466	.470	.467

Sources: Toyo keizai shimpo sha, *Kigyo keiretsu soran*, various years.

Notes: Conc. bank appt., a director concurrently holding a position at a bank; *past bank appt.*, a director who held a position at a bank earlier in his career.

the bank, and depended instead on that firm for his future income. Notions of "Confucian loyalty" do not reach that far, and the banks themselves do not locate future jobs for their officers once they leave. Instead, the bank would send a relatively young executive on the bank payroll who would forfeit his career if he proved disloyal.

Yet firms almost never appoint young bankers but appoint retired ones if they appoint any at all. Why *do* some firms appoint bankers? They do not appoint them because they have to appoint them. The main bank literature notwithstanding, banks do not have the power to name people to the boards of their debtors. They do not negotiate that right as a condition of their loans, and to our knowledge they do not demand board representation even implicitly. So why do the firms that name bankers name them?

Kaplan-Minton

According to the now-classic study by economists Stephen Kaplan and Bernadette Minton (1994), bankers appear on boards so that banks can control troubled borrowers. Banks name their men to a borrower's board when the firm hits hard times. When necessary, those bankers then fire the CEO.

To reach this conclusion, Kaplan and Minton compiled board composition and financial data on the 119 largest TSE-listed firms from 1980 to 1988. They then used the data to estimate the odds that a firm will appoint a new banker-director. They found that those odds rise if a firm earns low stock returns or posts a pre-tax loss.

One should wonder about those findings—at least according to our much larger database. (We surveyed all nonbank section 1 firms rather than just the biggest hundred.) In table 4.2, we identify for each half decade during 1980 to 1995 the number of firms that added or cut bankers from their

Table 4.2. Changes in the number of bankers and retired bankers on boards, by periods and profitability quartiles

	Decrease	No change	Increase	Fraction of firms w/ no bankers	Mean no. of bankers
A. Concurrent bankers					
1. 1980–85				(1980)	(1980)
Very low	24	228	13	.824	.281
Low	21	220	16	.767	.315
High	11	229	15	.821	.237
Very high	13	163	5	.871	.149
2. 1985–90				(1985)	(1985)
Very low	17	259	14	.862	.214
Low	11	245	15	.804	.280
High	13	238	17	.858	.187
Very high	10	183	8	.866	.169
3. 1990–95				(1990)	(1990)
Very low	16	256	27	.843	.231
Low	16	268	15	.833	.227
High	15	257	17	.869	.194
Very high	13	221	13	.879	.186
B. Retired bankers					
1. 1980–85				(1980)	(1980)
Very low	50	153	62	.386	1.184
Low	46	161	50	.427	1.100
High	40	186	29	.469	.962
Very high	23	141	17	.609	.644
2. 1985–90				(1985)	(1985)
Very low	48	186	56	.369	1.459
Low	62	165	44	.443	1.096
High	47	172	49	.496	.896
Very high	19	145	37	.602	.652
3. 1990–95				(1990)	(1990)
Very low	55	184	60	.395	1.369
Low	39	205	55	.448	.973
High	44	199	46	.526	1.017
Very high	34	163	50	.522	.842

Sources: Toyo keizai shimpo sha, *Kigyo keiretsu soran*, various years.

Notes: Firms are partitioned by quartiles on the basis of profitability. The sizes are uneven because not all firms with accounting data also have board composition data. Years in parentheses indicate that data were given for that particular year only rather than for the range of years shown in the far left-hand column.

board. If Kaplan and Minton are right, then the number of bankers should increase most at the troubled firms. From 1980 to 1985, however, only 13 of the firms in the least profitable quartile added current bankers to their board, while 24 firms cut them. Among the most profitable firms, 14 added such bankers while 17 cut them. Only for the period 1990–95 or for the data on retired bankers do we detect any pattern close to that asserted by Kaplan and Minton.

More generally, most firms (whether profitable or no) do not change the number of bankers on their boards either way. Although some firms increase bankers, about the same number cut them. Over the course of the period, most firms kept the number of bankers on their board unaltered. Apparently, most thought they had the number about right. When we use financial data to predict the net change in the number of banker-directors at a firm, we obtain the same result: whether a firm appoints more bankers seldom depends on how well the firm has done financially.

Rather than telling us something about how Japanese firms operate, Kaplan and Minton illustrate the way intellectual fables shape the production of academic research. For like Hoshi, Kashyap, and Scharfstein, Kaplan and Minton reached the conclusion they did because they set out to find it. They collected only data suggested by the fable—the appointments primarily of bankers rather than of all directors (Miwa and Ramseyer 2005a, tables 4 and 5).

Kaplan and Minton made two further missteps. First, they did not look to the appointment of *additional* bankers. Instead, they counted the appointment of new bankers, even when those new bankers merely replaced the old. In other words, rather than focus on firms in which a bank might have increased its influence, they studied all firms with new bankers—even when the firms merely replaced one ex-banker with another.

Second, to measure performance Kaplan and Minton did not use the usual accounting measure of operating income but instead used pre-tax income. To calculate its operating income (which is also before taxes), a firm simply takes its revenues and subtracts the cost of goods sold, direct selling expenses, advertising costs, and R&D. To calculate its pre-tax income, however, it makes a variety of adjustments over which it has discretionary control: nonoperating income and expenses and extraordinary gains and losses. A firm that hopes to avoid a loss can sometimes defer depreciation or sell appreciated property. One that hopes to wipe the slate clean can do the opposite.

Because of this discretionary element to its computation, pre-tax income typically shows a looser association to shareholder returns than does operating income. And because the board has that control over pre-tax income, it occasionally times the firm's losses to coincide with housecleaning. In the

United States, for example, when new senior executives take over troubled companies they sometimes accelerate discretionary expenses to post a "big bath."

Ultimately, Kaplan and Minton noticed that underperforming firms sometimes appointed new bankers, but because the myth of the main bank suggested that they collect board appointment data only on bankers, they missed the fact that those firms sometimes sacked almost their entire board. Kaplan and Minton interpreted the new appointments as "bank monitoring," but only because they primarily collected banker data and—as a result—failed to notice the other changes to the board. These firms did not appoint bankers to facilitate bank intervention. They appointed the bankers because they had fired their boards and wanted new bankers to replace the bankers they had just let go.

Shipbuilding Firms

Firms in the shipbuilding industry illustrate this phenomenon. Because listed firms did so well in the 1980s, not many posted pre-tax losses during the years Kaplan and Minton studied. One of the few industries in which there were such losses, however, was shipbuilding. And there, some firms did indeed time their pre-tax losses to coincide with board housecleanings.

The shipbuilding firms reported their numbers in a variety of ways. Some apparently decided to post losses. Kawasaki Heavy Industries, for example, had operating profits in 1984 and 1986 but reported pre-tax losses. Others tried to avoid them. Both Hitachi Shipbuilding and Mitsui Shipbuilding had operating losses in 1988 but used means such as "extraordinary gains" to report pre-tax profits.

When these shipbuilding firms did post losses, many installed new boards as well. Because Japanese directors generally serve about eight years, over a two-year period a typical firm would have replaced about a quarter of its board. During 1986–88, among our eight shipbuilding firms, all but one reported at least one loss year. Only Kawasaki, however, replaced fewer than 25 percent of its directors. Two firms replaced about 30 percent, and two replaced 40 percent. Mitsubishi (which did not post a loss) replaced half its directors, and two others sacked nearly all.

Even when shipbuilding firms responded to the hard times by replacing their directors, they did not necessarily add bankers. Two of the eight did increase their banker-directors by three, and one increased them by one. Three firms kept their number unchanged, however, and two actually reduced it.

The Puzzle

If banks do not post bankers to the boards of troubled firms, then the initial puzzle remains—why do some firms appoint bankers? To explore this issue, elsewhere we use firm financials and industry affiliation to predict the number of bankers at a firm. The procedure suggests some answers—but far more mundane ones than the notion that banks dominate and rescue troubled borrowers. Most basically, firms name bankers if they depend heavily on bank debt (Miwa and Ramseyer 2005c, 316, table 3; see Miwa and Ramseyer 2003c, table 5). The more they return to banks year in year out for loans, the more likely they will name someone who knows what the lender cares about.

Second, firms apparently name bankers (the evidence is weaker) if they have smaller stocks of mortgageable assets (Miwa and Ramseyer 2005c, 316, table 3; see Miwa and Ramseyer 2003c, table 5). A firm that can offer its bank a security interest will have less cause to worry whether the bank will renew its debt. Necessarily, it will have less to gain from appointing someone who knows what banks look for in their debtors. Instead, the firms that benefit most from having such a director are the firms without such security interests.

Last, firms name bankers if the firms themselves compete in the financial services industry (Miwa and Ramseyer 2005c, 316, table 3; see Miwa and Ramseyer 2003c, table 5). In short, bankers serve disproportionately in those firms whose business most resembles banking. These firms do not appoint bankers because banks want to monitor their work. They appoint them because bankers bring the background they need in their business.

Delegated Monitoring

In most societies, reason some main bank theorists, all banks monitor all of their borrowers. Does that not waste resources? Why should all banks monitor all borrowers? Why not split the borrowers among themselves and centralize their monitoring?

The answer, of course, is that real-world banks seldom trust each other. As potentially rival creditors, they hold fundamentally conflicting interests. And just as banks do not delegate monitoring in the United States, they apparently do not delegate it in Japan. If Japanese banks did delegate monitoring to main banks, and if (as observers claim) they monitored through the board, then virtually all banker-directors should come from a firm's main bank. By contrast, if firms occasionally appointed bankers to their boards because they valued their expertise, then many bankers would still come from the main bank. After all, because the firms (by definition) borrow the most from their main bank, they would often know the most bankers there. The firms would also, however, sometimes appoint other bankers.

In fact, banker-directors do most commonly come from a firm's main bank—but not exclusively. In 1985, firms recruited only about 57 percent of their banker-directors from their main bank. The rest they chose from other banks. On average, they appointed 1.1 retired banker-directors but only 0.6 who had retired from their main bank. They appointed 0.2 who concurrently worked at a bank but only 0.06 who concurrently worked at their main bank.

Main Bank Rescues

Typically, Japan specialists argue that main banks implicitly agree to "rescue" borrowers that fall into financial distress. As hypotheses go, it is a maddeningly intractable one. Firms routinely fail in Japan and always have. Yet because firms purportedly cut only an "implicit" deal, a main bank theorist, when asked about a firm that disappeared, can simply reply that the firm that failed must have been one of the few without a main bank.

Even the most enthusiastic partisans of the "main bank system" have not tried systematically to show that firms and banks enter these agreements. Instead, they merely tell stories about firms that banks rescued. Sometimes, they show, some Japanese banks offer some troubled firms loans and other assistance they might otherwise prefer not to offer.

Unfortunately, that some banks sometimes rescue some firms tells us nothing about what deals they cut at the outset. Even U.S. banks sometimes rescue some firms. A bank may try its hardest to avoid being stuck with an insolvent debtor, but like Brer Rabbit, sometimes stuck is what it is. And when stuck, it sometimes finds it profitable to cut the firm slack and try to nurse it back to health. The relevant question is not whether that happens in Japan—to our knowledge, it happens everywhere.

Instead, the relevant question is whether Japanese banks (implicitly) promise at the outset to help firms should they ever fall into distress. Basic logic suggests they would not make such promises. After all, a bank that did so would both attract the least healthy firms and induce its otherwise healthy borrowers to adopt higher-risk business strategies.

To test whether Japanese banks nonetheless do promise (implicitly) to help troubled debtors, we examined three measures. First, we asked whether troubled firms rely more heavily on their main bank than profitable firms do. Second, we asked whether troubled firms increase the fraction of the debt they borrow from their main bank more than profitable firms do. And last, we asked whether troubled firms switch their main bank affiliation less often than profitable firms do.

Main Bank Dependence

If main banks promise (implicitly) to lend borrowers extra funds when they fall into distress, then troubled firms should rely more heavily on their main bank than other firms do. More specifically, if a main bank will lend them funds other banks would not lend, then troubled firms should borrow a

Table 4.3. Reliance on main bank, by outstanding debt and profitability

	Profitability			
Outstanding debt	Very low	Low	High	Very high
1980–85				
Very low	.493 (12)	.412 (20)	.436 (46)	.492 (47)
Low	.330 (46)	.274 (40)	.326 (46)	.361 (34)
High	.271 (54)	.250 (60)	.267 (40)	.231 (21)
Very high	.215 (74)	.193 (59)	.205 (48)	.292 (11)
1986–90				
Very low	.588 (22)	.561 (42)	.503 (54)	.494 (58)
Low	.331 (44)	.285 (49)	.338 (55)	.354 (37)
High	.301 (63)	.267 (66)	.268 (48)	.276 (22)
Very high	.252 (78)	.214 (63)	.181 (43)	.286 (23)
1990–94				
Very low	.565 (24)	.449 (31)	.546 (52)	.515 (41)
Low	.392 (43)	.351 (38)	.301 (46)	.328 (37)
High	.294 (58)	.267 (53)	.288 (41)	.272 (23)
Very high	.277 (67)	.235 (76)	.242 (39)	.271 (17)

Sources: Nikkei QUICK joho, NEEDS, as updated; Nikkei QUICK joho, QUICK, as updated; Nihon shoken keizai kenkyu jo, various years; Toyo keizai shimpo sha, *Kigyo keiretsu soran*, various years.

Notes: The data are partitioned into quartiles, by profitability (operating income/total assets, by columns) and by the total amount of bank loans at the firm (by rows). In each case, we give the fraction of those bank loans that the firm borrows from its main bank for that cell, followed by the number of firms in that cell, in parentheses. Quartiles are uneven because we exclude firms that changed their main bank affiliation during the period.

higher fraction of their debt from their main bank than other firms borrow from their own main banks.

This does not happen. The most troubled firms do not owe a larger fraction of their loans to their main bank than other firms owe. In table 4.3 we divide the firms both by their profitability (the columns) and by the amount of their outstanding loans (the rows). Because we divide the firms by quartile, this process generates sixteen cells. For each cell, we then calculate the mean fraction of their loans that firms borrow from their main bank.[1] In 1980–85, for example, we find twelve firms that fell into the least-profitable quartile, fell into the quartile that borrowed the least from banks, and did not switch main banks. These twelve firms on average borrowed 49.3 percent of their bank loans from their main bank.

Because firms incur significant fixed costs to establish a borrowing relationship, those firms that borrow larger amounts will tend to borrow from

Table 4.4. Main bank stability and loans to distressed firms (mean values)

	1980–85	1986–90	1990–94
A. Increase in main bank loan fraction			
1. Bottom quartile firms, by profitability	.021	.033	−.023
2. Top three quartile firms, by profitability	.030	.034	−.012
B. Main bank switch rates			
1. Bottom quartile firms, by profitability	.281	.229	.266
2. Top three quartile firms, by profitability	.303	.201	.283

Sources: Nikkei QUICK joho, NEEDS, as updated; Nikkei QUICK joho, QUICK, as updated; Nihon shoken keizai kenkyu jo, various years; Toyo keizai shimpo sha, *Kigyo keiretsu soran*, various years.

more banks. In turn, they will tend to borrow a smaller fraction of their debt from their main bank. And so table 4.3 shows that the mean falls from the top row to the bottom.

If main banks (implicitly) promise to lend troubled firms money that other banks will not lend, then the least profitable firms should tend to borrow a higher fraction of their debt from their main bank than other firms borrow. If so, then the numbers in table 4.3 should fall from left to right. They do not: during 1980–85, firms in the least profitable quartile borrowed 27.8 percent from their main bank while the others borrowed 30.6 (the difference is not statistically significant at the 5 percent level). During 1986–90 they borrowed 32.0 percent from their main bank while the others borrowed 33.9 percent. Only during 1990–94 did the least profitable borrow more heavily from their main bank (34.4 percent) than the others did (33.8 percent).

Increases in Main Bank Loan Fraction

So, troubled firms do not owe a larger fraction of their debt to their main banks than other firms owe. But might the troubled firms at least borrow a larger fraction of any *increase* in their debt from their main banks?

To examine this claim, we first take the fraction of its debt that a firm borrows from its principal bank (that is, its main bank loan fraction) over the period and calculate the change in that fraction over time. We then compare that change in main bank loan fraction at the most distressed quartile of firms with the change at the other firms. To keep things simple, we do not partition the top three profitability quartiles. We give the resulting numbers in panel A of table 4.4.

If main banks (implicitly) agree to lend distressed firms funds that other banks will not lend, then the increase in a main bank's loan share should be larger at the distressed firms than among the other firms. It is not. Instead, during two of the three half-decades we examine, main banks increased their share of a firm's debt more among the healthier firms than among distressed firms. During the third period, it cut back its share less among the healthier firms than among the distressed (again, none of the differences is statistically significant).

Main Bank Stability

Last, compare the propensity of various firms to switch their main bank affiliation. If firms obtain (implicit) rescue insurance from their main bank, then the most troubled firms should switch main banks least often. After all, consider life insurance. A healthy thirty-year-old may switch his life insurance carrier. A terminally ill eighty-year-old will not. By hypothesis, the troubled firm has paid its (implicit) insurance premia for years.[2] At the very point at which it might start collecting on its policy, it will not cancel its coverage and look for another carrier.

Suppose the most troubled firms do switch main banks. That simple fact would suggest two possibilities: either their main bank reneged on its (implicit) rescue promise, or it never offered the (implicit) promise in the first place. In fact, the two possibilities come to much the same thing, for if main banks did regularly renege after the fact, they could not credibly promise to rescue in advance. If troubled firms regularly switch main banks, banks must not be offering (implicit) rescue insurance.

Troubled firms do indeed switch. In panel B of table 4.4, we again divide the firms into those in the least profitable quartile and all others. Then in each cell we give the fraction of firms that switch their main bank affiliation. In none of the cells does the probability that the more profitable firms will switch their main bank affiliation substantially exceed the probability that the bottom-quartile firms will switch. In no case are the differences significant at the 5 percent level, and in no period is the correlation coefficient between profitability and main bank switching statistically significant.

TESTING THE TALE: DISTRESSED FIRMS

The Exercise

If TSE-listed firms as a whole show no trace of any main bank rescue contract, consider whether the very most troubled firms (those not just in the bottom quartile but skirting bankruptcy) do. For this exercise we take two lists of distressed firms. Our first roster (the 1978 firms) dates from the mid-1970s. As the previous examples suggest, for Japan these were badly troubled years. The 1974 oil crisis had thrown the economy into recession, and by 1978 a wide variety of firms were under water. For this list, we take all 320 exchange-listed firms with a loss carryforward in 1978.

Our second list (the 1984 firms) dates from the first half of the next decade. As the massive late-1980s boom illustrates, these were healthier times for the economy as a whole. Nonetheless, the health was not uniform. Troubled firms remained, and for this second list we take all 134 exchange-listed nonfinancial firms with at least three consecutive loss years (after interest but before extraordinary gains and losses) as of April 1984.

The Japanese government gradually deregulated aspects of the financial services industry in the late 1980s. Some observers argue that this radically changed the main bank system. In fact, as we show in chapter 6, it did not. Because the regulations involved had not constrained bank–firm lending even in the 1960s, their relaxation could not have significantly affected loan patterns. For our purposes, however, note that the 1978 data set antedates any deregulation-induced changes to the system, and even the 1984 list antedated most of the changes.

Firm Failures

Firms fail in Japan, even big TSE-listed firms. Of the 320 troubled firms in 1978, 10.3 percent vanished immediately, and 20.9 percent still had not recovered six years later—that is, 33 firms disappeared within a year, and 67 remained sick enough to appear on the 1984 list. Of those that disappeared, 14 disappeared by merger, 9 through various bankruptcy-related legal proceedings, and 10 simply delisted (not all delisted firms failed, of course).

Were those firms with stronger main bank ties more likely to survive than those without? To examine some of the determinants of firm failure, we explored the effect of various firm characteristics on the probability that a firm in our 1984 data set survived on the TSE to late 2001 (Miwa and Ramseyer 2004a, 326, table 4). Two results appear. First, the more a firm depended on its main bank for its debt in 1984 or 1987, the *lower* the odds that it would survive to 2001. Second, whether it had many main bank representatives on its board or few had no effect on the odds it would survive.

Might those main bank–tied firms that disappeared have disappeared because the main bank "rescued" them through a merger? To examine this question, we similarly explored the effect of firm characteristics on the odds that a firm disappears through a merger (Miwa and Ramseyer 2004a, 326, table 5). Again, we found no effect of main bank ties: neither the main bank's loan share nor the number of main bank directors shows any relation to the probability of a merger.

In fact, the distinction between a liquidation and a merger is a distinction without substance anyway. On the one hand, that a firm is liquidated says nothing about what happens to its assets or employees. If its assets have economic value, another firm will buy and use them. If its employees have skills specific to those assets, then the firm that buys the assets will have an incentive to hire the employees as well.

On the other hand, that a firm is merged says nothing about what happens to its assets or employees either. If the acquiring firm cannot use the merged firm's assets as productively as another firm could, it will sell them. If it does not find the merged firm's employees cost-effective, it will discharge them. Fundamentally, whether a firm is liquidated or merged says nothing about what happens either to its assets or to its employees.

Main Bank Loan Share

According to the conventional accounts, in agreeing to rescue a troubled firm the main bank implicitly promises to lend it more funds as necessary. In fact, the main banks in the 1978 data show no willingness to increase their share of a troubled firm's debt. As of 1974, the main banks had lent a mean 24.2 percent of the debt to the firms involved. By 1977, that fraction had risen—but only to 24.7 percent.

Even that evidence misleads, for the main banks dramatically cut their risk at the most seriously troubled 1978 firms. Among the 324 troubled 1978 firms, 87 (26.9 percent) were insolvent. From 1974 to 1977, the main banks slashed the *amount* they lent to 19 of the insolvent firms (21.8 percent). They cut the *fraction* of the insolvent firms' loans they were willing to finance at 44 firms (50.6 percent).

To see the phenomenon more clearly, consider table 4.5. There, we trace the loan patterns to the firms in the 1984 data set. In the first line of each panel, we give the relevant figures for the data set as a whole. In the next lines, we partition the data set by the size of a firm's borrowings and include the relevant figures for each subset. Largely for informational purposes, in panel A we give the per-firm average total bank loans, in panel B the per-firm average growth in bank loans, and in panel C the per-firm average main bank loans.

In panel D, we trace the change in the distribution of bank loans between the firm's main bank and the other banks. During the 1970s, these firms had borrowed 18–20 percent of their funds from their main bank. As they hit hard times in the early 1980s, the main bank did not increase the amount it lent them. Instead, it cut the amount. From 18.1 percent in 1981, it had slashed the amount it shouldered to under 17 percent by 1983 and 1984. Only as the firms began to recover did the main bank increase the share again.

In table 4.6, we give the number of firms (partitioned again by loan size) in which the main bank raised or cut the fraction of the firm's debt it shouldered. Focus on the most troubled period for these firms, 1981–84. Among the firms with the most outstanding debt, the main bank raised the share it financed at only 3 firms but cut it at 10. Among the group with the

Table 4.5. Bank loans at the troubled firms

A. Total bank loans (per firm average; in million yen)

	1972	1978	1981	1983	1984	1987	1990	1996
All firms	16,182	32,055	37,876	41,870	39,775	40,153	38,972	48,608
By amount of bank debt								
Very large	88,730	191,977	250,569	271,031	255,853	266,234	229,873	273,926
Large	14,396	24,914	24,952	27,497	26,552	27,088	25,705	29,946
Small	3,528	6,592	6,224	7,189	7,202	10,841	19,069	35,020
Very small	2,096	3,658	3,021	2,745	2,562	3,199	7,008	10,362

B. Per firm average growth in total bank loans (100+%)

	1972–78	1978–84	1981–84	1984–87	1987–90	1990–96
All firms	198	124	105	101	97	125
By amount of bank debt						
Very large	216	133	102	104	86	119
Large	173	107	106	102	95	116
Small	187	109	116	151	176	184
Very small	175	70	85	125	219	148

C. Total main bank loans (per firm average; in million yen)

	1972	1978	1981	1983	1984	1987	1990	1996
All firms	3,219	5,823	6,874	7,056	6,692	7,351	8,021	9,955
By amount of bank debt								
Very large	12,539	29,394	39,084	38,514	36,063	41,613	43,458	56,535
Large	4,440	5,837	5,906	5,855	5,561	6,632	6,092	6,161
Small	1049	1,563	1,543	2,015	2,147	2,335	2,755	4,952
Very small	508	967	891	979	943	1,056	1,523	2,457

D. Main bank loan share (%)

	1972	1978	1981	1983	1984	1987	1990	1996
All firms	19.9	18.2	18.1	16.9	16.8	18.3	20.6	20.5
By amount of bank debt								
Very large	14.1	15.3	15.6	14.2	14.1	15.6	18.9	20.6
Large	30.8	23.4	23.7	21.3	20.9	24.5	23.7	20.6
Small	29.7	23.7	24.8	28.0	29.8	21.5	14.4	14.1
Very small	24.2	26.4	29.5	35.7	36.8	33.0	21.7	23.7

Sources: Toyo keizai tokei geppo, April 1978; *Shukan toyo keizai*, Aug. 11, 1984; Toyo keizai shimpo sha, *Kigyo keiretsu soran*, various years.

Notes: The firms are the 134 nonfinancial stock exchange–listed firms given in the Aug. 11, 1984, issue of *Shukan toyo keizai* as having had negative after-interest profits for three years in a row. A firm's debt size is defined as follows: very large, over ¥100 billion in bank debt as of March 1984 (15 firms); large, ¥10–100 billion in bank debt (40 firms); small, ¥5–10 billion in bank debt (25 firms); and very small, less than ¥5 billion in bank debt (54 firms). The average main bank loan share is calculated from the group loan amounts as a whole, rather than as an average of the per firm loan shares.

Table 4.6. Number of firms with increase or decrease in main bank loan share

	1972–78	1978–81	1981–84	1984–87	1987–90	1990–96
Very large group						
Increase	6	8	3	10	9	8
Unchanged			2			
Decrease	9	7	10	3	4	4
Large group						
Increase	15	23	17	22	24	21
Unchanged		1		2	1	1
Decrease	22	16	23	12	11	12
Small group						
Increase	9	14	13	12	12	14
Unchanged				1		
Decrease	15	11	12	9	9	5
Very small group						
Increase	33	31	27	27	18	28
Unchanged		2		3	1	1
Decrease	14	15	22	19	30	18

Sources: Toyo keizai tokei geppo, April 1978; Shukan toyo keizai, Aug. 11, 1984; Toyo keizai shimpo sha, Kigyo keiretsu soran, various years.

Notes: The firms are the 134 nonfinancial stock exchange–listed firms given in the Aug. 11, 1984, issue of Shukan toyo keizai as having had negative after-interest profits for three years in a row. A firm's debt size is defined as follows: very large, over ¥100 billion in bank debt as of March 1984 (15 firms); large, ¥10–100 billion in bank debt (40 firms); small, ¥5–10 billion in bank debt (25 firms); and very small, less than ¥5 billion in bank debt (54 firms).

second-largest amount of debt, the main bank raised its share at 17 firms but cut it at 23. Only with the next-smaller debt group did the main bank increase the share it financed more often than it cut it, but then only by 13 firms to 12.

Once more, we use firm characteristics to predict outcomes—this time to predict the increase in the share of a firm's debt that the main bank finances. By 1984, the firms in our sample already would have experienced at least three consecutive loss years. A main bank that intended to rescue such a firm should have begun to lend it extra funds by then. If main banks rescue the troubled firms closest to them, then both (1) the share of a firm's debt that a main bank finances and (2) the number of directors from the main bank on a firm's board should be associated with increases in the share of its debt that a firm borrows from its main bank.

In fact, the data show no such association (Miwa and Ramseyer 2004a, 333, table 8). For the period 1978–84, the share of its loans that a firm borrowed from its main bank is significantly *negatively* associated with changes in that loan share. For the 1981–84 period, the association is simply insignificant. During both periods, the number of directors from the main bank has no effect on any changes in the share of its debt that a firm borrows from its main bank. If anything, in short, the closer the ties a firm maintains with its main bank, the more the bank will *cut* the share of the firm's debt that it finances as the firm enters distress.

Total Bank Loans

Faced with evidence that main banks do not increase their debt share at distressed firms, readers may wonder whether main banks nonetheless help troubled firms by encouraging *other* banks to lend funds. To address this issue, we studied the effect of various firm characteristics on the increase in total loans at our 1984 firms (Miwa and Ramseyer 2004a, 335, table 9). Again, the result is insignificant: neither the main bank's share of the firm's loans nor the number of main bank directors has any effect on total bank borrowing.

Summary measures confirm the lack of any connection between main bank ties and total loans. Of the 131 firms in our 1984 database with *below*-median loan shares from their main bank in 1981, the amount of outstanding loans fell during 1981–84 at 13 firms; of the firms with *above*-median main bank loan shares, outstanding loans fell at 23 firms. Of the firms with a *below*-median number of directors with experience at the firm's main bank in 1981, the amount of outstanding loans fell during 1981–84 at 18 firms; of those with *above*-median main bank directors, outstanding loans similarly fell at 18 firms.

Main Bank Switch Rates

If main banks offered implicit insurance against distress, then those firms closest to insolvency should maintain the most stable main bank relationships. Among TSE-listed firms as a whole, 23–28 percent of those in the bottom quartile switched during the half-decades from 1980 to 1994. Among the 320 firms in our still more badly distressed 1978 database, 77 (24.1 percent) switched their main bank during the preceding three years. Among the 87 insolvent firms in the group, 32 (36.8 percent) had switched.

THE LOGIC OF BANK RESCUES

Bankers do not spend their careers running industrial firms. They run banks. Through their work, they do not learn to build cars or sell detergents. They learn how to operate a financial intermediary. They may indeed have been among the best students in their college class, but they need more than IQ to run a firm. Just as bureaucrats could not run the Eastern European economy, bankers cannot run Japanese firms.

Talent is not expertise. "The biggest problem with having a bank control management," complained one businessman, "is that bankers can't stop thinking like bankers" (Ginko kanri 1978, 87). As Mansaku Takeda (1978, 41), senior consultant to the Daiichi Kangyo Bank, put it, "banks are places to oversee loans. There's no reason to think a banker has any talent for running a firm, and there're precious few examples of firms that did better because a banker came to run them.... Sure, bankers may be smart. Whether they have any managerial talent is another issue."

Despite the broad claims about bank monitoring and intervention in Japan, bankers accomplished much less. As one late-1970s account (Ginko kanri 1978, 83) put it, bankers primarily intervened in firms with excessive investments. There, they did not need to run the firm. They needed only to arrive, to sell, and to leave.

Consistent with their slasher role, bankers, according to the same 1970s account, primarily intervened either where the industry had long-term excess capacity or where a strong company CEO had ruled autocratically. Newspapers called the late 1970s recession a "structural depression," and the structural changes fundamentally shifted Japanese comparative advantage. In many industries, firms were unlikely ever to recover their earlier levels: sugar, some steel sectors, aluminum, shipbuilding, textiles, chemicals, and paper, for example. Where the CEO had ruled autocratically, the firms had often gambled heavily in markets like real estate or built unnecessary plant capacity. Whether the firm was caught in a structural transformation or had suffered under a CEO who gambled and lost, it needed someone with a talent for numbers to come, sell unneeded assets, and leave. That much, bankers could do.

Given their limited ability, Japanese bankers avoid operating troubled debtors if possible. Like bankers elsewhere, they instead pull their loans when they can. As SHI and Hanasaki found, of course. When they needed extra money, the banks did not offer loans and volunteer to run the firm. Rather, they refused the money and pushed the firms toward bankruptcy. Whatever the pretext, explained one 1970s bank officer, "if a firm is in such bad shape that a bank will have to run it, banks will want to pull their loans if they can" (Ginko kanri 1978, 84).

At root, the notion that Japanese bankers rescue firms parallels the notion (one we discuss in chapter 6) that Japanese bureaucrats guide the economy. Traditionally, both banks and the government recruit smart college graduates, but IQ alone will not allow a graduate to build a car. If bankers from the Sumitomo Bank really knew enough to turn around Mazda, they would have done better to build cars themselves. They did not build their own cars, for the same reason they did not engineer Mazda's transformation: they did not know how.

CONCLUSIONS

Japanese firms sometimes appoint retired bankers to their boards. Yet most appoint none who holds a concurrent bank job; half have no bankers at all, few have more than one or two, and those in the financial services industry are far more likely to appoint bankers than are firms in other fields. Banks may sometimes take turns monitoring common debtors. Yet if they do, no trace of it appears in board appointment patterns. Japanese banks may sometimes bail out troubled firms. Yet they rescue very seldom, and doing so sometimes allows a bank to cut its losses after the fact. Fundamentally, the economywide data from the 1970s and 1980s show no evidence that banks ever promised (even implicitly) to support a debtor if it fell into distress.

The stories about the "main bank system" are good stories, but at root they are *only* stories. At root, the theory of the Japanese main bank system is a theory without a phenomenon. At root, the only charitable interpretation of the system is that it does not exist—and never did.

CHAPTER FIVE

And of Outside Directors

"Greed is good," yelled a triumphant, defiant Michael Douglas. Playing financier Gordon Gecko in the movie *Wall Street*, Douglas made the line quintessentially 1980s. His was a doomed triumph, a doomed defiance, of course, for Oliver Stone sent him to jail for his greed by the end of the film. Stone passed as countercultural at the time, but two decades later the didactically moralistic director has unambiguously gone mainstream—and greed has passed from good to bad. The rich do make nothing if not a convenient target. The rich you will have with you always, someone once almost said, and envy both sells newspapers and movies and elects politicians.

Wealthy insiders dominate the firms in which they work, we read. Already rich, in the United States they make themselves super-rich by stealing the guts of Enron and World.com. Already indolent, in Japan they steal their amenities in stability, security, and a refusal to make tough choices. Rather than take the risks and earn the returns that investors want and the country needs, they sleep on the job. Deadbeat borrowers they do not shut down. Redundant workers they do not fire. High-cost rivals they do not run out of business. Instead, they keep their world comfortable as it is. The country stays in recession, and they—the insiders—shoulder the blame.

Formally, whether in the United States or in Japan, directors rather than inside managers dominate corporate governance. Shareholders buy stock and take the rights to the residual interests in the firm. They earn high returns if it does well and lose their shirt if it flops. Creditors lend money and take less risk. If the venture succeeds, they collect only interest and principal, but if it tanks they still recover their claim before shareholders take anything at all. In exchange for bearing the greater risk, shareholders formally obtain ultimate control over the firm. Whether in the United States or in Japan, they pick the firm's directors, and those directors then hire and fire the men and women who run it.

Formally—but only formally. Whatever the case in the United States, declare most observers, in Japan this system does not work. Typically they make two arguments. First, powerful creditors manipulate the process to keep control. Second, insiders hijack the board to keep for themselves any power the creditors leave unclaimed. Of the two claims, the first follows from the tales observers tell about Japanese banks. For all the reasons we detail in chapter 4, this claim is not true. In this chapter 5 we explain why the second is no truer.

Whatever caused the 1990s Japanese recession, it was not bad corporate governance. By basic economic logic it could not have been bad governance, for (whether in the United States or Japan) competitive capital and product markets push firms to adopt efficient governance mechanisms or die. Without a governance structure that promotes investor returns, a firm would face higher capital costs. Unable to expand as cheaply as its rivals, it would incur higher product or service market costs. Eventually, its competitors would drive it out of business. In such a world, proposals to improve corporate governance are necessarily twenty-dollar bills on sidewalks: either they are ideas firms have already adopted, or ideas that would not work.

By basic economic logic, readers looking for the roots of the 1990s recession will have to look elsewhere, to causes (like politics) not subject to this market process (a point we examine in more detail in chapter 7). In this chapter 5, we explore the dynamics and details of corporate governance. To focus the inquiry, we investigate the composition of boards of directors. We begin by outlining the collective wisdom about these boards and the implications of market competition for patterns of firm governance. We use comprehensive data on large Japanese firms to explore which firms appoint what types of outside directors and what functions those directors might serve. Finally, we ask whether firms maintain observably inefficient ownership patterns.

THE REFORMIST AGENDA

The Need for Outside Directors
Both in the United States and in Japan, public intellectuals routinely champion outside directors. Firms need more of them, they declare. If firms do not name more on their own, the law should force them to name them. After all, explain they, directors monitor senior managers for shareholders. If they depend on those managers for their welfare, they will not monitor. If they take the job as part of a career at the firm, they will depend on the managers.

Directors are watchdogs, reformers explain. If they move into the position as "company men," they will lack the independence they need to watch adequately. Even less will they have incentives to push the firm toward the more "public-spirited" management that modern corporations so desperately need. For directors to do what society expects them to do so, they must come to the position from a lifetime outside the firm.

Of the activists, public-sector retirement plans have been among the most aggressive. By the late 1990s, CalPERS (1998) claimed that a "substantial majority" of board members should be independent. TIAA-CREF followed (2000), and old-line groups increasingly acquiesced. "It is important for the board of a large publicly owned corporation to have a substantial degree of independence from management," wrote the Business Roundtable (1999, 10) in 1999. "Accordingly, a substantial majority of the directors of such a corporation should be outside (non-management) directors." By mid-2002, even the New York Stock Exchange (NYSE Corporate Accountability and Listing Standards Committee 2002, 2) proposed to require that independent directors "comprise a majority of a company's board."

The Need in Japan

Like music videos and *anime*, intellectual fads hop the Pacific puddle, and this one has hopped as well. In Japan, public intellectuals champion the same rhetoric. Take the Corporate Governance Forum, headed at the time by a one-time university president and corporate law professor. Announced the Forum (Japan Corporate Governance Forum 1998), "a majority of the board of directors should be composed of outside directors." Sensing the way the wind blows (and voters vote), some politicians even proposed legislation to mandate outside directors.

Through avenues like the American Chamber of Commerce in Japan, Americans soon added outside directors to their weekly shopping list of changes they demanded of Japanese firms. But as with so much else on their list, one might wonder how much they really understood. CalPERS, for instance, excoriated Japanese firms for not appointing more outsiders. When asked for his "assessment of corporate governance practices in Japan," though, its representative tellingly added that a "simple first step would be to deliver proxy material to shareholders in English" (Japan Corporate Governance Forum 2003, 2). Excoriate first, read later, apparently.

Western observers, in turn, parrot the public intellectuals. Sociologist Ronald Dore (2000, 79) dismisses Japanese boards as "an 'insider system' over which shareholders exercise little monitoring control." Business scholar Christina Ahmadjian (2001) asserts that the directors "rarely play a supervisory role," few are outsiders, and "many outsiders are not independent." And quoting a United Kingdom study, reformers Robert Monks and Nell Minow (1995, 272) insist that Japanese boards "represent the interests of the company and its employees" rather than "the interests of shareholders."

Economic Logic

By basic economic theory, however, this corporate governance talk should leave one troubled. By definition, firms with underperforming governance arrangements will not maximize investor returns. If so, they will face higher costs in the capital market, and those capital costs will increase the cost of the goods and services they sell. Unable to match their rivals' prices, over time these firms should disappear. Given that market dynamic, any reforms academics might propose will be either ideas firms have already incorporated or ideas they have rejected for a reason—the ideas would not work (Demsetz and Lehn 1985).

Economic theory says nothing about what managers think. By that theory, they need not choose governance structures that maximize shareholder returns deliberately. They need not consider shareholder returns at all, and some may even ignore shareholder returns on purpose. Economic theory instead addresses which firms tend to survive. Its implications are unambiguous: whatever managers *claim* to be doing, those that do maximize shareholder returns will raise new capital more cheaply than their rivals. Their firms will tend to survive disproportionately. In equilibrium, the firms that persist will be those with governance structures that increase investor returns.

More outsiders are not always better than fewer. At some firms investors will choose outsider directors to protect themselves against managerial misbehavior. At others, however, they may use other means to monitor and constrain their managers, and want the sophistication and cohesion that an all-inside board brings. Given market pressures, the firms in which more outsiders would raise performance will either appoint those outsiders or lose customers to better-governed rivals. Given those pressures, the firms that survive with few outsiders will disproportionately be those in which outsiders would bring few gains.

For the scholar, this logic implies that observed board-composition patterns will bear no systematic relation to observed firm-performance levels. Recall the logic. Firms with inefficient structures will fail and drop out of the sample. If so, then a firm for which a given structure promotes shareholder returns will tend to persist, whereas a firm for which the same structure generates losses will tend to disappear. Although a particular structure may well lower shareholder returns at *most* firms, that point will not appear in the data since only the firms at which it increases returns will tend to survive.

And so empiricists find. Among Western companies, for example, they do *not* locate a positive association between outsider directors and firm performance. Instead, they generally report no relationship between observed performance and board composition. After a "meta-analytic" study of the results, one set of authors (Dalton et al. 1998, 278) concludes that "board composition has virtually no effect on firm performance." "No matter what variable is used to measure performance," writes Yale legal scholar Roberta Romano (1996, 287), "virtually all studies find that there is no significant relation between performance and board composition."

The point is not that boards do not matter—though the absence of any observable relation between board composition and performance is consistent with that conclusion. Rather, the point is that (1) the optimal board structure varies from firm to firm, and (2i) the firms that survive are those whose boards are close to the firm-specific optimum. As a result, the firms that would most benefit from outsiders will have them, while the firms without outsiders are those in which outsiders would do the least good. In such a world, if one looked for evidence that outsiders benefited a firm, one would not find it. The absence of that observable evidence does not necessarily mean outsiders bring no benefit. Instead, it may mean that those firms that did not appoint more outsiders when more outsiders would have helped likely underperformed their rivals and went out of business.

Although this does not make happy campers out of us empiricists, it is a situation we often face when markets work well. If markets clear, for example, competition will drive down returns and producers will rarely earn extra profits—but empiricists cannot prove the point through statistically significant results. If markets impound information quickly, stock prices will reflect all available information about the firm—but empiricists again will not have significant results to prove it. Rather, in both cases the dynamics imply that empiricists will *not* observe significant results. When we note that firms choose governance structures that align managerial and shareholder incentives reasonably well, we make exactly such a claim. We merely claim, in short, that markets work effectively.

The Application to Japan
Whether this market logic applies to firms in the United States, argue many area-studies scholars, it cannot apply to Japan. Most basically, claim they, capital markets there do not function. The logic depends on a smoothly functioning stock market, but that Japan does not have. Japanese firms insulate themselves from stock market pressure through cross-shareholding arrangements and do not raise their funds through stock markets anyway.

In fact, of course, the claim is false. As noted earlier, Japanese firms maintain substantial equity capital—roughly comparable to the funds U.S. firms raise there (chapter 4). The cross-shareholding arrangements do not exist and never did (chapter 2). Popular claims to the contrary notwithstanding, the stock market in Japan provides exactly the same incentives for efficient management that it does in the United States.

Financial Disclosure

The Japan specialists continue that the economic logic ignores the level of financial disclosure in Japan. The disclosure is so bad there, they argue, that market signals will not reflect whether a firm maintains good governance or bad. For the stock market to discipline firms as the logic implies, investors must be able to gauge the relative performance of various firms. That, claim the specialists, Japanese investors cannot do.

Alas, Japan specialists again miss the logic of the market. Investors need information, but they have multiple ways to obtain it: most basically, they can gather it individually or invest in a firm that gives the information to everyone. Because neither procedure is free, shareholders pay the price either way. Even if they invest in a firm that collects, assembles, and disseminates the information for them, they pay for the work. If either the production of the information entails scale economies or the information is a firm-specific public good, they gain by having the firm produce the information collectively. If not, the procedure yields no net benefits.

Because information is not free, however, more is not necessarily better than less. Even if the production of information involves scale economies or public goods, investors will not want all information. They will want only cost-justified information. Beyond that point, they incur a net loss.

Crucially, the firms themselves have incentives to provide investors with cost-justified information. Disproportionately, the firms that provide that information will tend to survive, and that process itself will tend to eliminate the firms that do not provide it. As a result, the optimal level of disclosure is not the level demanded by regulators or professional shareholder activists. It is the level generated in competitive, unregulated securities markets.

All this holds true even when the information is unfavorable. If a firm refuses to produce information that investors would ordinarily value, investors will presume the worst—and their competitors will encourage them to adopt that presumption. To avoid their doing so, firms will even produce information that is negative. If shareholders do not believe the information that a firm volunteers, it will hire outsiders (such as accountants) to vouch for the information.

Accordingly, in competitive markets like those of the United States and Japan, the firms that disclose information up to but only up to the cost-justified level will incur the lowest capital market costs. They will produce and expand most cheaply. In markets such as those of the United States and Japan, firms that produce either too much information or too little will suffer a capital market hit. Eventually (and unless regulatory constraints otherwise require the information—as they currently do), they will change their strategy or go out of business. Firms in Japan may or may not produce less information than firms in the United States—but either way (and except in those cases in which the regulatory framework *stops* firms from disclosing information they want to disclose) they do not produce less information than investors need.

The Corporate Control Market

The Japan specialists are not done. Economic logic hinges on a viable "corporate control market," claim they, and Japan lacks that market. For the economic logic to work, they explain, badly run firms must run the risk that a T. Boone Pickens will take them over. Yet Japan lacks many hostile acquisitions. Necessarily, the corporate control market must not function. Absent a functioning market for that corporate control, the stock market cannot discipline inefficient firms.

This objection is no truer than the last. Takeovers or no, a firm sells good products cheap or—eventually—dies. To make those products it needs capital, and to raise the capital it must convince investors to part with their money. Whether as debt or as equity, however, investors will invest only if it promises them a return as attractive as that offered by its rivals. Absent efficient governance, it will find that promise hard to keep. As much as the prospect of a takeover may help constrain managers, firm efficiency does not hinge on it. Ultimately, the hostile takeover is not a prerequisite to efficient management. Instead, it merely constitutes one mechanism among the several by which market competition moves assets to more productive uses.

In any case, the Japanese government never imposed high costs on tender offers anyway. Until 1971, it regulated them not at all. Since then, it has merely imposed on acquirers a framework modeled on that in the United States. Although the framework does raise the cost of an acquisition, it raises it little (if any) more than it raises it in the United States. Yet the incentive effect of the corporate control market hinges on the cost of an acquisition, not on its numbers. After all, if most firms are well managed, acquirers will make few takeovers even if takeovers are cheap—simply because they will find few plausible targets. Ultimately, the incentive effect hinges only on the potential for takeovers. Sans regulatory interference, that potential will remain high.

In terms of allocating assets to their most effective users, moreover, hostile takeovers and friendly mergers are substitutes, and Japan has always had plenty of mergers. In 1994, Japanese firms engineered 1,917 mergers and 1,153 sales of all or substantially all their assets (Kosei torihiki iinkai 1994a, 181). In a hostile takeover, a would-be acquirer obtains the target shares by paying target shareholders a premium. In the merger, it does so by bribing target managers to deliver the firm. The bribe is a fiduciary duty breach, to be sure. Disguised as a consulting agreement or other high-salary low-work contract, it is also unpoliceable. Suppose an acquirer could more efficiently run a firm than its incumbent managers. Whether it offers the target shareholders a premium or those senior managers a consulting contract, it will obtain the firm. Either way, the target's assets will move to the entrepreneurs who can most efficiently exploit them.

Banks Are Different

Some Japan specialists will object that whatever the logic's applicability generally, it does not apply to banks. Banks were central to the 1990s recession, and for several reasons the logic about market-driven governance does not apply to them: (a) regulators have severely restrained competition in the industry; (b) mutual (i.e., not stock) insurance firms have held bank shares; and (c) the government maintains deposit insurance. In fact, the market logic does apply to banks.

Regulatory Constraints

The regulatory constraints never substantively restricted competition. Not only do they not bind in the post-1980s deregulated environment, but they did not bind in the 1960s or 1970s. As we show in chapter 6, for example, the controls on the loan interest rate never bound. From time to time, observers suggest that banks circumvented the controls by requiring debtors to maintain low-interest deposits at the bank. In fact, the loan interest-rate caps were so porous that banks rarely demanded the "compensating balances." Even without the deposits, they charged market-clearing rates.

Nor did the limits on new entry restrict competition. As of the early 1990s, Japanese firms chose from among 140-plus banks. With that many rivals, the industry was competitive, new entrants or no. To be sure, only the three long-term credit banks (and a few other financial institutions) could issue debentures, and only the seven trust banks could serve as trustees. Otherwise, however, the market was largely open to all—hardly what some scholars (e.g., Milhaupt and Miller 1997, 6) characterize as "extreme compartmentalization." Regional banks may have "specialize[d] in local lending to small business" (1997, 7), but (other than the effects of the government's approval process for branches), regulations did not drive the specialization.

Mutuals as Shareholders

Mutual insurance firms may have held bank stock, but their ownership structure does not affect the market logic outlined here. Stock or mutual, insurance firms compete for customers. At any given level of contractual benefit, those customers choose from among insurance contracts by price. A mutual insurance firm can offer a given level of benefits at a competitive price, though, only if it effectively invests the premiums it receives. If it systematically buys underperforming stock, it will earn a lower return than a firm that invests in market-performing stock. Over time, the former will offer less attractive prices and benefits than the latter. Over time, competition in the insurance product market will tend to drive the former out of business.

Deposit Guarantees

That the government guaranteed deposits and allegedly promised to rescue troubled banks affects none of this either. In the late 1980s, it insured deposits of up to ¥10 million per depositor (Nihon ginko 1995, 124). Simultaneously, claim many observers, it informally promised not to let banks fail. One might wonder about the latter, as it did let them fail once it faced hard times in the 1990s—but never mind.

According to economists Masaharu Hanazaki and Akiyoshi Horiuchi (1998, 15–16), these government guarantees eviscerated corporate governance. The deposit insurance and promised rescues "deprived investors," they write, "of incentives to monitor the performance of individual banks." In the process, they "hindered the development of market mechanisms to discipline bank management."

In truth, the policies did nothing of the sort. To be sure they raised the possibility—indeed, probability—that banks would adopt higher-risk strategies. If times are good the shareholders make money, but if bad the government foots the bill; under such an arrangement, shareholders obviously have an incentive to increase risk. Crucially, shareholders do not have any reduced incentive to monitor their bank. The government may have changed the risk level that maximized bank profits, but shareholders still face incentives to ensure that their managers select that (now higher) profit-maximizing risk level.

So, Why Are There So Many Outside Directors in the United States?

Why then the cross-national difference? U.S. firms typically have appointed many more outsiders than Japanese firms have. According to one study (Herman 1981, 35), the fraction of manufacturing firms in the United States with a majority of outsider directors "rose from 50 percent in 1938, to 61 percent in 1961, to 71 percent in 1972, to 83 percent in 1976." By 1973 the median large manufacturing firm had only 40 percent inside directors, and by 1988 that figure had fallen to a mere quarter (1981, 35). If product, factor, and corporate control markets in the United States and Japan drive firms toward their firm-specific optimal governance structures, why do U.S. firms appoint so many more outsiders than do their Japanese rivals?

U.S. firms do not hire the outsiders to improve their governance. If they did, capital market pressure would have induced them to hire the outsiders decades ago. Instead, although they long appointed a few outsiders, they only recently switched to outsider-dominated boards. They switched because of the increasing receptivity that U.S. judges show toward derivative and shareholder class-action litigation. Virtually all such suits involve extortionate claims that generate attorneys' fees but no shareholder returns (Romano 1991). For firms facing such claims (which is to say, any exchange-listed firm), outside directors offer substantial benefits: by routing potential conflicts of interest through a committee of nominally independent outsiders, the firms can insulate themselves from virtually all conflict of interest claims. For such firms, outside directors offer cheap insurance against trial lawyers.

Until recently, Japanese law imposed on derivative claimants a formidable set of costs, and virtually no shareholders filed suit (West 1994). The law still bars class actions, but over the past few years courts and legislators have begun to dismantle the obstacles to derivative litigation (West 2001). Given that change, even if the proposed legislation to require outside directors does not pass, Japanese firms may well start hiring outsiders anyway. They would not be hiring them because outsiders improved management. They would be hiring them because outsiders helped insulate them from fraudulent shareholder claims.

WHO APPOINTS THEM?

The Literature
Despite arguing that Japanese firms should appoint more outsiders, few observers claim they appoint none. Instead, they note two types of outsiders appointed by Japanese firms: bankers and retired bureaucrats.[1] The former they tie to the main bank myths we detailed in chapter 4. The latter (a phenomenon popularly known as *amakudari*) they alternately tie to the myths about industrial policy we discuss in chapter 6 or to newspaper accounts of corruption.

Bankers
Writers on the Japanese economy do not just observe that Japanese firms sometimes appoint bankers to their boards. They also claim that the bankers dominate the firms. Take economists Randall Morck, Masao Nakamura, and Anil Shivdasani (2000, 540). According to the trio, in Japan "corporate governance rights rest primarily with banks." Investment banker Paul Sheard (1996, 181) describes the banks and large shareholders as "the principal agents of direct corporate governance in Japan." And reformers Monks and Minow (1995, 265) assert that at large Japanese firms, "outside directors usually represent major lenders."

According to such writers, many of the bankers on Japanese boards come from the firm's main bank. Harvard business professor Karl Kester (1993, 70), for instance, claims that "one or more members of a typical (21-member) Japanese board frequently are former executives of the company's main bank(s)." And according to economists Benjamin Hermalin and Michael Weisbach (1998, 112), representatives of a main bank "usually serve on the company's board."

Once on that board, the bankers serve not the firm's interests but the bank's. Fundamentally, each uses his board slot to monitor the firm on behalf of a bank. As Sheard put it (1996, 181), in "supplying managers to the board," the "main banks directly exercise 'voice.'"

Retired Bureaucrats

Most scholars assert that retired bureaucrats have a prominent place on Japanese boards as well. Given the "high number of *amakudari* board members," writes political scientist Ulrike Schaede (1994, 290–91), "ex-government officials constitute an important factor in the Japanese governance structure." Indeed, "the CEOs of *many* major city banks were retired government ministry officials" (ital. added).

Yet if scholars agree about the presence of the ex-bureaucrats, they do not always agree about their role. Instead, they offer cross-cutting theories about these bureaucrats-turned-directors. Several argue that the retired bureaucrats retain their loyalty to the government and help it regulate the firms. Aoki (1988, 266), for example, writes that retired bureaucrats allow the government to "extend its visible and invisible influence throughout its jurisdiction." Schaede (1995, 316) claims that they "contribute directly to [the] alignment" of "corporate decisions with government interests." Economist Takeo Hoshi (1998, 862) writes that they reflect "the influence of the government over private firms" and give it a way "to intervene in the management if necessary." And political scientist Daniel Okimoto (1989, 162) then adds that MITI sends its ex-bureaucrats "to the very sectors identified as most central to the development of Japan's economy."

Others suggest that the firms and banks appoint the ex-bureaucrats to obtain favored access to regulatory perquisites. Horiuchi and Shimizu (2001) claim banks that accepted ex-bureaucrats maintained riskier loan portfolios than did their competitors. Schaede and Aoki apparently see the influence going both ways. Claims Schaede (1995, 309), construction firms accepted them to obtain "access to price and project information in the bid-rigging process." And argues Aoki (Aoki, Patrick, and Sheard 1994, 32), not only did the ex-bureaucrats allow the government to influence firms, but firms accepted them "as a means of gaining access to valuable information from, and to exert influence on, the regulatory authorities."

Outside Appointments at Firms Other Than Banks

Turn, then, to actual board appointment patterns at large Japanese firms. To explore those patterns, we assembled information on all nonbank firms listed on section 1 of the Tokyo Stock Exchange (the largest 1,000+ firms).

Observers rightly note the most obvious characteristic of the boards: they are big. At the section 1 firms in 1985, boards ranged from 6 directors to 54, with a median of 18 and a mean of 19.5. By contrast, in 1988 the mean size of the board of a large U.S. manufacturing firm was about 12. Given the large board size, most of the firms appointed a subset of the directors to an executive board. At our 1985 Japanese firms, the executive directors ranged from 1 member to 32, with a median of 7 and a mean of about 8.

Outsiders

Observers also rightly note the source of most directors—firm ranks. Again among our firms in 1985, 14 of the mean 19 directors were career firm employees, and 6 of the mean 8 executive directors were as well. Put another way, at the mean 1985 firm, 26 percent of the directors and 27 percent of the executive directors had either past or concurrent appointments at other institutions (our definition of an outsider). The mean varied widely by industry: from fewer than 3 outside directors in light industry to nearly 9 in (nonbank) service and finance.

These outside director ratios are higher than those reported in other studies. They are higher because we survey all section 1 firms, where most writers canvass only the very largest (typically the largest hundred-odd firms). Because in Japan the biggest firms appoint the fewest outsiders, those who focus on the largest necessarily bias the outside-director figures downward.

Few firms named a majority of outsiders, but most did appoint some. On the one hand, only 15 percent of the firms had at least half of the board composed of outsiders, and 23 percent had at least half of the executive board composed of outsiders. On the other, only 10 percent of the boards had no outsiders. Appointment patterns again varied widely by industry: only 6 percent of the firms in light industry had a majority of outsiders, while 51 percent of those in service and finance did; only 2 percent of the construction firms had no outsiders while 20 percent of the light industry firms had none. Among large U.S. manufacturing firms, in recent years nearly three-quarters of their board members have been outsiders (Agrawal and Knoeber 2001, 182, table 1).

Of the outsiders, those with a past career beyond the firm (as opposed to those with a concurrent career outside) dominated. At our mean firm in 1985, 1.8 of the 19.5 directors were former executives at other firms, while 1.1 currently held such positions; 1.1 were former bankers, while 0.2 currently worked at banks; 0.5 were former bureaucrats, while legal

Table 5.1. Numbers and types of outside directors

	N	Full board				Executive directors			
		Min.	Median	Mean	Max.	Min.	Median	Mean	Max.
A. Boards and outsiders, all firms									
1. Total directors									
1985	1,029	6	18	19.49	54	1	7	7.91	32
1990	1,134	6	19	21.16	59	1	8	8.66	34
1995	1,197	7	19	21.26	60	1	7	8.23	34
2. Total outsiders									
1985	1,029	0	4	4.70	24	0	1	1.95	9
1990	1,134	0	4	4.90	29	0	2	2.15	11
1995	1,197	0	4	5.14	23	0	1	1.96	10
B. Boards and outsiders, by industry (1985)									
1. Total directors									
Construction	101	11	23	24.98	51	2	10	11.45	32
Trade	117	7	17	19.68	54	2	6	7.84	28
Service/financial	43	9	19	19.07	32	2	6	6.54	13
Utilities	87	7	20	20.52	39	1	8	8.48	20
Light industry	131	9	17	17.85	40	2	6	6.92	19
Chemical	156	8	18	19.13	41	1	7	7.73	23
Metals	119	6	17	18.79	52	2	7	8.14	29
Machinery	275	8	17	18.44	54	1	6	7.13	20
2. Total outsiders									
Construction	101	0	7	8.21	19	0	4	4.46	9
Trade	117	0	3	4.14	19	0	1	1.82	8
Service/financial	43	0	8	8.63	21	0	2	2.91	6
Utilities	87	0	4	4.82	24	0	1	1.62	7
Light industry	131	0	3	2.84	12	0	1	1.06	6
Chemical	156	0	3	3.75	15	0	1	1.44	7
Metals	119	0	3	4.14	14	0	1	1.72	8
Machinery	275	0	4	4.65	17	0	1	1.86	8

	1985	1990	1995	1985	1990	1995
C. Mean percentage of outsiders, by outsider category						
Past banker	5.87	5.27	5.50	7.38	6.86	6.16
Past other firm	10.49	11.12	11.85	14.74	15.62	15.75
Past bureaucrat	2.41	2.13	2.16	2.48	2.64	2.56
Con. banker	1.06	0.96	0.91	0.25	0.19	0.08
Con. other firm	5.87	5.39	5.35	1.89	1.91	1.41
Total outsiders	25.60	24.86	25.78	27.22	27.23	25.95

Sources: Toyo keizai shimpo sha, *Kigyo keiretsu soran*, various years.

Notes: Past banker, a director who had earlier worked at a bank; *past other firm*, a director who had earlier worked at another firm; *past bureaucrat*, a director who had earlier worked for the government; *con. banker*, a director who concurrently holds a position with a bank; *con. other firm*, a director who concurrently holds a position with another firm.

restrictions prevented current officials from holding board posts. Of the 7.9 executive directors at the mean firm, 1.0 were former executives at other firms, while 0.1 currently held such positions; 0.5 were former bankers, while 0.01 currently worked at banks; and 0.3 were former government officials. More generally, at the mean firm 6.9 percent (and 2.1 percent of the executive directors) concurrently held other posts. At only three firms did such directors comprise at least half the board, and at only nine did they comprise at least half the executive directors.

The law mandates none of these appointment patterns. Should they have wished to do so, Japanese firms could long ago have appointed men and women who held full-time jobs elsewhere. Notwithstanding, they generally choose not to do so. Instead, they opt to give their directors full-time positions instead.

Change over Time

As the firms left the booming 1980s for the depressed 1990s, they did not change the type of directors they appointed. One might have thought they would pick different kinds of directors in expansionary and recessionary times—but apparently not so, or at least not observably so. In 1985 the firms chose outsiders for 25.6 percent of their directors, and in 1990 for 24.9 percent. In 1995 they still chose outsiders for 25.8 percent.

Of their outsiders, the firms consistently chose 6–7 percent from banks, 16–17 percent from other firms, and 2–3 percent from the government. From 1985 to 1990, 34 percent of the firms kept the number of outsiders they named to their boards unchanged. Sixteen percent added one outsider, and 17 percent added two or more; 18 percent cut one outside director, and 15 percent cut two or more. From 1990 to 1995, 29 percent made no change in the number of outside directors, 22 percent added one, and 20 percent added two or more; 16 percent cut one outsider, and 14 percent cut two or more.

Bankers

Of the banker-director appointments, several facets are straightforward, as we detailed in chapter 4 (Miwa and Ramseyer 2005c, 316–17, table 3). First, directors with banking backgrounds tend to serve on the boards of firms with more bank debt. The more heavily a firm relies on banks for its funds, the more likely it will appoint a banker to its board. Second, they are less likely to serve on the boards of firms dominated by a major shareholder. Third, they are also more likely to serve on the boards of firms without a large stock of mortgageable assets. Apparently, firms that can raise funds by offering their creditors a security interest find bankers less helpful.

Although bankers are common, they do not dominate. Indeed, about half the firms have none. In 1985, 47 percent had no ex–banker director, and

Table 5.2. Type of outside directors by industry, 1985

	Full board				Executive directors			
	Min.	Median	Mean	Max.	Min.	Median	Mean	Max.
A. All industries (N = 1,029)								
Past bankers	0	1	1.06	19	0	0	0.54	6
Past other firm	0	1	1.83	15	0	0	0.98	8
Past bureaucrat	0	0	0.53	11	0	0	0.30	8
Con. banker	0	0	0.22	6	0	0	0.01	2
Con. other firm	0	0	1.06	11	0	0	0.12	6
B. Construction (n = 101)								
Past bankers	0	1	1.18	6	0	0	0.69	3
Past other firm	0	2	3.50	13	0	1	1.95	8
Past bureaucrat	0	2	2.57	11	0	1	1.71	8
Con. banker	0	0	0.07	1	0	0	0.01	1
Con. other firm	0	0	0.89	8	0	0	0.09	2
C. Trade (n = 117)								
Past bankers	0	0	0.91	6	0	0	0.50	4
Past other firm	0	1	1.90	15	0	0	0.97	6
Past bureaucrat	0	0	0.26	3	0	0	0.09	2
Con. banker	0	0	0.12	4	0	0	0.12	2
Con. other firm	0	0	0.95	8	0	0	0.21	6
D. Service and finance (n = 43)								
Past bankers	0	1	2.42	19	0	0	1.12	6
Past other firm	0	1	2.51	12	0	1	1.09	4
Past bureaucrat	0	0	0.67	7	0	0	0.28	2
Con. banker	0	0	0.60	6	0	0	0.05	1
Con. other firm	0	2	2.42	8	0	0	0.37	2
E. Utilities (n = 87)								
Past bankers	0	0	1.01	15	0	0	0.51	5
Past other firm	0	1	1.24	8	0	0	0.66	5
Past bureaucrat	0	0	0.53	5	0	0	0.30	4
Con. banker	0	0	0.49	4	0	0	0.01	1
Con. other firm	0	1	1.54	8	0	0	0.15	2
F. Light industry (n = 131)								
Past bankers	0	1	0.97	5	0	0	0.46	3
Past other firm	0	0	0.85	9	0	0	0.41	5
Past bureaucrat	0	0	0.18	4	0	0	0.08	2
Con. banker	0	0	0.15	3	0	0	0.02	2
Con. other firm	0	0	0.69	4	0	0	0.08	2
G. Chemical (n = 156)								
Past bankers	0	1	1.08	7	0	0	0.60	6
Past other firm	0	0	1.24	12	0	0	0.72	4
Past bureaucrat	0	0	0.13	3	0	0	0.08	3
Con. banker	0	0	0.28	2	0	0	0.01	1
Con. other firm	0	0	1.02	11	0	0	0.04	1

(continued)

Table 5.2 (*continued*)

	Full board				Executive directors			
	Min.	Median	Mean	Max.	Min.	Median	Mean	Max.
H. Metals (*n* = 119)								
Past bankers	0	1	0.80	5	0	0	0.39	3
Past other firm	0	1	1.71	9	0	0	0.98	8
Past bureaucrat	0	0	0.36	3	0	0	0.25	3
Con. banker	0	0	0.14	3	0	0	0.01	1
Con. other firm	0	0	1.13	8	0	0	0.08	3
I. Machinery (*n* = 275)								
Past bankers	0	1	1.03	7	0	0	0.49	4
Past other firm	0	1	2.13	13	0	0	1.13	7
Past bureaucrat	0	0	0.32	4	0	0	0.13	3
Con. banker	0	0	0.19	3	0	0	0.01	1
Con. other firm	0	0	0.98	10	0	0	0.11	3

Sources: Toyo keizai shimpo sha, *Kigyo keiretsu soran*, various years.

Notes: Past banker, a director who had earlier worked at a bank; *past other firm*, a director who had earlier worked at another firm; *past bureaucrat*, a director who had earlier worked for the government; *con. banker*, a director who concurrently holds a position with a bank; and *con. other firm*, a director who concurrently holds a position with another firm.

63 percent had no ex–banker executive director. The mean firm had 4.7 outside directors, but only 1.1 with a background at a bank. According to one study (Cable 1985, 119), at the largest hundred German companies, banks held 9.8 percent of all board seats. By contrast, at the largest hundred Japanese firms, ex-bankers held 5.5 percent of the board seats and 5.9 percent of the executive board seats.

Most of the banker-directors are *ex*-bankers rather than men currently working at banks. Again as we explained in chapter 4, the distinction matters for understanding what the bankers might be doing. A banker who keeps his post at the bank owes his future career and livelihood to the bank. Even though as director he legally owes his fiduciary duty to the industrial firm, he plausibly might use his spot on the board to promote the interests of the bank. By contrast, a banker who has retired from the bank owes his livelihood to the firm to which he has moved. He has nothing to gain by promoting the bank's interests over those of the firm. As a result, if (as the conventional wisdom asserts) banks place bankers on boards to monitor on behalf of the banks, they would not place men who had cut all ties to the bank. Instead, they would appoint younger executives who could expect a long and profitable bank career if they proved loyal. Notwithstanding those dynamics, only 15 percent of the 1985 firms had a director with a concurrent bank position. Fewer than one in a hundred had an executive director with a concurrent bank post.

What is more, the bankers tended not to serve at the manufacturing firms anyway. Conventionally, observers envision the bankers going to manufacturing firms. In fact, they went to firms in those related industries where they could best use their financial expertise. In the (nonbank) service and finance industry, the mean 1985 firm had 2.4 ex–bank directors and 1.1 ex–bank executive directors. By contrast, in the chemical industry the mean firm had only 1.2 ex–banker directors and 0.6 ex–executive directors; in the machinery industry it had 1.0 ex–bank directors and 0.5 ex–executive directors; and in metals it had 0.8 ex–bank directors and 0.4 ex–executive directors.

"Main banks" were hardly the "exclusive" source of the directors. If (as the conventional wisdom asserts—see chapter 4) the main bank served as the exclusive monitor for all other banks, *only* bankers from the main banks should appear on boards. In fact, only a bit over half the ex–bank directors are from the main bank.

Nonbank Outside Executives
Firms that invest heavily in a company will demand a way to influence it. Consistent with that logic, the firms that appoint the most outside business executives to their board (nonbank, nonbureaucrat outside directors) are those with a large shareholder. Consider a shareholder who owns at least a quarter of a firm's stock to be a dominant shareholder. On the Tokyo Stock Exchange, about a fifth of the firms have such a dominant shareholder—and such firms are substantially more likely than other firms to appoint at least one retired outside business executive to their board.

Although 57 percent of all TSE firms had a nonbank retired (i.e., not concurrent) outside director, 81 percent of the firms with a dominant shareholder had one. Although 45 percent of the TSE firms had such an officer as an executive director, 78 percent of the firms with a dominant shareholder did. Among all TSE firms, retired executives constituted 9.4 percent of the board (12.4 percent of the executive directors). At those firms with a dominant shareholder, they constituted 24 percent (36 percent of the executive directors).

Predictably, these outside directors often came from the dominant shareholder itself. Of the 1,884 retired executives from other firms serving as directors at the TSE firms, 39.3 percent were from a dominant shareholder. Of the 403 serving as executive directors, 39.9 percent were. Other relevant factors held constant, the presence of a dominant shareholder increased the number of retired business-executive directors at a firm by about 2.4. It raised the number of retired executive directors by 1.5, and the number of directors with concurrent (i.e., not retired) posts in other firms by 1.4.

Retired Bureaucrats

For all the pages academics have lavished on them, the retired-bureaucrat directors are few. Our 1,000+ 1985 firms had a mean 0.5 ex–government directors and 0.3 ex–government executive directors. Seventy-four percent of the firms had no ex–government directors at all, and 83 percent had no executive directors.

What is more, few of the firms with ex-bureaucrats were in any of the industries that drove the postwar economic growth. Academics to the contrary notwithstanding, firms in industries "central to the development of Japan's economy" did *not* recruit ex–bureaucrat directors. In the machinery industry in 1985, nearly 80 percent of the 275 firms had no former government officials on their board, and 90 percent had none as a executive director. In the chemical industry (156 firms), 89 percent had no government officials on their board, and 93 percent had none as an executive director. Indeed, the average machinery firm had only 0.32 ex–bureaucrat directors, and the average chemical firm only 0.13.

Instead, retired bureaucrats served in the construction firms. Where the average TSE firm had half an ex-bureaucrat on its board in 1985, the average construction firm (101 firms) had 2.6. Where a quarter of the TSE firms had ex–bureaucrat directors, 71 percent of the construction firms did. Where 17 percent of the TSE firms had ex–bureaucrat executive directors, 63 percent of the construction firms did. Of the 542 ex–bureaucrat directors at all nonbank TSE firms, nearly half (260 directors) were at the construction firms. Of the ex–bureaucrat executive directors, 55 percent were.

Even banks were no more likely to hire ex-bureaucrats than were the construction firms (see also "Outside Appointments at the Banks," below). In 1986 only two of the big money center banks had a former Ministry of Finance (MoF) official as an executive director, and only three had any executive directors from the Bank of Japan (BoJ). The regional banks had more ex-bureaucrats than did the city banks, but no more than the construction firms. Of the 56 regional banks, 48 percent had a MoF director and 50 percent a BoJ director; 36 percent had a MoF executive director and 39 percent a BoJ executive director. Replicating the construction firm ratios, 71 percent of the regional banks had *either* a MoF or a BoJ director, and 63 percent had either a MoF or a BoJ executive director. Of the 43 nonbank firms in the services and finance industry, 74 percent had no ex–bureaucrat directors, and 81 percent had no ex–bureaucrat executive directors.

Construction Firms

If the construction firms hired half the ex-bureaucrats, they also hired many of the outside business executives. All told, 18.7 percent of the retired business executives served at construction firms in 1985, and among the executive directors 19.5 percent did. If the average construction firm had about 2 more ex-bureaucrats on its board than TSE firms in general, it had 1.7 more retired business executives.

Within the construction industry, board appointments reflected expected revenues. Among the firms, those that focused on public-sector projects appointed more ex-bureaucrats. Those that focused on large private-sector projects may have appointed more retired executives from other firms.

To show this effect, in regressions reported elsewhere (Miwa and Ramseyer 2005c, 322, table 4) we estimated the number of ex–bureaucrat directors (or executive directors) in 1985 as a function of (inter alia) the fraction of its revenues a construction firm generated from (1) construction projects (both public and private sector) and (2i) civil engineering projects (almost entirely government funded). The more a firm relied on civil engineering projects, the more ex-bureaucrats it named to its board and executive board. Conversely, the less a firm relied on civil engineering projects, the more retired business executives (sometimes from its principal customers) it named to its board.

Confronted with evidence that construction firms hire retired government bureaucrats, observers typically assume corruption. Given the bid-rigging scandals on public-sector projects, the assumption is superficially plausible enough. Some writers claim that the firms name bureaucrats to their boards as a form of deferred compensation for their help in colluding on past bids. Others claim the ex-bureaucrats use their connections and reputations to help rig future bids.

As much as the hypotheses appeal to the Philip Marlowe in us all, they raise more logical problems than they resolve. In Japan as in the United States, bid rigging is a serious crime. When in 1976 a mayor's campaign staffer solicited funds from a contractor in exchange for favorable treatment on a city housing project bid, he found himself prosecuted and convicted for bribery.[2] When in 1991 a construction firm executive director bribed a mayor for a contract on the city's new sports facility, he found himself sentenced to two years in prison (suspended) and civilly liable to the firm to boot.[3] And when a director at a real estate firm bribed a governor for regulatory clearance and favorable treatment on a bid, a court convicted them both: two years in prison for the governor and two and a half for the director, neither term suspended.[4]

Although heavy penalties will not eliminate crime entirely, usually they both reduce its incidence and induce criminals to cover their tracks more carefully. In Japan the high penalties for bid rigging will not make all politicians as honest as the day is long, but they ought to induce those firms determined to bribe politicians to negotiate and pay their bribes covertly.

Hiring ex-bureaucrats either to negotiate the crime or to compensate coconspirators, however, makes the Russian mob look subtle.

In fact, ex-bureaucrats probably would not help rig many bids anyway. Because of the stiff penalties, most bureaucrats will not rig bids unless they know well the person propositioning them. An official from prefecture X will not likely take a bribe just because the man approaching him once worked for the Ministry of Construction. Even less will he care whether the man once worked for prefecture Y. Perhaps a retired bureaucrat from city Z will help rig a bid at city Z. He will hardly help cheat anywhere else. The retired bureaucrats at the construction firms, however, come from a wide range of national and local government offices.

Crucially, the Ministry of Construction does not auction public-sector projects nationwide, and neither does anyone else. Instead, for any given project the government unit involved solicits its own bids. Cities solicit bids for city projects, and prefectures solicit those for their own. The national government itself solicits less than 12 percent of all public-sector projects. Prefectural and municipal governments each solicit another 30 percent, and assorted public entities solicit the rest.

Consider instead a more mundane explanation for the hiring patterns: construction firms appoint directors who will help them identify the services their principal customers want to buy. If they sell heavily to the public sector, they appoint men with experience in government. If they sell heavily to the private sector, they appoint executives with experience in business.

Manufacturing firms need to learn about customer preferences too, of course, but for them it involves information they can cheaply obtain elsewhere. If a firm sells standardized products (tractors, DVD players) into the general retail market, it can learn buyer preferences by surveying customers or auditing sales patterns. Kubota need not appoint a farmer to its board to learn which plow its customers want to buy. It can simply watch which plows sell.

By contrast, construction firms sell small numbers of nonstandardized service packages (the construction of airports or office towers) to specific customers. To sell successfully, they need to tailor the packages they offer to buyer preferences. Surveys and sales audits will only haphazardly enable them to do that. To tailor their packages, they instead recruit men with a lifetime of experience at the types of organizations to which they hope to sell.

Outside Appointments at the Banks

Among the banks, most boards did include some outsiders, but at few could those outsiders have dominated the bank (see also the section titled "Outside Appointments at Firms Other Than Banks"). Of the 87 banks in our database, only 8 had no outsiders on the board, but at none did

Table 5.3. Outside directors in banking

A. No. of banks with any director from MOF or BOJ, 1986

	No. of banks	Any MOF	Any BOJ
City banks	11	3	3
Regional banks	56	27	28
Type-2 regional	10	6	5
Long-term-credit banks	3	3	2
Trust banks	7	1	1

B. Mean number, mean percentage, and maximum percentage of outsiders, 1989

	No. of banks	Mean no.	Mean %	Max. %
City banks	11	1.502	4.001	11.765
Regional banks	56	2.929	15.405	31.579
Type-2 regional	10	4.200	21.555	46.429
Long-term credit banks	3	2.667	8.713	17.857
Trust banks	7	1.429	4.717	11.111

Sources: Toyo keizai shimpo sha, Kigyo keiretsu soran, various years.

Note: Bank categories are explained in the text.

they constitute a majority. That said, board composition varied by sector. Although the distinction between the big money center banks (called *city banks*) and smaller local banks (called either *regional banks* or *type-2 regional banks*, depending on whether the bank had been a bank or credit cooperative before the war) reflects customary usage rather than regulatory policy, the local banks appointed more outsiders than did the money center banks. As we discussed earlier, of the 11 money center banks, 7 had no retired bureaucrats (1986), and 3 had no outsiders at all (1989). Among the 56 regional banks, half had a Bank of Japan retiree and half a Ministry of Finance retiree. Only 16 had neither, and only 2 had no outsiders.

WHAT DO THEY DO?

For all the reasons given earlier, in competitive capital, product, and input markets, firms with governance mechanisms approaching their firm-specific optimum should tend to survive, while those with bad governance mechanisms disappear. Given that market process, any attempt to find an observable association between firm performance and board composition should yield insignificant results. Obviously, insignificant results will not prove that firms adopted optimal structures. Insignificant results never will.

Instead, what testing for the association between performance and governance structure will do is to check whether firms maintain observably *in*efficient boards. According to the public intellectuals, they do: Japanese firms appoint few outside directors to what are therefore inefficient boards. If so, however, then firms with more outside directors should observably outperform firms with fewer.

Outside Directors at Firms Other Than Banks

In regression analyses reported elsewhere (Miwa and Ramseyer 2005c, 328–29, table 6), we asked whether board structure predicts firm performance. Toward that end, we held constant industry affiliation and a variety of financial variables and measured performance by several distinct indices—shareholder returns, accounting measures, and firm growth.

We used data from two distinct periods, 1986–90 and 1990–94. We broke the data in 1990 because of the dramatic break in economic performance. If competition does push firms toward their optimal board structure, then the 1990 shift allowed us to ask whether that optimum varies by economic environment. As noted earlier, Japanese firms did not change the types of directors they appointed from 1985 to 1995. Yet suppose that optimal board structure depended on the macroeconomic context. Even if board composition had no observable impact on performance in the 1980s, it might plausibly have had such impact in the early 1990s. Suppose instead that good board structure does not vary by macroeconomic health. If so, then the two periods should produce similar results.

For both periods, the results contradict the reformist literature: in neither 1986–90 nor 1990–95 did firms maintain observably inefficient governance structures. Instead, the results confirm the logic of basic economic theory: board composition shows no observable association with firm performance. If firms did have inefficiently few outsiders, then the calculated coefficients on the number of outsiders would be significantly positive. They are not. Most such coefficients are statistically insignificant. Where the calculated coefficients on board composition variables are significant, they sometimes run in the opposite direction from what the reformists predict; in others, they are not robust to alternative specifications. As explained earlier, however, if competition does push firms toward their firm-specific optimal patterns of board composition, this result is exactly what one would expect.

Outside Directors at the Banks

Again in regressions reported elsewhere (Miwa and Ramseyer 2003d, 370–72, tables App-3, App-4, App-5), we ran analogous tests on banks. We used slightly different financial variables. And because of the variation within the industry, we focused on the single largest segment—the fifty-six regional banks. We obtained two results of note.

First, we again found no evidence that outside directors improve performance. Instead, we obtained mostly insignificant coefficients on the board composition variables. Where we did locate significant coefficients, they showed no coherent pattern. If the reformers were right, those banks with more outside directors should observably outperform those with fewer. They did not.

Second—and noncontroversially—we confirmed the effect of real estate prices on bank performance. During the 1980s, real estate prices climbed. After 1990, they plummeted. More importantly, however, metropolitan prices rose more dramatically than did rural prices in the 1980s, and fell more precipitously in the 1990s. Because the urban banks loaned to borrowers who then invested in metropolitan real estate, they did better than rural banks in the 1980s. As urban borrowers defaulted on their debt and banks found themselves saddled with collateral now worth substantially less than the loans, urban banks did worse than rural banks in the 1990s. More specifically, banks headquartered in the greater Tokyo and Nagoya areas earned high returns in the early 1980s. By the 1990s, those headquartered in Osaka earned low returns, and those in Tokyo incurred more bad loans.

OWNERSHIP PATTERNS

The Issues
Might ownership patterns affect firm performance? Might Japanese firms act as they do because of the people and institutions that own their stock? Commentators do so argue, though somewhat schizophrenically. From time to time they cite two potentially crosscutting effects.

Costs
On the one hand, observers sometimes argue that Japanese managers trade large blocks of stock with their business partners in order to cut the stock market pressures they would otherwise face. With less market pressure, they face less reason to work hard. If skittish investors held their stock for immediate returns, they would need to worry about quarterly returns. By parking shares with friendly business partners, they ensure themselves an easier life.[5]

By swapping stock with friendly colleagues, observers continue, managers can also more readily divert resources to their personal benefit. In the language of the academic flavor of the month, they can more effectively "tunnel" the firm, more completely capture "private benefits of control." In the language of the street, they can more easily steal. Thus, economists Randall Morck and Masao Nakamura (2003, 28) write that the pre-war "*zaibatsu* pyramids were designed to facilitate tunneling." The families organized the firms as they did to extract "private benefits of control" (101), and the managers of the postwar *keiretsu* have done the same. "There is," they claim (101), "considerable evidence for the existence of large private benefits of corporate control." Within Japan, these "private benefits of control certainly figured large in the formation of *zaibatsu* and *keiretsu*" (102).

Benefits
On the other hand, by concentrating larger blocks of stock in a single shareholder, the firms potentially increase the odds that someone will aggressively police their performance. Because that shareholder may hold a less diversified investment portfolio and a big enough stake to influence the shareholder vote, he is better able and has a stronger incentive to intervene when appropriate. Fearing his intervention, managers will run the firm more carefully from the start.

More than anyone else, continue some observers, banks and insurance companies perform this function in Japan. Until 1977 Japanese banks could own up to 10 percent of a firm's stock, and they can still hold up to 5 percent. By owning stock, they add to the incentives they already have as creditors to ensure that managers perform. The argument obviously draws on the main bank literature in chapter 4. In part, main banks monitor because of the loans they have made, argue main bank buffs, but they also monitor because of the equity stakes they hold.

Misleading Implications
Although both offsetting effects potentially matter, these observers fundamentally mislead. In part, they mislead on the facts. Japanese firms and banks do not hold the quantities of stock that observers claim (as we detailed in chapters 2 and 3), and banks do not intervene in governance (as we detailed in chapter 4). Yet the offsetting effects also mislead on the theory. Although both effects matter, they matter differently from firm to firm, and—crucially—those with inefficient ownership structures will less often survive than those with more appropriate ownership patterns.

The logic obviously tracks the logic about outside director appointments. Firms with suboptimal board structures will tend to fail. As a result, in equilibrium, those that stay in business will tend to have board structures suited to the firm. Similarly, firms with suboptimal ownership structures will disproportionately tend to fail as well. In equilibrium, those still in business will tend to have firm-specific appropriate ownership patterns. Just as board composition should show no observable association with firm performance, neither should ownership structure.

Evidence from the Zaibatsu Dissolution
History helps illustrate this equilibrating process, for the postwar zaibatsu dissolution program offers a natural experiment. As explained in chapter

3, in 1946–49 the U.S.-run Occupation dissolved the zaibatsu shareholding networks. By the logic discussed earlier, because the Occupation forced the owners of the zaibatsu but not the nonzaibatsu firms to sell their shares, the latter would have kept their firm-specific appropriate ownership structures while the zaibatsu firms would not have.

In turn, this process suggests several testable implications. First, because the nonzaibatsu firms would have kept their firm-specific optimal ownership structures, their ownership structures should bear no observable association to firm performance. Second, among the zaibatsu firms, the government disrupted the equilibrium and forced the owners of the largest blocks to sell. Among them, the firms in which the occupation forced owners to sell the largest blocks would have shifted farthest from their firm-specific optimum and thus should have performed the worst. Third, over time the ex-zaibatsu firms should either have restructured their ownership successfully or have disappeared. As they did so, even among them any observable association between ownership and performance should have disappeared.

All this is exactly what the data show (Miwa and Ramseyer 2003b, 79, 82, 86, tables 2, 3, 5, respectively). In 1953, the ex-zaibatsu firms did perform worse than those firms whose ownership the government left intact. Over the next five years, those ex-zaibatsu firms then restructured their ownership. Some of the stock exchange–listed firms had already done so before 1953. Because the unlisted firms often needed to negotiate sales individually, many of them had not. As a result, among the unlisted firms, those with the most dispersed ownership still performed worse than the others. Those firms then continued to restructure after 1953, and as they did, the association between ownership and profitability disappeared. By 1958, the data show the predicted market equilibrium: no observable relationship between ownership structure and firm performance even among the ex-zaibatsu firms.

Contemporary Evidence

If market competition forces firms to select their firm-specific optimal ownership structure, then among contemporary firms too we should see no relation between ownership concentration and performance. And again, so we see. Elsewhere we took all nonbank, large TSE-listed firms and asked whether firm performance bears any relation to the presence of a shareholder owning at least a quarter of the stock. In virtually all regression specifications, we found no statistically significant association (Miwa and Ramseyer 2005c, 328–30, table 6). Because banks seldom have a single dominant shareholder, we asked whether bank performance shows any association with the fraction of its stock held by the top ten shareholders. Again, we found no such observable association (Miwa and Ramseyer 2003d, 370–72, tables App-3, App-4, App-5).

The point is basic. Ownership structure may indeed matter. Some firms may indeed perform better with more (or less) concentrated ownership, but that effect should vary from firm to firm. If so, then those firms with ownership structures best suited to the firm will tend to produce their goods and services more efficiently than their rivals do and to raise their funds more cheaply. Over time, they will then face higher odds of surviving. In equilibrium, those firms that do survive will disproportionately include those with ownership structures suited to those particular firms. In Japan, this is exactly what the data show.

CONCLUSION

Idolized and feared for much of the 1980s, Japanese firms were ridiculed and shunned for much of the 1990s. Rather than cite their management practices as models, observers now blame their corporate governance—particularly their board structures and ownership patterns—for the depression. Logic suggests not.

Like U.S. firms, Japanese firms face competitive capital, service, product, and labor markets. Govern themselves badly, and they incur higher production and capital costs. Govern themselves badly, and they find it harder to sell good products and services cheap. Given the obvious market constraints, those that do survive disproportionately will have governance and ownership structures suited to their markets, their industries, their personnel. Given those constraints, blaming the firms for the depression is blaming the victim all over again.

Consider the reforms academics propose: unwind cross-shareholdings, hire outside directors—and if firms refuse, legislate them offers they cannot refuse. A draconian litany that embodies nothing so much as the old government-can-do-no-wrong tradition, it leaves unanswered (indeed, unasked) the classic Chicago workshop question: if the reforms are so wonderful, why did firms that ignored them so thoroughly earn so much for so long? If inside boards and cross-shareholdings hurt investors, why did Japanese firms that indulged them succeed so spectacularly for decades? Should they not have found themselves penalized in the capital market? Unable to raise funds competitively, should they not have disappeared?

What logic suggests, the data confirm. Firms with more outside directors (whether banks or nonbanks) do no better than those with fewer. Firms with more concentrated shareholding networks do no worse than those with less. Bad governance did not cause the 1990s depression. Statutes to change that governance would do nothing to end it.

Legends of Government Guidance

It was October 1971. Motoharu Yamada stormed into the mayor's office in the suburban Tokyo city of Musashino. Musashino had boomed over the last decade, and Yamada, as head of the local Yamaki construction firm, was playing his part. He built condominium buildings. Now, however, the city wanted his money.

As Mayor Kihachiro Goto explained it, the city wanted developers like Yamada to do two things: to get their neighbors' consent before they built new buildings and to donate money for school facilities. If they might block a neighbor's access to sunlight, they should make sure the neighbor did not mind. If they packed more students into the already overcrowded schools, they should do their part to build more. Many Musashino voters opposed the new construction projects, and Goto owed his position to local voters.

To Yamada, the requirements simply meant more money. If neighbors could veto a new project, he would have to "buy" their consent—regardless of whether his new building blocked much light at all. If the city could demand cash—well, that meant less cash for himself.

The city government had not made its demands by statute. It could not. Although obviously responsible for local welfare, it faced strict national limits on the range of legislation it could pass. Absent a closely related regulatory program, neither could it make its demands by formal regulation.

Unable to legislate or regulate, the Musashino government had demanded the money informally. More specifically, it had demanded the money through what many observers characterize as the peculiarly Japanese practice of "administrative guidance." Such ostensibly voluntary and nonbinding bureaucratic "suggestions," they explain, effectively bind but are legally unreviewable. They constrain the firm but leave unrestrained the government. They favor some, ruin others. They "can often result," declared prominent UC Berkeley and San Diego political scientist Chalmers Johnson (1995, 79), "in rampant lawlessness in favor of those enterprises and interests that enjoy privileged access to the bureaucracy."

Yamada was not about to pay. As the two later recalled, he taunted Goto. "You've made something that's not a statute or a regulation," he shouted. "And you're forcing it on us. That violates the separation of powers, it does. You've got a problem? Fight it out in court."[1]

Fight Yamada did. He continued to build his condominiums. Although he occasionally took modest steps to placate his neighbors, he seldom gave on issues that mattered and sued those neighbors who tried to block his crew. Sued? Apparently, he had not read the dozens of English-language articles about the social norms against litigation in Japan. Luckily for him, the judges had not read the articles about unchallengeable Japanese government power either. Rather than enforce the guidance, the judges forthrightly ordered Yamada's obstructionist neighbors to pay him damages.[2] Rarely did Yamada give to the city's school fund either. When the city stalled his requests in response, he sued it too.

Yet if Yamada could play to the courts, Goto (quintessentially, a politician) could play to the cameras. When Yamada proved particularly obdurate, Goto went to the construction site personally. With a handful of wet cement, he plugged Yamada's water pipes. Not that that stopped Yamada. He simply marched back into court. The city had a legal duty to provide the water, he demanded, regardless of whether he paid his neighbors or gave to the schools. The court agreed and ordered Goto to unplug the pipes.[3]

Alas for Goto, apparently the local prosecutors too had not read the articles about Japanese government power. Rather than commend him for promoting the local welfare or enforcing norms of politeness, they thought his behavior criminal. He had a legal duty to run water to Yamada's apartments, they reasoned, whether Yamada talked to his neighbors or not, whether he gave money to the schools or not. In plugging the water, Goto had committed a crime. Forthrightly, the prosecutors filed criminal charges. The Tokyo District Court convicted, and the Tokyo High Court affirmed. By 1989, so did the Supreme Court.[4] Make no mistake: by enforcing administrative guidance Goto did not just break the law; according to the Japanese Supreme Court, he committed a crime.

Yamada, however, was not finished. Under Japanese law, taxpayers can sue derivatively, on behalf of their community, those local officials who misuse funds. When the prosecutors filed charges against Goto, Musashino had paid his defense costs. After all, Goto was responsible for promoting the town's welfare. He had made his demands on the contractors to carry out that responsibility. To Yamada, however, the administrative guidance was illegal—and if Goto broke the law in enforcing the guidance, then the city broke the law in paying his legal fees. As a Musashino taxpayer, Yamada filed a taxpayer derivative suit to force Goto to refund his attorney's fees. Again Yamada won, and again the High Court and Supreme Court affirmed.[5]

And still Yamada continued. When Musashino had tried to force administrative guidance on him, Yamada argued, Yamada incurred a variety of costs. For those costs, the city owed him damages. To the court, the case was a no-brainer. It had already held the city's actions illegal. If Yamada had lost money, the city had a duty to pay. This time, Musashino did not even bother to appeal.[6]

To any lawyer who reads U.S. cases but not the English-language literature on Japan, what Musashino did should not surprise. The city of Tigard, Oregon, tried much the same thing a few years ago when it told Florence Dolan she could expand her retail store only if she donated land for a bicycle path. Neither should the court's response to Musashino surprise. As Justice Scalia put it in a similar case, such a scheme is just an "out-and-out plan of extortion."[7] It was illegal in Oregon. And it was illegal in Tokyo.

To readers steeped in conventional English-language accounts of Japan, the Musashino dispute will indeed surprise. Most obviously, Yamada should not have sued. By those conventional accounts, the Japanese government routinely guides the economy. It hires the best and the brightest; they gather elaborate amounts of information, and they then tell firms where to invest and what to produce. Raised on Confucian precepts, executives and their firms duly obey. When they do not, the government punishes. But courts—what courts? Japanese do not sue, and if they did the courts would not find against the government anyway.

Yet men like Yamada do flout the government. They contest orders they do not like. Sometimes they sue, and sometimes the courts rule in their favor. In this chapter we trace the implications of the resulting legal principles for understanding the roles Japanese bureaucrats have played. We begin by summarizing the literature on the power of the Japanese government and explore three prominent case studies). We then outline how Japanese courts treat bureaucratic intervention and how the government regulated (and did not regulate) the financial markets. Finally, we discuss the loan program and limits on foreign exchange transactions that the government purportedly used to enforce its will.

LEGENDS OF GOVERNMENT GUIDANCE

They Planned It

It is an old legend, a venerable one, and a resilient one. In the English-language press it dates at least to the 1970s and probably much earlier. The tale begins by positing a nearly omniscient corps of elite bureaucrats who determine which firms should invest how much in which industries. When in the 1950s and 1960s these bureaucrats did their job well, the economy boomed to double-digit growth. When in the 1990s they misjudged (or by some accounts, when politicians tied their hands), the economy stagnated in a decadelong malaise.

To many American readers, Harvard sociologist Ezra Vogel (1979, 65, 71) introduced the legend in 1979 with his best-selling *Japan as Number One*. A "bureaucratic elite," declared Vogel, had catapulted Japan to riches. "Boldly," they work "to restructure industry, concentrating resources in areas where they think Japan will be competitive internationally in the future."

The legend was not specific to sociology. In political science, Johnson (1982) famously fashioned his theory of the "plan-rational" "developmental state" on these tales of omniscient and omnipotent bureaucrats. Even Harvard economist (and later dean) Henry Rosovsky (1972, 244) could—apparently with a straight face—describe Japan as "the only capitalist country in the world in which the Government decides how many firms should be in a given industry, and sets about to arrange the desired number."

And the legend persists today, resplendent still in its pan-disciplinary gloss. Sociologist Ronald Dore (2002, 23–24)—winner of the Japan Foundation Award for lifetime contributions to the field of Japanese studies—listed among the "main characteristics of the Japanese economy" a "strong role for the state" in "the promotion of economic growth and national competitiveness." Columbia and Michigan law professors Curtis Milhaupt and Mark West (2002, 44) characterized the postwar economic environment as one of "bureaucrat-orchestrated economic management." In his now-standard text on the Japanese economy, University of Tokyo economist Takatoshi Ito (1992, 201) attributed "Japan's rapid economic growth" to its "successful industrial policy." And one historian even claimed the government "intervened to shape how ordinary Japanese thought" (Garon 1997, xiv).

Given the apparently impeccable academic credentials of the tales, politically ambitious U.S. intellectuals sometimes put them to domestic use. Ira Magaziner and Robert Reich (1982, 6) used Japan to advocate an industrial policy in the United States. In Japan, they declared, that policy "enhance[s] the creation of wealth by improving the international competitiveness of a number of growing businesses and by easing the transition of declining businesses." Both landed top jobs in the Clinton administration.

Laura D'Andrea Tyson (Tyson and Zysman 1989, xvi) claimed that in "the Japanese variant of capitalism," people emphasized markets "as a source of growth rather than of short-run efficiency." As a result, "a primary role of government is to supply incentives to promote growth through markets." Under Clinton, she bagged the chair of the Council of Economic Advisors. Even as recently as 2003 the *New York Times* would complain that the United States was losing its lead in computer technology over its hostility to "industrial policies" (Markoff and Schenker 2003).

They Enforced It

Culture

In guiding the Japanese economy, bureaucrats could enforce their will. Why could they do so? In the English-language version of the legend, the question is nothing if not overdetermined: firms obeyed the government because, given their Confucian culture, they could imagine nothing else; because the government would reward them if they did; and because it would punish them if they did not.

In the West, even scholars not otherwise given to cultural analysis stress the importance in Japan of non-Western norms. "Japan is a fuzzy kind of society," Princeton economist Paul Krugman (1990, 119–20) declared, where firms behave out of "habits of deference to central authority" rather than by "the hard-edged legalisms that Americans...expect." Almost as fuzzily, University of Washington economist Kozo Yamamura (1972, 170) explained that "any discussion of the effectiveness of the ministerial administrative guidance of an industry...based solely on economic motivations is woefully inadequate."

And anyway, wrote legal scholars David Litt, Jonathan Macey, Geoffrey Miller, and Edward Rubin (1990, 435), "open conflict is anathema to" Japanese bureaucrats. They would "regard a public challenge to their announced decision as either an insult or a disgrace." But as far as Rosovsky (1972, 244) was concerned, the risk of insult and disgrace was all academic anyway. Claimed he, "no Japanese would dare ask" a MITI bureaucrat what legal basis he had for his instructions.

Credit Market Benefits

Despite these endless bows to Japan as a land governed by a different cultural logic, most observers add that Japanese bureaucrats motivated reluctant firms by rewarding those that obeyed. The bureaucrats did so, they write, by favoring such firms in the credit market. There, they both lavished low-interest government loans on compliant firms and ensured them access to banks.

The argument proceeds in several steps. First, bureaucrats controlled access to generously subsidized government loans—particularly from the Japan Development Bank. Harvard and University of Tokyo economists Richard Caves and Masu Uekusa (1976b, 150), for instance, claimed that MITI "offer[ed] positive inducements through its influence over access to the generous lending facilities of the public Japan Development Bank."

Second, bureaucrats in the 1950s and 1960s influenced (or by some accounts controlled) the loans made by private banks. "There is no question," wrote Krugman (1990, 120), "that before the early 1970s the Japanese system was heavily directed from the top, with the MITI and the Ministry of Finance influencing the allocation of credit and foreign exchange in an effort to push the economy where they liked."

To control the allocation of credit, the government took three further crucial steps. First, it disabled the securities markets. According to economists David Weinstein and Yishay Yafeh (1998, 636), "capital markets in Japan were highly regulated and immature." As a result, "firms could raise only limited amounts of capital through commercial flotation of debt or equity." Corporations simply "did not have alternative sources of funding until the mid 1970s," explained Ito (1992, 119); "the domestic securities market was underdeveloped, and loans from abroad were not allowed." Consequently, "Japan's financial system was one of the most regulated and administratively controlled in the world" (Ito 2000, 95–96). Declared University of California–San Diego and University of Chicago economists Takeo Hoshi and Anil Kashyap (2001, 310), banks "were the only game in town."

Second, the government used its control over foreign exchange to insulate the Japanese market from international competition. As University of Washington legal scholar Dan Henderson (1986, 132) put it, through the exchange controls it "shield[ed] from international market forces Japan's high savings managed by a controlled banking system, fixed interest rates, and preferential credit allocations."

Last, the government capped loan interest rates. According to Columbia economist Hugh T. Patrick (1972, 114), for example, the "interest rate structure [was] extremely inflexible." What is more, the rates were "set below that which would have resulted solely if market forces had been relied upon to determine them."[8]

In short, the government forced firms to raise capital primarily through banks, and kept interest rates at levels lower than those that would clear the market. By pressuring banks, it could then determine which firms borrowed and which went without. As a recent Harvard Business School case study (Schaede 2000, 3) put it, through all this the Japanese government could generate a "fabulous tool to orchestrate a system of corporate finance that would ensure both low financing costs and the political allocation of funds to strategic industries."

Foreign Exchange Controls

Culture, carrots—but also sticks. To motivate the truly recalcitrant firm, the legend continues, bureaucrats in 1950s and 1960s controlled brutally powerful penalties. Of these, the strongest involved foreign exchange. As Johnson (1982, 194–95) put it, the foreign exchange law constituted "the single most important instrument of industrial guidance and control that MITI ever possessed." With it, declared one historian (Allinson 1997, 93),

MITI obtained "the legal authority to channel often-scarce foreign currency toward large firms that would use it most effectively in pursuit of national economic goals."

Or take Caves and Uekusa. MITI held "a general implied administrative responsibility and authority that [went] well beyond what is customary in the United States," explained the two (1976a, 487–88). "A major sanction until the mid-1960s was the MITI's authority over the allocation of foreign exchange for the purchase of essential inputs." Indeed, added they (489, ital. added), "controls over international transactions have *often* served as a club when gentle persuasion failed."

Yamamura (1972, 173) echoed the argument. "During most of the rapid growth era," claimed he, MITI "had the power to allocate selectively foreign exchange for the purchase of imports; because nearly every Japanese industry relied heavily on imported raw materials, this discretionary power gave MITI a valuable 'stick' for prodding business." Crucially, he continued (with co-author, in Eads and Yamamura 1987, 433), it was discretionary: "uncooperative or recalcitrant firms [could] expect, immediately or at a later date, indirect retribution from a disappointed or displeased ministry."

By some scholars, this restrictive regime continued into recent memory. According again to the Harvard case study (Schaede 2000, 2), MITI could reward cooperative firms "through preferential access to foreign exchange, whereas resistance could result in severe penalties." Importantly, "the most important revision of the Foreign Exchange Law occurred in 1980, when its basic logic was reversed: whereas before, everything that was not explicitly allowed by MITI was prohibited, after the 1980 revision everything that was not explicitly prohibited was allowed." Yet even after 1980, MITI retained its restrictive approach. Although "trade and foreign finance controls were gradually reduced," at least into the early 1980s MITI "maintained a long list of limitations and restrictions."

Unfettered Discretion

Bureaucrats could use these exchange controls so powerfully because courts deferred to them so completely. More precisely, bureaucrats could use the controls to direct the economy because courts gave them such wide-ranging discretion. As University of California–San Diego political scientist Ulrike Schaede (1994, 290) wrote, a ministry faced with "noncompliance with administrative guidance [had] numerous options to obstruct the business of the party concerned." It could and would, as the Japanese aphorism more colorfully put it, "take Edo's revenge in Nagasaki."

Observers give two reasons why bureaucrats had the discretion they did. First, when courts reviewed the actions bureaucrats took, they found for the government. They may not have quite rubber-stamped the bureaucracy, but they came fairly close. Second, as New York University law professor Frank Upham put it, the very informality of the bureaucratic action precluded judicial review. "The Japanese Supreme Court [had] limited [review] to administrative acts that immediately and directly create or delimit private rights and duties," explained Upham (1987, 171). "Under this definition, most of industrial policy [was] beyond judicial review."

THREE CASES

As with so much of Western scholarship on Japan, the scholarship on Japanese government power depends heavily on anecdote. Given the massive government power the legend posits, one might have expected a similarly massive number of anecdotes—or at least several. Not so. Instead, in the English-language press the legend hinges almost exclusively on a single anecdote: the mid-1960s confrontation between MITI and Sumitomo Metals Industries. In the Japanese press, observers add two others: the disputes involving MITI and the Nisshin spinning and Idemitsu oil firms. Consider, therefore, these central anecdotes—both the tales as the legend recounts them and the disputes as they actually happened.

Sumitomo Metals

The Legend
In explaining the power MITI wielded, no English-language source has had more impact than Upham's award-winning 1987 book, *Law and Social Change in Postwar Japan*. To Upham as to most Western observers of the Japanese government, the clearest evidence of MITI power lay in its 1965 dispute with Sumitomo Metals. MITI's "legal powers were at their height in the 1960s" (1987, 176), explained Upham, and those powers rested on the foreign exchange control statutes. The "overriding characteristics" of those statutes, in turn, were "the wide scope of authority delegated to MITI and the vagueness of the standards by which MITI [was] to exercise that authority" (169).

According to Upham, MITI leveraged this power over foreign exchange into control over completely unrelated issues. It used its foreign exchange powers, in other words, to force firms to comply with other directions it might give. The courts then broadened that power further still: "the doctrines governing judicial review of administrative action" left MITI "virtually unrestrained legally" (176).

Consider the battle between Sumitomo Metals and MITI, as Upham (1987, 177) tells it. Through early 1965, Japanese steelmakers had faced "a severe decline in the demand for steel." To coordinate their response, they "created a committee to develop strategies" through their trade association, the Iron and Steel Federation. "By May 26 the committee decided that a reduction in production was necessary to maintain appropriate prices." By the end of the next month, "MITI's Heavy Industries Bureau requested that the Federation immediately organize a production cartel."

This MITI-coordinated group proposed production restraints. Although most industry members planned to comply, Sumitomo Metals wanted to produce more. It declared it would ignore its quota. "MITI's response was swift, harsh, and public," wrote Upham. "On the afternoon of November 19, Vice-Minister Sahashi Shigeru announced that MITI would use its formal legal power . . . to limit Sumitomo's import of coking coal" (178–79). When "Sumitomo responded that such public coercion violated its right as a private company to manage its own affairs and threatened to take legal action" (179), the battle was joined.

According to Upham, the battle was one Sumitomo Metals lost. Indeed, it was not even close: "by leaving the system of industrial cooperation, Sumitomo had become a pariah and had to be totally boycotted by the other firms" (179). By December, its president found himself reduced to making the rounds of "the presidents of the major steel makers to pledge his future cooperation" (181). The firm did convince MITI to include "a wider choice of reference periods for the FY66 quota." But this was only "a minor concession" and "turned out to be of little significance economically because the informal cartel was discontinued in August 1966" (254n21).

"Sumitomo Metals' refusal to cooperate [had] threatened," explained Upham, "the 'orderly competition' that [was] the preeminent norm of the Japanese steel industry" (182). It was a norm MITI actively maintained. "Although the bureaucrats may [have said] that the resolution of intraindustry disputes [was] up to the industry members themselves," claimed Upham, it was "the relevant MITI bureau that set[] limits, facilitate[d] coordination, and approve[d] and enforce[d] the final agreement." Through this "oversight role," it helped "ensur[e] that the final outcome [was] consistent with [its] perception of the national interest" (183).

Given Japanese standards of judicial review, it was a norm Sumitomo could not realistically have challenged. Not until MITI refused its application to import coal could it "have had its day in court." It would have been a day to rue. "At that point, it would have had to prove that MITI had used illegal criteria or violated statutory standards in withholding Sumitomo's import permit. Given the lack of clear [statutory] standards . . . , such a showing would have been difficult indeed" (183).

Firms seldom challenged MITI's authority, explained Upham, and for good reason: they would have lost. By making an example of Sumitomo Metals, the ministry had shown any firm with dreams of independence that it could and would manipulate its "abstract legal powers" to "ensure compliance" (176). Graphically and brutally, it had shown the business community that it faced "virtually no statutory restrictions on [its] regulation of foreign trade" (179).

The tale Upham told is one with canonical status. Scholars of Japanese regulation routinely cite the Sumitomo Metals dispute and routinely tell the same story: MITI issued its informal directives; Sumitomo refused to comply; MITI threatened to punish it (or actually punished it, in some accounts) through its foreign exchange powers; and Sumitomo caved.

"When a 1964 recession led the steel makers to negotiate output quotas among themselves, Sumitomo initially refused to go along with the low quota dealt to it," wrote Caves and Uekusa (1976b, 149–50). Yet a "major sanction until the mid-1960s was MITI's authority over the allocation of foreign exchange for purchasing essential inputs." Accordingly, MITI "retaliated by limiting the firm's access to imported coking coal." As a result, "when the "company's president was summoned to" MITI, "wisdom prevailed." To Johnson (1974, 958), the outcome was clear: challenged by Sumitomo Metals, MITI "stuck to [its] guns and won."

The History

As critical a role as the tale of Sumitomo Metals may play in the legend of bureaucratic power, the tale is too tall by half. MITI never used its foreign exchange powers to punish Sumitomo Metals. Sumitomo never backed down. To our knowledge, at *no* time before had MITI even threatened to use those powers to enforce unrelated policies.

First, begin with the question of why MITI intervened. Did it do so to implement any "industrial policy"? In fact, it did not. Instead, it merely enforced a private cartel.

For several years, the six biggest steel producers had met regularly to pool capacity expansion plans. In early 1965, facing lower demand, they discussed the possibility of coordinating production cuts. Although they (including Sumitomo Metals) agreed on the general principle, they disagreed on specifics. Sumitomo wanted to produce more than the others would allot it, but—ostensibly as an emergency measure—the company acquiesced anyway. Once Sumitomo had agreed, the firms adopted production restraints for the second fiscal quarter (July–September 1965; the fiscal year for most Japanese firms begins in April). In doing so, they keyed the restraints to 90 percent of the production they had each maintained during October 1964–March 1965.

The firms now needed to decide how to proceed. They did not want a private agreement. The agreement would not bind any of them and potentially subjected them to criminal antitrust penalties besides. Neither did they want a statutorily authorized "depression cartel." Although it allowed them to skirt criminal liability for price-fixing, it would not bind (*Asahi*, Nov. 20, 1965).[9] Instead, they opted to approach MITI (*Asahi*, July 13 and Dec. 12, 1965). If the ministry endorsed their plans, they reasoned, they could both avoid criminal liability and bind each other to the cartel (wrong on both counts, as we explain below).

Sumitomo Metals remained unhappy. It had invested aggressively in new equipment and now sold abroad more than the others. To continue this strategy, it needed a quota that excluded exports (*Asahi*, July 13, 1965; *Mainichi*, Nov. 16, 1965). Toward the end of obtaining that exclusion, it continued to negotiate these issues through the summer. Apparently it hoped the others would acquiesce by the end of the third quarter (December).

When by November the other firms still refused to exclude exports, Sumitomo announced it would no longer comply. MITI immediately ordered Sumitomo to cut production to the level demanded by the other firms. "Production cutbacks should be decided strictly by agreement among the firms," an indignant Sumitomo replied (*Mainichi*, Nov. 16, 1965). Barely seven years before Harvard dean Henry Rosovsky would declare that "no Japanese would dare ask" a MITI bureaucrat what legal basis he had for his instructions, Sumitomo publicly announced that should MITI try to punish it, "we intend immediately to file suit" (*Nikkei*, Nov. 28, 1965).

Did MITI try to punish? For all the attention scholars lavish on MITI's supposed powers, did it punish Sumitomo Metals? In fact, it did not. Although it talked of doing so, it never did. Once Sumitomo Metals threatened to sue, MITI promptly caved.[10]

To force Sumitomo's hands, MITI would have needed to take far more draconian measures than observers typically relate. Crucially, Sumitomo held two months' coal in reserve (*Nikkei*, Nov. 20, 1965). Under its own plans, it hoped to produce about 10 percent more than the industry quota allowed it. Suppose MITI allotted it the coal it needed for its cartel allocation. By even the crudest of calculations, Sumitomo could have ignored the cartel and produced as planned for twenty months.

To induce Sumitomo Metals to comply with the cartel, MITI would have needed to exhaust its coal reserves. To exhaust them in six months, it would have needed to cut the amount it allocated Sumitomo by a full third. Yet even that ploy Sumitomo Metals claimed ready to outlast. Let MITI starve it of coal, it declared. It would simply import pig iron directly (*Nikkei*, Nov. 20, 1965). After all, by the mid-1960s, pig iron imports (like most imports, as we detail later in this chapter) were subject to no restrictions. MITI controlled coal imports only because of the role that mining villages played in keeping the ruling party in power.

These draconian measures were measures MITI never adopted. Ultimately, it never tried to exhaust Sumitomo's reserves. Instead, it allocated

Sumitomo the full amount it needed for its cartel quota (*Nikkei*, Nov. 27, Dec. 8 and 27, 1965; *Asahi*, Nov. 20, 1965).

Last, did Sumitomo lose? The most unnerving aspect of the legend is the notion that MITI largely obtained what it wanted. It did not. Instead, Sumitomo did. Most basically, Sumitomo Metals wanted steel exports outside the quotas. Although it favored a cartel in principle, it wanted one only in the domestic market. Ultimately, that was exactly the position MITI and the steel industry adopted.

Already by early December, MITI announced that it would consider placing exports outside the cartel (*Mainichi*, Dec. 3, 1965). When it finalized its deal with Sumitomo in mid-January, it did just that. During the third quarter (October–December 1965), Sumitomo had exceeded its cartel allocation by 88,000 tons. Of this amount, it had exported 55,000 tons. For the fourth quarter, the industry ignored the 55,000 exported tons and cut Sumitomo's quota by the remaining 33,000 (*Nikkei*, Jan. 12, 1966). Barely six weeks after Sumitomo declared that it would no longer abide by the cartel, MITI had caved.

By its own behavior during the next several months, Sumitomo Metals showed what it had learned from the confrontation: firms that flout MITI get what they want. Come mid-1966, it repeated exactly the tactic it had used the previous November. The demand for steel had increased, and Sumitomo now wanted the quotas—the very limits to which it had just agreed—abolished. Its rivals refused and insisted it keep its end of the deal. Up yours, Sumitomo seemed to reply. "Even if the industry decides to continue the crude steel adjustments into October," announced its president, "we do not intend to comply" (*Nikkei*, Aug. 25, 1966).

The ploy had worked for Sumitomo in 1965, and it worked in 1966. The second quarter would have lasted through September but not the production quotas. Faced with Sumitomo's announcement that it would renege on its deal, MITI ended the quotas at the close of August (*Nikkei*, Aug. 30, 1966).

Nisshin Spinning

According to Japanese versions of the legend, in the mid-1960s MITI not only intervened to enforce its policies on a noncompliant Sumitomo Metals but it enforced them on the Nisshin cotton-spinning firm as well. Through early 1966, 174 spinning firms had maintained a "depression cartel" authorized by the Antimonopoly Act. With the cartel expiring at the end of March, MITI proposed to extend it. When Nisshin refused to cooperate, MITI intervened and pressured the firm to comply. Nisshin recanted, and MITI obtained its cartel.

In fact, MITI did not actively pressure Nisshin. The textile industry was widely dispersed. In the cotton-spinning industry, 350 legal firms competed (the black market firms are excluded here and discussed below), and the top 13 produced only half the industry output (1966 figures; Tsusho sangyo sho 1966a, 24). In this environment, MITI had no obvious way to compel compliance. At least in steel MITI could plausibly threaten to cut Sumitomo's coking coal. In cotton spinning Nisshin had been able freely to import what it wanted since 1961.

In truth, on a long-run basis MITI did not want to cartelize the industry anyway (*Nikkei*, Jan. 26 and Feb. 3, 1966). Through the 1950s, it had allocated the foreign exchange for raw cotton imports among the spinning firms according to the number of spindles they had registered. In 1961 it voluntarily abandoned that power.[11] It did not do so because it had to abandon it. It abandoned it to further the largely free market policies of the ruling Liberal Democratic Party (LDP).

Although the LDP relied in part on small firms for political support, it set its small-business policies within a capitalist, free market context. Japanese voters did not want an interventionist government, and the LDP knew that. Socialist and Communist candidates regularly offered voters interventionist alternatives, and they regularly rejected them. Reflecting their policy preferences, the LDP instead maintained a fundamentally noninterventionist course. As its faithful agent, so did MITI.

Nisshin opposed the planned cartel but for the same reasons that the other big firms opposed it too (*Mainichi*, Jan. 21, 1966; *Nikkei*, Jan. 23 and 26, 1966). First, the cartel favored the less-efficient firms. Fundamentally, the industry had too much capacity. Of the 12.8 million total spindles, industry insiders estimated that only three-quarters would survive in a competitive market. The cartel mandated production cutbacks, but because it mandated them uniformly they fell on the efficient and inefficient alike. If the industry could eliminate the cartel, market competition would instead force the cutbacks on the inefficient firms—eventually driving them out of business. What the larger firms (and MITI) wanted were policies that tracked that market competition (*Nikkei*, Feb. 15, 1966).

Second, the cartel favored the black market shops and the legal firms that had not joined the cartel. Since the 1950s, firms had been able legally to spin cotton thread only on those spindles they registered with the government. That ban, however, the government had enforced haphazardly, if at all— resulting in an estimated 500,000 unregistered spindles in the mid-1960s (*Mainichi*, Jan. 21, 1966). Yet the cartel applied only to participating firms. The black market firms obviously did not participate, and neither did over 170 legal firms—who probably used another half-million spindles (Tsusho sangyo sho 1966a, 24). By requiring only the participating firms to cut back, the cartel effectively expanded the market into which the black market and nonparticipating legal firms could sell.

At least before 1961 the black market firms could not import raw cotton directly. Because they had not registered their spindles, MITI would not allocate them foreign exchange. Once MITI abandoned its control over cotton imports, though, they could freely obtain their raw materials. In truth, even under exchange controls MITI had not stopped firms from reselling the cotton they imported. As a result, the less-efficient legal firms had simply re-sold the cotton they imported to more efficient black market firms. Even before 1961, black market firms had been able to obtain the cotton they needed.

Although Nisshin eventually acquiesced to the cartel extension, it did so only after the trade association and MITI gave it much of what it wanted. It had hoped to remove the cartels, and the association and MITI agreed to work toward that end. Even the structure of the cartel reflected Nisshin's aims. In exchange for Nisshin's cooperation, the association and MITI specified in the cartel that firms could sell on the market only 70 percent of their output (*Nikkei*, Mar. 10, 1966). Because the larger firms maintained vertically integrated weaving operations, the limit left them largely untouched (none of the ten largest firms sold 70 percent of their output on the market; *Mainichi*, Mar. 4, 1966). It hit instead the independent smaller firms.

True to the LDP's noninterventionist policies, MITI never seriously tried to sway Nisshin. When Nisshin first announced that it would not comply with a new cartel, MITI talked to Nisshin. Yet it only talked and made no threats. Fundamentally, MITI agreed with Nisshin, but the smaller firms stood in its way. By making its compliance with the cartel contingent on market-liberalization reforms, Nisshin gave MITI the leverage it needed to pursue policies it supported anyway.

As had Sumitomo Metals, Nisshin soon put the lessons it learned to further good use. In the rayon fiber industry as well, in 1966, several firms wanted to coordinate capacity cuts (Nisshin 1969, 930). Nisshin refused to cooperate, and the group dropped its proposal (Tsusho sangyo sho 1966b, 132). When they raised it again the next year, several remaining firms agreed to scrap facilities. Nisshin scrapped none (Tsusho sangyo sho 1967, 142–43).

Idemitsu Kosan

Because English-language accounts of government power in Japan rely so heavily on the tale of Sumitomo Metals, not only do they ignore the dispute around Nisshin but they ignore the one around the Idemitsu kosan oil company as well. Japanese accounts do not. Instead, they use Idemitsu kosan to tell the now-familiar story: MITI ordered the firms to cartelize, Idemitsu kosan refused, MITI threatened to punish, and Idemitsu kosan complied. That story did not describe Sumitomo, did not describe Nisshin, and does not describe Idemitsu kosan.

Through the 1950s MITI controlled crude oil imports through its foreign exchange powers. In October 1963 it lifted those controls. In exchange, it substituted the authority it gained through one of the few industry-specific postwar control statutes—the 1962 Petroleum Industry Act.[12]

The Petroleum Industry Act gave MITI dubious control over short-term production. Under the act, the ministry could set five-year supply plans. On the basis of those plans, it could then issue refining licenses and new facility permits. The act also required refiners to submit annual production plans to the ministry. It authorized MITI to recommend changes if those plans seemed excessive and to determine nonbinding standard sales prices.

Crucially, the act did not authorize MITI to force firms either to follow its production recommendations or to follow its standard prices. The recommendations were instead just that—recommendations. To force an adamant firm to comply, MITI would thus have needed to take Edo's revenge in Nagasaki—and use its power over new investments to penalize noncompliance. Hence the questions: could it have done so, and did it try?

For its suggested production plans, MITI sought to use quotas developed by the industry trade association, the Petroleum Federation. As in the cotton-spinning industry, however, the trade association was split. Being more efficient and aggressive, the larger firms wanted a looser structure that rewarded firms for new investment—if they wanted quotas at all. Many firms, like Idemitsu kosan, wanted none. The smaller less-efficient firms wanted a straightforward cartel. With the firms unable to agree among themselves, MITI found itself in a quandary.

For the October 1963–March 1964 period, MITI adopted quotas that largely tracked its April–September 1963 numbers. Idemitsu kosan promptly refused to comply. It was the second biggest firm in the industry and one of the most aggressive. It had just opened a new plant in February, yet the quotas ignored the plant almost entirely. "Open conflict is anathema" to Japanese bureaucrats, claim legal scholars Litt, Macey, Miller, and Rubin (1990, 435). They would "regard a public challenge to their announced decision as either an insult or a disgrace." Maybe so, but it was a disgrace with which they had to learn to live. We will "produce as much as we can sell," declared company president Sazo Idemitsu in response to MITI's quotas. The quotas "completely ignore our special circumstances" (Nikkei, Oct. 6, 1963).

Idemitsu kosan did not just refuse the quotas. Rather than battle the smaller firms in the Petroleum Federation, it simply quit. It cancelled its federation membership and on November 29, 1963, announced its withdrawal (Nikkei, Nov. 30, 1963). Repeatedly, MITI pleaded with Idemitsu to rejoin and follow the quotas. Repeatedly, Idemitsu refused. Declared its president, the production restraints potentially violated the Antimonopoly

Act (he was right, as we note below). Let MITI pressure him. He would never comply. After all, the Petroleum Industry Act gave MITI no authority to make him comply (*Nikkei*, Dec. 12, 1963). We "oppose the production adjustments themselves," he explained. "Unless those adjustments are themselves abolished, we cannot agree to any compromise" (*Nikkei*, Jan. 12, 1964).

MITI talked and pleaded, but—crucially—that was all it did. Never did it threaten to penalize Idemitsu when next it applied for approval of new facilities. Never did it threaten otherwise to take Edo's revenge at Nagasaki. Instead, it recognized that it could not force Idemitsu kosan to comply. As then–MITI minister Hajime Fukuda told the press, he hoped Idemitsu would compromise. If it refused, he would issue a ministerial recommendation under the Petroleum Industry Act. If it ignored the recommendation, well then he was plain out of luck. He would have no choice but to plead with the politicians for a stronger statute (*Nikkei*, Jan. 14, 1964). "Because a ministerial order carries no penalty or other legal force," explained the *Nikkei* newspaper, "MITI believes that Idemitsu would ignore it and continue with its own production plans" (*Nikkei*, Jan. 19, 1964).

Yet a few days later, Idemitsu kosan did agree to quotas—for the time being (*Nikkei*, Jan. 25, 1964). To induce it to agree, MITI promised to recalculate the quotas to incorporate Idemitsu kosan's concerns and to hike its allocation from 113,000 barrels a day to 131,000 (*Nikkei*, Jan. 24, 1964). Provided it cut output during the low-demand summer months, calculated the *Asahi* newspaper, Idemitsu kosan could now produce almost what it could with no cartel at all (*Asahi*, Jan. 26, 1964). As a further part of the deal, Idemitsu kosan demanded that MITI agree to abolish production restraints as soon as possible.

Yet "as soon as possible" is not now—and the persistence of the restraints proved the deal's undoing. From the outset, MITI refused to say when it would actually abolish them (*Nikkei*, Jan. 24, 1964). Neither would Idemitsu kosan rejoin the Petroleum Federation until it did. Instead, when sailors struck the next year, Idemitsu kosan used the pretext to cancel the deal. Consumers needed its oil, it declared. With supplies now uncertain it would again produce whatever it could sell. Over the intervening year MITI had raised its quota to 192,000 barrels a day. It would produce 240,000 (*Mainichi*, Jan. 21, 1966).

MITI begged, but President Idemitsu seemed determined to kill the cartel. "Ever since freeing crude oil imports," he complained (*Mainichi*, Jan. 21, 1966), "MITI has used administrative guidance to control production. Our firm left the federation because we opposed this. . . . We cooperated only on the condition that MITI promise to abolish the production controls. . . . That promise it still has not kept."

This time MITI did keep its promise. As soon as the sailors returned to work, Idemitsu agreed to the cartel (*Nikkei*, Feb. 1, 1966)—and MITI dropped the price controls at the end of the month (*Nikkei*, Feb. 2, 1966) and the production restraints at the end of the next biannual period. The restraints died at the end of September, and Idemitsu kosan rejoined the federation in October.

JUDICIAL REVIEW

Something is wrong with this picture.

The scholars in the Japan field tell the stories we have just recounted to show the bureaucracy's power, but the stories they tell are fiction. The legend of bureaucratic power hinges on the stories, yet the stories do not fit the facts. Does the account of the law in the first section of this chapter fit any better? To explore the issue, we ask whether bureaucrats had the power scholars attribute to them.

We first examine any limits courts may have imposed: their willingness to review informal regulatory measures, the case law on administrative guidance, and any potential criminal liability for complying with illegal guidance. We then turn to the regulation of financial markets: to the restrictions on equity issues, to the restrictions on bond issues, to the barriers between domestic and overseas capital markets, and to the loan interest-rate caps. Finally, we discuss the subsidized government-loan programs and the foreign-exchange controls.

Judicial Review of Informal Regulation

Although MITI regulated informally, it did not regulate informally to avoid judicial review. Instead, it regulated informally for the same reason most regulators everywhere regulate informally: informality saves costs.

MITI could not have stayed informal to avoid judicial review because informality would not have stopped that review. If a Japanese firm wants to contest an informal instruction in court, it need simply ignore it. By doing so, it forces the government's hand. To induce the firm to comply, the government will then need to take more formal steps. When it does, in most cases courts will review what it does.

This is not peculiar to Japan. Rather, it is as true in the United States as in Japan. If an American firm wants to contest an informal government action, it must first force the government's hand. Until it does, U.S. courts will not review the action. When it does, they generally will review.

Judicial Review of Local Administrative Guidance

When Japanese courts do review administrative guidance, scholars claim they favor the government.[13] "There are no cases directly on point in the industrial policy context," wrote Upham in 1987, "but there are cases in other contexts that indicate that the range of permissible criteria is much greater in Japan than in the United States." Oddly, he then added, "most instructive is a series of land use planning cases" (174).

Land use planning? Already in 1975, the Tokyo High Court had told Musashino not to use Yamada's refusal to comply with its land-use-planning guidance to stop his condominium projects. By 1984 the Tokyo District Court had convicted Mayor Goto on *criminal* charges for trying to enforce that guidance.

"See one cockroach, you've got a hundred," promises a Japanese aphorism. Like cockroaches, like lawsuits—at least sometimes. Musashino's policies (make developers compensate neighbors, give to the schools) were not unusual: city governments adopted them the country over. Nor was the Tokyo District Court's response (declare attempts to enforce the policies flatly illegal): courts adopted it everywhere too.

One developer applied to the Tokyo government for construction permits on a couple of condominium buildings. The government cited opposition from his neighbors and stalled. The developer sued and in 1982 won.[14] Another developer applied to the Kyoto prefectural government for a hotel building permit. When the government told him to negotiate, he refused— and this court declared the stalling illegal too.[15]

By 1985 the Supreme Court entered the fray and announced that developers could freely ignore administrative guidance. When they did, city governments could not use their intransigence to delay their applications.[16] To be sure, it left open the possibility that a developer might act so obstreperously that a city could withhold its services after all. Over the next several years, however, the courts made it clear it was a possibility in theory only. Obstreperous developers came and went, but the courts refused to let cities stall applications.

By the early 1990s, developers had themselves become veritable courthouse cockroaches. When a firm applied to Tochigi prefecture for a permit on an industrial waste plant, the government told it to obtain its neighbors' consent. The developer refused, sued for its permit, and won.[17] Another developer applied to Yamanashi prefecture for a construction permit on vacation condominiums. The prefecture stalled on grounds that he had not cooperated; he sued, and he won.[18]

A developer in northern Kyushu wanted a condominium complex in suburban Fukuoka. The city told him to reduce the complex's size. He refused, sued, and won.[19] Still others found their plans for a golf course or pinball parlor stymied by administrative guidance, sued, and won.[20] And the disputes continued even into the next decade—when a resort condominium developer contested a local administrative guidance program and in 2001 won.[21]

In turn, these suits generated a variety of related claims. Suppose a mayor stalled a developer's applications to induce him to cooperate with the city's administrative guidance. Time is money, and when developers sued for their damages, they won. In a further extension, local taxpayers adopted the tactic Yamada had used: bring a taxpayers' derivative action against the mayor to force him to reimburse the city for those damages the city had had to pay developers. Naturally, they won too.[22] In yet another move, developers who had earlier donated money under the guidance began suing for refunds. Although nominally they had "donated" the money, they explained, they had done so only because they thought they had no choice. Now that the courts had made it clear they could have refused, they wanted their money back. The courts (including the Supreme Court) agreed: the cities owed refunds.[23]

Judicial Review of Guidance over Foreign Exchange

Although in their contests over administrative guidance plaintiffs most commonly sued local governments, not all did. Sometimes they sued MITI, and in the 1960s at least one set of plaintiffs sued MITI over foreign exchange. In deciding the case, the court did not tell MITI it could take Edo's revenge in Nagasaki. It told MITI (and we know of no cases telling it anything else) the opposite: MITI could *not* use the foreign exchange controls to enforce its unrelated policies.

The dispute involved militarily sensitive exports to China.[24] With the cold war in progress, the United States hoped to keep military technology out of the communist block. It would not sell communists the technology, and it did not want its allies selling them the technology either. To coordinate the boycott, it organized the Coordinating Committee for Export Control (COCOM), an unofficial agreement among its allies not to sell specified products into the Soviet block.

Notwithstanding COCOM, in the late 1960s a Japanese group decided to ship sensitive material to trade fairs in Beijing and Shanghai. Some of it appeared on COCOM's banned list. When the Japanese group applied to MITI as required by the foreign exchange statute, MITI said no. Shipping the equipment would violate the COCOM agreement, and that the ministry did not intend to let it do.

The group then sued MITI on the application, and the court held MITI's denial illegal. It noted that if the group exported the equipment, the United States might retaliate. Indeed, the United States did exactly that when, twenty years later, a Toshiba-related firm flouted COCOM by selling the

Soviets submarine screw technology. The court further noted that such retaliation could hurt the Japanese economy.

Despite the resulting risks to the public welfare, the court refused to
let MITI deny the group its export license. In general, reasoned the court,
the government could regulate private conduct only by the "principle of
administration according to law." Here, article 22 of the Japanese Consti-
tution protected a citizen's right "to choose his occupation." As a result,
MITI could regulate in ways that limited an individual's ability to choose
his business only if a statute clearly authorized its regulation.

Granted, the foreign exchange statute delegated the question of whether
exports harmed the national economy to MITI's discretion. Nonetheless,
reasoned the court, that discretion extended only to "direct economic" factors. It did not allow MITI to consider such real but indirect effects as
American retaliation. If MITI denied the application because of those indirect concerns, it violated the law.[25]

Criminal Liability for Regulatory Compliance

Not only did courts let firms challenge guidance they hated, they refused
to let firms use guidance they liked to avoid criminal liability. Take the
oil firms. Since the 1960s they had—haphazardly, given the opposition of
firms like Idemitsu kosan—cut production and fixed prices. They had managed their deals in the Petroleum Federation and delegated enforcement to
MITI.

In turn, MITI had implemented the cartel through informal directives.
To the Fair Trade Commission (FTC; the agency charged with enforcing the
antitrust laws), however, the arrangement was criminal. To be sure, MITI
had authority under the Petroleum Industry Act to set standard prices and
review production plans. It had then enforced the industry's arrangements
through administrative guidance. Price-fixing was still price-fixing, declared
the FTC, and violated the Antimonopoly Act. The prosecutors agreed and
launched criminal prosecutions.

In 1980 the trial court straightforwardly convicted the firms.[26] Never
mind that MITI had told them to follow the price-fixing schedule, explained
the court. Never mind either that the Petroleum Industry Act authorized
MITI to advise firms to cut output or to set resale prices. Informal advice
and guidance do not bind, and the firms could have ignored MITI had they
wanted. In using the guidance to enforce their cartel's terms, they fixed prices
in violation of the antitrust statute—and that violation constituted a crime.

On appeal, in 1984, the Supreme Court duly affirmed.[27] Firms need not
follow administrative guidance, it noted. And precisely because compliance
is voluntary, the guidance will shield no one from criminal prosecution.

FINANCIAL MARKET REGULATION

In claiming that MITI had carrots to dispense to firms that cooperated with its instructions, scholars typically cite the credit market. There, they argue, MITI could both influence private-sector loans and make subsidized public-sector loans. Yet the claim should trouble. In financial markets, traders arbitrage away the effect of many government programs. If they arbitraged here too, MITI could have influenced the allocation of private credit only if lenders rationed credit.

Put another way, MITI could not have influenced the allocation of bank loans if financial markets cleared at market prices. (How much effective influence it could have had even in rationed markets, of course, is unclear.) Given that traders arbitrage prices not only within financial markets but across them as well, MITI could have done so only if *no* substantial financial markets in Japan cleared. And so scholars routinely assert: that the government restricted equity issues, that it virtually banned bond issues, that it insulated the financial markets from foreign competition, and that it created the venue for credit rationing by capping loan interest rates at sub-market levels. In fact, however, by the 1960s the financial markets cleared, banks lent at market rates—and MITI did not influence the allocation of private credit.

Equity Issues

The Japanese government never seriously regulated domestic equity issues. Indeed, despite the pervasive references in the English-language literature to highly regulated Japanese securities markets (e.g., Weinstein and Yafeh 1998, 636; Allinson 1997, 92), the government never even tried to restrict equity issues. Subject to routine corporate (e.g., par value) and securities (e.g., registration and disclosure) rules, it allowed firms to sell stock as they pleased. And sell stock the firms did. In 1964, Tokyo Stock Exchange–listed firms raised ¥531 billion through 533 issues, in 1970 ¥681 billion through 537 issues, and in 1975 ¥1,001 billion through 285 issues (through 1970 the dollar traded for about ¥360/US$; in 1975 it traded for about ¥305/US$).

Although cross-country comparisons typically suggest that Japanese firms rely less on equity issues than American firms do, the typical comparisons badly mislead. According to the recent consensus, the lower U.S. debit/equity ratios instead reflect "differences in accounting" (Myers 2001, 83; see Rajan and Zingales 1995). If U.S. firms apparently have a book debt/capital ratio of 37 percent (1991 data) compared to 53 percent among Japanese firms, adjusted for basic accounting differences the ratios fall to 33 percent (United States) and 37 percent (Japan). If U.S. firms apparently have a market debt/capital ratio of 28 percent compared to 29 percent among Japanese firms, adjusted for accounting differences the ratios fall to 23 percent (United States) and 17 percent (Japan) (Myers 2001).

Nor is this convergence recent. Instead, the modern consensus just brings to English-language readers what Iwao Kuroda and Yoshiharu Oritani (1979) showed Japanese scholars over two decades ago. On the basis of their study of mid-1970s firms, Kuroda and Oritani (1979) estimated equity/asset ratios of 33.0 percent for U.S. firms and 47.4 percent for Japanese firms. Once one adjusted the numbers for the differing accounting treatment of such items as leases and lines of credit, U.S. firms relied on financial intermediaries at least as heavily as Japanese firms did.

Bond Issues

Nor did the government itself restrict the bond market. To be sure, the major banks tried collectively to limit the firms that could issue bonds. Yet even they succeeded only haphazardly. Despite the collective efforts by banks, many large companies still raised enormous amounts on the bond markets. In 1965, Tokyo Stock Exchange–listed firms raised ¥324 billion through 467 bond issues, and in 1970 ¥509 billion through 306 issues. By 1975, they had raised ¥1,406 billion through 306 straight bond issues, ¥408 billion through 57 convertible issues, and ¥372 billion through 52 foreign issues (Tokyo shoken torihiki jo, *Shoken tokei nempo* 1985, 111).

What is more, those firms that could not meet the bank-organized requirements could—and did—readily circumvent them. Rather than sell bonds, they just borrowed directly from the institutional investors that would otherwise have bought their bonds. In the United States, investors such as insurance companies traditionally bought most of the bonds that firms issued. In Japan, the industrial firms simply borrowed from them directly (Kuroda and Oritani 1979, 19).

The Overseas Market

Throughout the 1950s and 1960s, the government did "regulate" foreign investment in Japan. It banned it in principle and then made assorted exceptions. The question is whether the residual restrictions prevented foreign firms from investing in Japan and arbitraging away the effect of any domestic policy measures.

From 1952 to 1960, foreigners invested relatively little. All told, they brought in only $1.01 billion, and only 16 percent of that as equity. Of the debt, the World Bank loaned 43 percent (the largest amounts to electrical utility firms) and the Washington-based EXIM Bank 21 percent (Tsusho sangyo sho 1990, 402–10).

Come the 1960s, foreigners began to see serious economic potential in Japan. Quickly they came to invest amounts that swamped the earlier levels. In 1961 alone foreigners invested $581 million, in 1963 $904 million, in 1965 $549 million, and in 1967 $880 million. By the 1970s, they had hiked their investment levels higher still and increasingly took equity (and thus long-term) positions: $3.5 billion in 1969 (71 percent as equity), $4.3 billion in 1971 (63 percent equity), and even $2.9 billion in recessionary 1973 (70 percent equity) (Nihon ginko 1974, 210). "The Foreign Exchange Law prescribed that companies needed special permission to go abroad for financing, and such permission was in principle denied," declares a Harvard Business School case study (Schaede 2000, 2). Well yes, "in principle." By the 1970s, that "principle" stood subject to an annual $3–5 billion exception.

Interest Rate Caps

Whether the government could allocate credit depends crucially on whether the credit market cleared. If banks lent at market interest rates, anything the government did to direct funds would simply have produced offsetting shifts elsewhere. Because the marginal cost of funds would generally have stayed at market levels, even loan subsidies would seldom have affected investment patterns.

During the 1960s, Japanese banks faced a cap on the interest they could charge their commercial borrowers: subject to a variety of qualifications, a maximum of about 8.4–9.2 percent on loans of more than ¥1 million for less than one year. In addition, they faced a potentially more binding limit imposed by the banking industry association (again on loans of more than ¥1 million for less than one year). The cap applied to all banks and ranged from about 5.5–8.4 percent during 1960–68.

It was a bizarre cap indeed. One can imagine banks trying collectively to impose an interest rate floor. One can imagine firms trying collectively to obtain an interest rate cap. Why *banks* would want a *cap* is a tougher question.

Perhaps, however, it is also a needless question. For perhaps they imposed no such thing. If the cap bound lenders, observed nominal interest rates should have bunched at the mandated level. They did not. Instead, they varied broadly. In 1965, the money center banks charged modal rates of 8.0–8.4 percent within a range of 6.2–9.5 percent. With their smaller clients, the regional banks charged modal rates of 8.4–8.8 percent, given a range of 6.2–9.9 percent. In no case did lenders tie lower-interest loans to whether a firm followed "government policy"—whatever that might mean.

Despite those lower modal rates, banks did charge higher rates to some firms. From 1960 to 1968, the money center banks lent a third to a half of their loans at rates above the highest trade-association-imposed cap. With their smaller customers, the regional banks charged even more. From 1960 to 1968, they lent a full half to three-quarters of their loans at rates above that cap.

Observed interest rates exceeded the "mandatory" caps because the banks could so easily avoid them. Most basically, the caps applied only to large, short-term loans. Suppose a bank wanted to charge a firm more than the maximum. First, for a small client it could simply cut the amount of the loan. It could either split it into several smaller loans or lend some of the money and tell the firm to go elsewhere for the rest.

Second, the bank could extend the loan term beyond a year. The one-year term was arbitrary, after all. Most banks regularly rolled over short-term loans. Given the porous character of these regulations, money center banks made only 60–80 percent of their loans on terms that formally subjected them to the caps. Regional banks made only 50–60 percent on such terms.[28]

GOVERNMENT LOAN PROGRAMS

Loans in Ocean Shipping

The Japan Development Bank (JDB) offered subsidized loans, but primarily it offered them to firms in ocean shipping (Nihon zosen 1980). From 1961 to 1970, the JDB routed to firms in this field over a third of its entire loan base (an average of ¥204 billion a year). To shipbuilding firms preparing vessels for export, the government routed nearly half its Export-Import Bank loans (a loan base averaging ¥247 billion a year).

Through the loans, the government transferred enormous wealth. The JDB raised its funds from government-run financial institutions such as the postal savings system. It then lent the funds to private firms at 6.5 percent (Nihon senshu kyokai 1970, 177). To shipping firms on approved projects, it lent 60–80 percent of the cost of a ship and spread repayment over eleven to thirteen years—a period so generous that it exceeded the expected life of the ship (166, 173).

The subsidies did not stop there. First, the government used the general budget to cut the cost of JDB loans further. For much of the 1960s, it forgave 2.5 percent of the 6.5 percent interest rate and charged shipping firms only the remaining 4 percent (Nihon senshu kyokai 1970, 177–78). Second, it informally guaranteed private-sector loans for the rest of the cost of a ship. In exchange, the banks loaned shipping firms the necessary funds at 8.4–9.1 percent and extended repayment over eight years (166).

Third, usually the government paid 2–3 percent of the stated interest rate on the private-sector loans. As a result, shipping firms borrowed from private banks at 6–7.1 percent net (Nihon senshu kyokai 1970, 176–79). In effect, those firms that complied with the government program borrowed most of the cost of a ship from the JDB at 4 percent and the remainder from private banks at 6–7 percent.

Last, if a shipping firm was financially troubled, the government allowed it to defer repayment even beyond the (already generous) contractual terms. When shipping firms found themselves in distress after the Suez Canal reopened in the late 1950s, for example, the government deferred their JDB obligations. It then induced private banks to defer theirs as well.

Sanko Steamship

If the program's structure is clear, its effect is less so. Reflecting the standard wisdom, Hoshi and Kashyap (2001, 159) argue that the program increased government power: through the program, the government could "tightly regulate[] the number of new vessels that could be produced each year." Yet to do so the government would have needed to stop firms from both (1) borrowing at market rates on nonapproved projects and (2) arbitraging funds from approved projects to the nonapproved.

If the government could stop both unapproved loans and arbitrage, it had at least a shot at regulating investment. If it could not, it would seldom have affected a firm's returns on its marginal investments. Not changing marginal calculations, it would seldom have affected either the level or direction of investments. Not affecting output, for better or worse it could not have implemented any "industrial policy."

So—did the government regulate the number of new vessels?

Among the shipping firms, none was more outspoken than the Sanko steamship firm. Before the early 1950s, Sanko had taken government subsidies and complied with government mandates. In the mid-1950s it decided to go it alone. Rather than take and comply, it would raise its own funds and follow its own plans. While its rivals stayed within the government's orbit, it repaid its JDB loans and turned exclusively to private sources.

In Sanko's eyes, the subsidies brought too much control. Loans always come with terms, of course—whether in Japan or in the United States, whether from the government or from private banks. Sanko was willing to accept the terms private creditors and investors imposed. It was not willing to accede to the government's.

For Sanko, the government loans presented several problems (Miwa and Ramseyer 2004b). First, the government pushed obsolete services. Because regular, scheduled freight liners had been central to the industry pre-war, the government focused the postwar program on liners as well. Yet as Sanko saw it, the industry had shifted. The future lay not with standard liners but with industry-specific ships such as oil tankers, operating on shipper-specific schedules. If Sanko accepted the subsidies, it would need to focus on services it considered obsolete.

Second, the government imposed a long and cumbersome loan application process but promised funding only year by year. Again as Sanko saw it, to offer its clients what they needed it had to be able to plan over several years. Rather than apply annually for funds it might not obtain, it had to be able to work with its clients long term.

Third, through its loan covenants the government demanded a veto over new projects. To Sanko, this posed trouble on two fronts. On the one hand, to help the industry earn monopoly rents, the government often wanted to block construction just when Sanko wanted to expand. On the other, the government wanted Sanko under the control of (and perhaps a mere division of) a larger, more compliant shipping firm. To reduce competition, the government had decided to consolidate the industry into six firms (or firms under the control of the six), and Sanko was not to be one of the six.

Sanko jettisoned the government subsidies all the way to the bank (Miwa and Ramseyer 2004b). It had opened the 1950s with virtually nothing. It closed the 1960s as the most profitable firm in the industry. During the last half of the decade, it earned shareholder returns of 32 percent a year, and by the early 1970s 62 percent. Its closest rival during the late 1960s was Showa, but it earned only 17 percent and in the early 1970s only 32 percent. Its closest rival during the early 1970s was Japan Lines, but it earned only 50 percent and in the late 1960s only 9 percent.

OPEC transformed the industry with its 1973 embargo, but by then Sanko had grown from the sixth-ranked firm (in 1964) to the largest. From a stock market capitalization of ¥3.59 billion in 1964, it had boomed to ¥514 billion by 1973, three times that of its nearest rival. Despite making no government-"approved" vessels, it commanded a shipping capacity second only to that of Japan Lines. Despite collecting no government-subsidized loans, it serviced the third largest debt in the industry.

Flout as it did government policy, Sanko raised funds straightforwardly. First, it sold stock and retained its earnings. In 1952, it had paid-in capital of only ¥420 million. By 1956, it had ¥1,300 million, by 1964 ¥4,700 million, and by 1974 ¥31,000 million (Sanko 1968; Kyoiku sha 1980, 76).

Second, it leased. From 1963 to 1971, Sanko increased the number of ships it controlled from 13 to 108. It did not buy them all. Instead, about half of the 108 it leased (Sanko securities filings). Depending on the contractual terms, leasing can have identical economic effects as borrowing. For Sanko, the identity presented a standard financing strategy.

Third, it borrowed. On the one hand, Sanko borrowed from banks. Sometimes it borrowed from a single bank, sometimes from multiple banks (Sanko securities filing, March 1961, 496ff.). Generally it arranged for its client— the firm on whose behalf it would eventually operate the ship—to guarantee it business (Sanko 1968, 99).

On the other, Sanko bought on credit. Often it negotiated deferred payments to the builders from which it bought its ships (Sanko securities fillings,

September 1966, 14). The trick involved arbitrage. Even if the government could discourage banks from lending directly to Sanko, it did not try to prevent banks from lending to shipbuilding firms that sold to Sanko. If those firms then let Sanko defer its payments to them, they effectively arbitraged their own credit. Suppose a firm obtained a subsidized loan through the Export-Import Bank to sell ship A abroad. If it then deferred payment on the ship B it sold Sanko, it even arbitraged the government loan on the exported ship.

The moral is simple. During the 1960s, the government intervened heavily in the ocean shipping industry. It paid Sanko's competitors subsidies but not Sanko itself. It lent Sanko's competitors money but not Sanko. It encouraged private banks to lend to Sanko's competitors but not to Sanko. All this Sanko flouted to spectacular success. By the early 1970s it had raised enough funds to catapult itself into preeminence and earned high-enough profits to assure its investors huge returns.

Tanker Firms

Nonconformity neither started nor stopped with idiosyncratic Sanko. Sanko may have been the most visible shipping firm to buck national shipping policy, but it was hardly alone. If it questioned the government's unwillingness to promote tankers, so did many petroleum refining firms. Rather than defer to national policy, some bought their own tankers or formed transportation subsidiaries that did.

Through such policies, the refining firms integrated vertically into transportation. And internationally, vertically integrated tanker operations were the norm (Okaniwa 1981, 125). Sometimes Japanese refiners did buy the tankers in conjunction with foreign firms. These foreign firms could borrow abroad, of course. Arbitrage being what it is, Japanese firms that entered joint ventures with them could finance both their refineries and their tankers abroad.

Yet even Japanese firms not tied to foreign firms borrowed abroad and bought their own tankers. From 1955 to 1963, independent Idemitsu kosan borrowed $56 million from Bank of America and Esso ($6 million of that for tanker capacity). Independent Maruzen sekiyu borrowed $61 million from the Bank of America, Unoco, and Continental Illinois (also $6 million for tankers). And independent Daikyo sekiyu, Nihon kogyo, and Shin Ajia sekiyu each borrowed lesser amounts abroad (Sangyo keikaku kaigi 1965, 71–73). Indeed, from 1960 to 1963, only 16 of the 41 tankers built were funded by the government, and 11 were funded abroad (Tonen tankaa 1979, 315).

Petroleum refiners built considerable transportation capacity. By 1978, Tokyo Tanker had 8 tankers carrying 749,000 tons. Idemitsu (with its own tanker subsidiary) owned 10 tankers (1.2 million tons), Daikyo (also with a tanker subsidiary) owned 3 (189,000 tons), and Maruzen 2 (46,000 tons). The firm with the most tanker capacity, however, remained the Sanko shipping firm: 23 tankers carrying 2.6 million tons (Nihon tankaa kyokai 1980, 220–21).

Of all new ships in 1965, private firms produced 36 percent of the shipping capacity (18 percent of total capacity) beyond official government programs. Like Sanko, they apparently found few financing barriers they could not circumvent. To fund these ships, they borrowed 15 percent from banks, 41 percent from trading partners (such as shipbuilding firms), and 26 percent from abroad (Nihon senshu kyokai 1970, 172–73; Ginko kyokai 1965, 361).

OPEC

Come OPEC, all this changed. Facing radically higher oil prices, Western firms now cut the amount of oil they consumed—and shipped. They also began looking harder for oil outside of the Middle East—and further cut the amount they shipped. Firms that had invested heavily in tankers suffered, and Sanko as much as any. By 1985 it filed for bankruptcy. It had gambled and lost. Gambles that go bad *ex post* can still be good *ex ante*, of course. At least investors seem to have thought Sanko a good gamble *ex ante*. And in losing *ex post*, Sanko also had good company. Even government-favored firms lost heavily. Among the government's anointed six, Japan Lines had failed by 1988.

Subsidized Loans in Other Industries

Despite the predominant role that the shipping industry played in the government loan programs, a few scholars (most recently and elaborately Pekkanen 2003) go to enormous lengths to show that the government also subsidized firms in several higher-growth fields. Unfortunately, they miss the fact that such subsidies need not (and in Japan almost certainly *did* not) increase investment.

To see why the programs would not have increased investment, take figure 6.1. The downward-sloping line gives the investment function for a hypothetical firm—$I(\rho)$, the amount of which depends on the imagined rate of return on investment. At the market interest rate of r_m, for example, it will invest I^*. With access to cheaper funds, it will invest more. Hence the obvious intuition: by lending money at submarket rates, the Japanese government could promote investment in targeted industries.

Unless the government either lends *all* the funds a firm needs or makes its loans explicitly conditional on a firm making investments it would otherwise find unprofitable (and the Japanese government seldom did either),

Figure 6.1 Investment relative to interest rate for a hypothetical firm

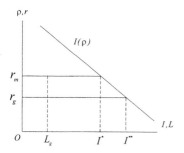

the intuition is wrong. Suppose the government agreed to lend a firm all amounts it wanted at rate r_g (below r_m). The firm would expand its planned investment from I^* to I^{**}. Suppose instead, however, that the government will lend only L_g (below I^*) at r_g. The firm will happily borrow the cheap money from the government, but it will merely pocket its savings (given by $[r_m - r_g] \times L_g$). It will not expand investment and thereby its productive capacity. Because it cannot borrow all the money it needs from the government, to expand it must borrow on the market. For that money, however, it must pay r_m. Because it borrows on the margin at r_m, it still invests only I^*.

FOREIGN EXCHANGE CONTROLS

Did MITI rely on its foreign exchange control powers? As noted earlier, Johnson thought the power "the single most important instrument of industrial guidance and control that MITI ever possessed." The Harvard case study claimed firms that cooperated "with the country's growth strategies would be rewarded through preferential access to foreign exchange, whereas resistance could result in severe penalties" (Schaede 2000, 2). And Harvard and Tokyo University economists Richard Caves and Masu Uekusa asserted that "controls over international transactions have *often* served as a club when gentle persuasion failed" (1976a, 489; ital. added).

To the best of our knowledge, before the Sumitomo Metals dispute MITI *never* used its powers over foreign exchange and trade to enforce unrelated policies (*Nikkei*, Nov. 20, 1965). To be sure, it did eventually try the ploy once—in 1969, to enforce COCOM. When it did, the Tokyo District Court declared the ploy flatly illegal.

Yet by 1969 the issue was moot anyway. By then, MITI had few foreign exchange control powers to wield, for the Japanese government had already freed virtually all imports. The shift had begun in the late 1950s, when it decided to integrate Japan more fully into the international economy. In 1960, measured by volume, 44 percent of all imports were unrestricted.

By 1963 that fraction had climbed to 92 *percent*.[29] MITI's "single most important instrument" was nothing but a hall of mirrors.

MAKING SENSE OF THE LEGEND

Resolving the Dilemma

The conventional story about "industrial policy" presents an intellectual puzzle. On the one hand, Japanese voters endorsed a half century of what Pulitzer Prize winner John Dower (1993, 14) called "conservative hegemony"; on the other, the conservatives they chose gave their hired hands in government what sociologist Ronald Dore (1986, 25) called "developmental state control over the long-term growth and structure of the economy." On the one hand, voters chose politicians committed to a capitalistic framework; on the other, those politicians hired men who implemented a nearly socialist industrial policy. On the one hand, voters rejected socialist and communist candidates for politicians who promised to leave the economy alone; on the other, those politicians appointed bureaucrats who intervened relentlessly.

The dilemma is easy to resolve. It requires no special theory, no oddball cultural norms, no Japan-specific analysis—not even Krugman's "Japan is a fuzzy kind of society." Instead, the conventional story is just wrong on the facts. Japanese bureaucrats never heavily intervened. They never intervened because politicians rarely gave them the means to intervene. Politicians seldom gave them the means because voters did not want interventionist government. Reflecting those preferences, LDP politicians instead kept their decidedly capitalist and noninterventionist approach front and center to economic policy.

That Japanese voters did not want heavy-handed state control should surprise no one except self-styled intellectuals. From 1950 to 1990 American voters elected Republican presidents seven out ten times. Why expect rich voters elsewhere necessarily to want anything else? Reflecting those voter preferences, the Japanese government did not promote growth through interventionist policy. Neither did it try such a policy but fail. It never tried. Having lived through the war and the early Occupation, voters knew the perils of government planning. They wanted none of it and elected politicians who would give them none of it.

The Genesis of the Legend

Although LDP politicians maintained a fundamentally hands-off-the-economy approach, that never stopped them from taking credit for the boom market that coincided with their tenure. *Of course* the economy doubled in less than a decade—had not their prime minister announced his plan to do just that? To make their claims plausible, LDP politicians turned to their bureaucrats for the appropriate white papers. Dutifully, the bureaucrats wrote them by the score. Not having studied economics at Chicago, they did not write the Friedmanesque essays they might have written. Instead, they wrote essays that reflected the training they had received. As we explained in chapter 3, on matters economic that was an almost exclusively Marxist training. The economy grew, they explained, because they in the government had led the private sector so adroitly.

Predictably, their Marxist professors showed inimitable skepticism toward everyone in business and virtually none toward the men on the government payroll. If the Japanese economy grew, it must have grown because their students in the bureaucracy had guided it so well. Reflecting that academic background (and perhaps his own ego), the top bureaucrat at MITI even compared his team to Napoleon and Clausewitz. In the quarter of a century since World War II, he declared (quoted in Trezise and Suzuki 1976, 793), MITI had created on Japan's "cramped land area a giant economy that ranks second in the free world."

In effect, the bureaucrats wrote their political pamphlets as best they knew how. Through Western observers looking for variously congenial anecdotes, their pamphleteering then emigrated to the United States as scholarship. For those observers, the myth was congenial to a fault. Some used it to push an "industrial policy" domestically. Many saw it as ammunition in their interminable campus brawls over the cultural relativity of economic theory—as yet another example of how their rivals in the economics departments had gotten it all wrong. Still others used it to motivate their latest models of "market failure" or "strategic" trade theory. Unfortunately for them, the legend of Japanese government guidance tells us nothing about Japan. Like the best urban legends, it tells us only about ourselves.

CONCLUSION

The story of Japanese industrial policy is not a story about the virtues of an interventionist bureaucratic policy. Nor is it a story about its vices. It is not a story about interventionist policy at all. This should not surprise. In lacking such policies, Japan was not the exception. Among the advanced capitalist economies, it was instead the norm.

Given that politicians never empowered their bureaucrats to try to grow the economy through intervention, the debate over the effectiveness of Japanese industrial policy misses the point. Voters elected politicians committed to free market principles, and those politicians largely implemented that commitment. They implemented the usual pork barrel programs too, of course. When observers talk of industrial policy they merely confuse the cover for pork with actual policy.

There is a moral here, and it goes to the perils of relying on either government publications or secondary research. For their accounts of 1950s and 1960s Japan, modern Western scholars rely on exactly those sources. Yet those were the days when Marxists ran the Japanese social science departments. Predictably, they told tales that suited their doctrinal requirements: markets fail, planning works.

Their students in the government did the same. Electoral exigency required that they celebrate the importance of keeping the current politicians in power. The theory they learned in college taught them to celebrate it by championing government intervention and leadership. Had modern scholars done more than recount the conclusions in government publications and the secondary literature, they would have noticed they were merely adding social scientific gloss to political sloganeering and 1960s-vintage Marxism. Unfortunately, they rarely tried.

CHAPTER SEVEN

The Cost of Kipling

"Surely," some readers will complain, "Miwa and Ramseyer might have tried harder to reconcile their story with what went before." Surely the extant accounts of Japan could not be so radically wrong. Surely Japan does not fit standard economic microtheory so closely as they claim.

Yet conventional microtheory with its profit-maximizing firms buying and selling in competitive markets does describe Japan. It always did. The fables about Japanese bureaucrats, keiretsu, main banks, and systematically misgoverned firms are just that—fables. At root the Japanese economy differs little from the American economy (or, we suspect, from any economy anywhere else). To learn about the Japanese economy one does not need Japan-specific accounts of corporate groups, main banks, and government-led growth. One does need economics. "The Japanese" are "different from you and me," F. Scott Fitzgerald once almost remarked. Well, yes, Hemingway once almost replied—they speak Japanese.

We conclude with a few thoughts on the economic malaise in 1990s Japan and a short summary of our argument.

THE SCOPE OF THE MALAISE

Although the Japanese economy hit a recession in the early 1990s, one can—and most observers do—overstate the problem. Firms did not earn as little as often asserted. During the late 1980s, investors had dramatically bid up the price of Japanese real estate. Why they did so we will not guess. Perhaps they hoped to play a bubble. Perhaps they had updated their information about future rental streams. Perhaps some investors did one, some the other, and some a bit of both. Whatever the reason, prices rose.

Come late 1990, prices plummeted. In the six largest cities (with prices indexed at 100 for March 1990), they rose from 24.5 in March 1980 to 33.6 in March 1985. After hitting 100 in March 1990, they fell to 54.7 by March 1995. Prices fluctuated most radically for commercial real estate: from 16.7 in 1980 to 25.6 by 1985, 100 in 1990, and then to 54.7 by 1995. By 2003, indexed metropolitan real estate prices stood at 27.8, and for commercial property at 14.3 (Nihon fudosan kenkyu jo 1998).

Within the real estate industry, the fall caused massive losses. Obviously those who bought high and sold low lost money, but their loss was a simple transfer: wealth moved to those who had sold high. Unfortunately, many investors had started long-term projects on the basis of projections keyed to late 1980s prices. They, at least, did not think the high prices a speculative bubble. On the basis of the high expected cash flows, they had begun golf courses, hotels, office towers. When expected future demand fell, many of them found their finished projects unmarketable and their unfinished ones not worth completing. For the economy, they generated a deadweight loss.

Not only did developers and construction firms lose when the demand for real estate fell, but so did those who had lent them the money they lost. Particularly when firms borrowed nonrecourse by pledging the real estate, they could walk away from the loan—and did. Effectively, they forced a sale to their creditors. Those creditors then lost additional funds if—after the price collapse—they lent extra money to try to help the developers recover.

Despite these real estate–driven losses, Japanese GNP continued to grow during the 1990s (Hayashi and Prescott 2001). Other than the firms that either bought real estate or lent to those that did, many firms remained healthy at the core. Consider indexed stock prices for Tokyo Stock Exchange (TSE)–listed firms. The effect of the real estate collapse appears directly: of the ten sectors with the lowest share prices in 1998 relative to 1986, firms in four had invested directly in real estate (agriculture, mining, real estate, and construction), and firms in two others (securities and banking) had invested heavily in firms that did.

By contrast, firms in several sectors more central to the Japanese economy enjoyed substantial stock-price growth over 1986–98. Stock prices in the automobile (transportation equipment) industry, for example, rose 86 percent between 1986 and 1998, and tire firms grew more rapidly still. Machinery, pharmaceuticals, and electrical products posted less dramatic results (9 percent, 16 percent, and 18 percent, respectively), but positive increases nonetheless. Economists Fumio Hayashi and Edward Prescott (2001) find no evidence that banking-sector problems prevented firms from exploiting profitable investment opportunities. And firms in the most profitable two quartiles during 1990–94 earned annual profits of 4.8 and 8.6 percent— only slightly less than their 5.4 and 9.3 percent profitability rates during 1986–90 (see table 7.2). All this hardly shows a boom, but neither does it suggest an economy in crisis.

Figure 7.1 explores the recovery through another metric: the performance of the nonfinancial firms from 1963 to 2002, *net the cost of capital*. To measure performance, we first divide operating profits by total assets.

Figure 7.1 Net rate of return for Japanese firms

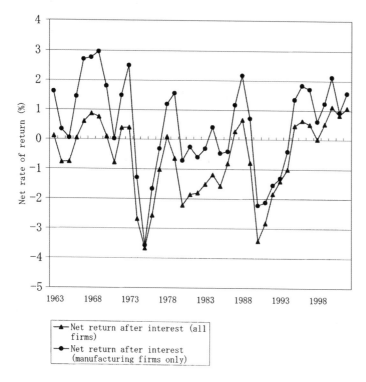

Note: This figure shows the average operating profits/total assets for all nonfinancial firms, and for all manufacturing firms, less the short-term interest rate on business loans (P/TA-Int).

Source: Okura sho, various years, Bank of Japan.

We then subtract the cost of capital—here proxied for by the average interest rate (on loans of one year or less) for business loans.[1]

The moral is simple: after a recession in the first half of the decade, firms outside the financial and real estate sectors recovered. Among nonfinancial firms, operating profits on total assets have not been negative since 1994 and among the manufacturing firms have ranged from 0.6 to 2.1 percent. Since 2002, firms have continued to do well. At the close of March 2003, the nonbank TSE-listed Japanese firms posted operating profits 72 percent above the previous year. By the close of 2004 they reported profits up yet another 21 percent (*Nikkei,* Mar. 7, 2004). Manufacturing firms did particularly well: from March 2002 to 2003, they boosted profits 104 percent; from 2003 to 2004, they hiked them yet another 25 percent.

Indeed, by the metric of figure 7.1, nonfinancial firms today perform at rates comparable to those of the 1960s. Two factors explain this surprising result. First, by using operating profits we exclude unrealized capital gains and losses. In the process, we capture a firm's current operating performance more accurately than do many routinely used accounting measures. Second, by using profitability net of the cost of capital, we measure the extent to which firms put the capital they raise to good use. Because they can obtain funds so cheaply, Japanese firms undertake projects they would not pursue under higher-interest-rate regimes. Undertaking these lower-expected-return projects, they earn lower profits on total assets—but profits that still let them recover their cost of capital. During 1995–2002, as a fraction of total assets, operating profits ranged from 2.5 to 3.9 percent.

Suppose they gave a party and no one came? Japanese firms gave a recovery. Because they focused so exclusively on the financial and real estate sectors, most Western observers missed it entirely.

DID GOOD FIRMS ABANDON THEIR BANKS?

Many commentators trace the 1990s malaise to the 1980s financial deregulation rather than the 1990 real estate collapse. Some argue that the deregulation caused the banks to lend to high-risk borrowers by letting the best corporate firms abandon bank loans for bonds (hypothesis A). Others argue that it allowed the firms to gamble wildly in the speculative bubble by freeing them from the constraints of main bank monitoring (hypothesis B).

We have already explained why the 1980s deregulation could not have caused the 1990s malaise—the government had no significant regulatory program to dismantle (chapter 6). The changes in the 1980s involved little more than the liberalization of the bond market and the elimination of caps on deposit interest rates. We have also explained why the end of main bank monitoring could not have caused the malaise—banks never dominated firms anyway (chapter 4). In this section we ask whether the best firms did abandon their banks during the 1980s (hypothesis A). In the following section we ask whether the firms that invested most aggressively during the 1980s boom disproportionately failed in the 1990s (hypothesis B).

Hypothesis A

Economists Takeo Hoshi and Anil Kashyap nicely outline hypothesis A. The 1980s deregulation, they explain, caused banks to shift their loan strategy. By facilitating bond issues, deregulation allowed the blue chip firms to raise disintermediated funds. Those firms then abandoned their banks, and the banks responded by turning to riskier firms that then failed. "Between 1983 and 1989," Hoshi and Kashyap write, "the Japanese bond market blossomed, permitting many internationally known companies to tap the public debt markets for the first time" (1999, 143–44; see Miyajima 1998, 53; Milhaupt and Miller 1997, 29). As a result, the banks "lost many of their borrowers in a very short period of time." To replace the lost business they turned to real estate developers; when the market crashed those developers failed, and as they failed banks found themselves saddled with losses.

To show how blue chip firms left banks, Hoshi and Kashyap (1999, 148, table 5) examine the ratio of bank debt to assets among the biggest listed manufacturing firms. That ratio, they note, fell from 36 percent in 1970 to 32 percent in 1980. From 32 percent, it fell to 13 percent by 1990, and there it has roughly remained since. "As the banks started to lose their customers to capital markets, they went after small firms," they reason. The result was a "portfolio shift: increasing loans to the real estate industry" (Hoshi and Kashyap 1999, 163).

The Evidence

Ratios mislead here, for the banks did not lose their customers, and bond issues do not explain the shift into real estate loans. Many of the loans they did lose were among firms in weaker sectors: oil, nonferrous metals, and steel. These sectors were retrenching, and they lost equity capitalization as well. Among the listed manufacturing firms, any decline in loans was simply too small to have driven any substantial shift in lending policy. During 1983–89, bank loans to all listed manufacturing firms fell only ¥6.6 trillion (see table 7.1).

From 1983 to 1989, banks increased monotonically the total loans they made by ¥174 trillion. Even the loans to the TSE-listed firms they increased year by year. At the money center banks alone, they increased their total loans by ¥71 trillion. Banks did not shift into real estate because their loans to their traditional clientele fell, for traditional clients as a whole did not cut their loans. Banks shifted because they captured huge increases in loanable funds.

DID DEREGULATION LEAVE FIRMS UNMONITORED?

Hypothesis B

Other observers argue that deregulation caused the malaise by freeing firms from the control of their main banks. Before the late 1980s, reason they, main banks had carefully kept their firms in line. By monitoring the firms assiduously, they had ensured that they promoted shareholder welfare. In the process, however, they also freed investors from the need to develop alternative market-based monitoring institutions. Main banks had "obviat[ed] a

Table 7.1. Bank loans, by borrower category

	All firms			Listed firms				Manufacturing						
	Total	Construct.	Manufact.	Total	Construct.	Retail	Real Estate	Total Manufact.	Chemical	Oil & Coal	Steel	Mach.	Elect. Goods	Train Equip.
1980	1,346	73	430	564	33	116	13	267	40	27	55	15	21	36
1981	1,484	80	468	604	33	120	14	285	42	32	56	16	22	39
1982	1,640	88	501	641	33	131	16	295	43	29	61	16	22	42
1983	1,810	100	523	657	34	139	16	293	43	24	64	15	22	43
1984	2,021	114	553	665	36	150	16	280	42	21	63	15	20	40
1985	2,228	127	582	675	39	154	18	280	43	17	65	16	22	37
1986	2,444	135	576	690	40	158	20	282	41	17	66	16	25	37
1987	2,686	140	550	717	41	184	25	268	38	17	60	16	28	34
1988	2,882	148	539	770	45	242	30	252	35	17	46	16	27	36
1989	3,551	192	591	813	44	298	35	227	30	18	35	16	26	32
1990	3,760	200	592	857	52	288	45	255	32	27	33	18	34	35
1991	3,857	216	600	899	71	279	50	275	37	25	33	20	38	39
1992	3,930	234	592	932	81	275	52	293	40	23	37	21	40	42
1993	4,776	298	766	937	92	242	54	296	43	21	41	20	36	44
1994	4,784	307	748	937	93	240	54	290	42	20	42	19	38	39
1995	4,845	311	726	928	90	232	54	279	41	19	38	20	36	36

Sources: Toyo keizai shimpo sha, *Kigyo keiretsu soran*, various years; Nihon ginko, various years.

Notes: Figures are in ¥100 billion. Figures for "all firms" give the loans and discounts through the banking accounts of all banks. They thus exclude loans through trust accounts and loans from such sources as life insurance companies and government institutions. Note that in 1990, when manufacturing firms borrowed ¥59.2 trillion through their banking accounts, they borrowed only ¥2.2 trillion through trust accounts. Figures for "listed firms" include (nonsecuritized) loans from all sources.

need" for "more arm's length market-oriented" governance mechanisms to develop, explain the authors of a World Bank study on main banks (Aoki, Patrick, and Sheard 1994, 5). Because investors could count on the main bank to monitor, they "disengage[d] from these activities with little fear of adverse consequences" (Flath 2000, 288).

In the 1980s, continue these observers, the deregulation in the capital market enabled large Japanese firms to escape the constraints of their main banks. Because they could borrow directly on the market, they no longer needed to do as their main bank said. And because they borrowed from so wide a variety of places, the main bank no longer had the information it needed to tell them sensibly what to do.

Freed from their main bank, the firms found themselves freed from monitoring altogether. In response, they gambled wildly, played the stock and real estate bubbles, and failed when the bubbles eventually burst. Caught with now-uncollectible loans, the banks that had loaned them the funds they lost now suffered as well.

The account appears in a variety of sources, but economist Masahiko Aoki (2000, 91) articulates it as well as any.[2] The 1980s bond market, he explains, cut the ties between a firm and its main bank. As those ties vanished, the firms became "freed from the bank's implicit and explicit intervention." This, in turn, "diminish[ed] the flow of information from firms to city banks and consequently the bank's ability to keep track of the firm's business" (Aoki 1994, 137). In the process, the deregulation triggered "a negative incentive effect on the insiders of the firm, as they became free from any external discipline" (Aoki 2001, 91).

The Evidence

Never mind the problematic premises to the hypothesis. Never mind that the government had maintained few stringent regulations to dismantle, that Japan had maintained an active corporate control market even before 1990, and that large firms had always diversified their borrowing broadly. Consider instead whether, as these theorists assert, the firms that aggressively expanded in the 1980s failed in the 1990s.

They did not. The firms that expanded most aggressively in the late 1980s were the firms that were *least* likely to fail in the early 1990s. At root, the data tell a mundane tale. The best firms in the 1980s were the best firms in the 1990s. They had the best projects in bull times and the best projects in bears. They expanded the most in the late 1980s and contracted the least in the early 1990s.

The phenomenon appears directly in table 7.2. In panel A, we partition nonbank TSE-listed firms into quartiles by their growth rate in asset base during the late 1980s. We then calculate a variety of attributes for each

Table 7.2. Growth and profitability quartiles

	1. Growth (%)			2. Profitability			3. Main bank loan fraction		
	1980–85	1986–90	1990–94	1980–85	1986–90	1990–94	1980–85	1986–89	1990–94
				A. By 1986–90 growth quartiles					
Very low	19.493	11.463	10.848	.058	.036	.033	.277	.290	.294
Low	25.203	39.043	17.017	.066	.052	.042	.290	.306	.319
High	30.096	63.656	18.827	.072	.053	.042	.296	.330	.327
Very high	33.346	157.153	30.379	.084	.071	.052	.319	.381	.383
				B. By 1990–94 profitability quartiles					
Very low	27.956	54.474	3.481	.053	.025	.009	.292	.322	.312
Low	22.620	59.021	15.960	.060	.041	.033	.274	.301	.298
High	28.061	65.077	24.989	.070	.054	.048	.285	.323	.337
Very high	29.069	94.780	42.896	.101	.093	.086	.331	.366	.382

Sources: Nikkei QUICK joho, NEEDS, as updated; Nikkei QUICK joho, QUICK, as updated; Nihon shoken keizai kenkyu jo, various years; Toyo keizai shimpo sha, *Kigyo keiretsu soran,* various years.

Notes: Growth, percentage growth in total assets; *profitability,* operating income/total assets; *main bank loan fraction,* fraction of bank loans borrowed from the bank lending the firm the largest amount. In panel A, we partition the data by their 1986–90 growth rates (%) and calculate the other indices given; in panel B, we partition the data by 1990–94 profitability rates and calculate the other indices given.

quartile. For example, take the quartile of firms with the slowest growth rate during 1986–90. On average, these firms grew 11.5 percent during 1986–90 and 10.8 percent during 1990–94. They earned annual profits (operating income/total assets) of 3.6 percent during 1986–90 and of 3.3 percent during 1990–94.

During the late 1980s the firms in the fastest-growing quartile grew spectacularly fast (157 percent). Although they grew more slowly during the next half decade, they still grew faster than the firms that had invested more conservatively during the late 1980s. The firms that grew most slowly in the early 1990s (at 10.8 percent) were instead the firms that had grown the most slowly in the late 1980s (11.5 percent).

Firms in the fastest-growing quartile in the late 1980s also made the highest profits in the 1990s. Those fastest-growing firms earned 7.1 percent profits during the late 1980s and 5.2 percent in the early 1990s. The slowest-growing firms in the 1980s earned mean profits of only 3.6 percent in the late 1980s and only 3.3 percent in the 1990s. Note that the fastest-growing firms were not the firms with the weakest ties to their main bank (defined as the bank from which they borrowed the most). Instead, they borrowed the most from their principal bank during the late 1980s (38.1 percent) and continued to borrow the most in the early 1990s (38.3 percent).

In panel B we view the data backward: we segment the firms by their profitability during 1990–94 and calculate the same indices. The most profitable firms in the early 1990s grew the most dramatically in the late 1980s (94.8 percent) and continued to grow the most in the early 1990s (42.9 percent). The least profitable firms in the early 1990s grew the least during the late 1980s (54.5 percent) and continued to grow the least during the early 1990s (3.5 percent).

The firms skirting the margins of insolvency in the early 1990s were not the firms that had gambled with aggressive investments in the late 1980s. Instead, those closest to bankruptcy in the 1990s had been the least profitable and least aggressive in the 1980s. Necessarily, they were the firms least able to tap the bond market in the late 1980s as well.

THE COST OF KIPLING

"East is east, and west is west, and never the twain shall meet, till earth and sky stand presently at God's great judgment seat." As politically incorrect as Sylvester "Rambo" Stallone and Mae "Peal-Me-a-Grape" West, Kipling nonetheless remained a cultural relativist to the end. Dumb down his verse six levels and it captures most of what passes for "theory" among modern cultural relativists and much of what passes for analysis about Japan. And stripped of their political baggage, the modern cultural relativists and the old-school colonialists like Kipling fascinate for the same reason: they indulge our lust for the exotic and free us from the rules of social science.

Only in Kipling do mongooses talk. And only in books do firms sacrifice profits for the sake of cultural norms, do banks implicitly agree to rescue firms, or do governments guide economies to double-digit economic growth. The story of Japan's economic emergence is not a story about leadership by the government. It is not a story about coordination by banks. And it is not a story about some indigenous "group" or "Confucian" mentality. It is a story about competition among profit-maximizing firms in decentralized markets.

Keiretsu

By legend, most large exchange-listed Japanese firms work within a keiretsu conglomerate group. They send their presidents to monthly meetings to plan collective strategy. They protect themselves from outside acquirers, from stock market pressure, and from bilateral opportunism by swapping stock in each other. And they buy and sell the bulk of their supplies and output from and to each other.

In fact, the keiretsu do none of this and never did. They do not significantly trade with each other. They do not hold stock in each other. Most of them do not meet with each other. In fact, most do not even consider themselves part of a group.

At root, the keiretsu are not groups that firms formed. Rather, they are groups that academics invented. Fictitious even in the 1960s and 1970s, they are not currently in decline—for there was no phenomenon from which to decline.

Instead, the keiretsu constitute the quintessential academic urban legend. From the 1950s through the 1970s, Japanese economists were overwhelmingly Marxist. According to Marxist theory, they needed to find a "monopoly capital" that dominated the Japanese market. Japan had no monopoly capital, of course, but no matter. An independent think tank created their capital for them by sorting exchange-listed firms by the source of their loans. It called the lists the keiretsu and sold economics departments an annual subscription for a tidy sum.

In turn, the scholars who dominated the field of Japanese studies in the West came from departments other than economics. Not only were they not economists; many of the most prominent were actively hostile to economics and used Japan to fight what they saw as the incursions of economic logic into their own disciplines (political science, for example, or sociology). For them, the Marxist-invented keiretsu promised to be a godsend—noneconomic institutions that determined the very structure of the world's second-largest economy. They took the godsend, and the rest is history.

The Zaibatsu

Unlike the keiretsu, the pre-war zaibatsu did once function as conglomerates. Owned by a few very wealthy families, sometimes they did indeed operate as groups. Crucially, however, they did not thrive or succeed because they were zaibatsu.

Instead, the groups became the zaibatsu because they thrived and succeeded. More to the point, the groups became known as the zaibatsu because they happened to be making their owners rich in the early 1930s, when muck-raking journalists came looking for someone to blame for the depression. "Financial clique" may be the standard translation of *zaibatsu* but it misses the point. A more idiomatic translation would be "robber baron."

The zaibatsu firms had succeeded for all the reasons that a few firms in any competitive economy succeed while many fail and most just survive. As they earned their owners profits, those owners diversified into new industries. In the process, they necessarily created conglomerates. Alas, in the troubled 1930s journalists needed someone to blame. That bill these successful industrialists fit to a tee.

Main Banks

Japanese firms do not maintain a "main bank system" and never did. Ask a Japanese businessman whether his firm has a "main bank" and he will probably say "sure." By that, however, he does not mean what academics mean by the "Japanese main bank system." He does not mean his firm borrows all its money from the bank. He does not mean the bank dominates his firm, places officers on its board, forces it to borrow, or tells it what products to sell or factories to build. He does not mean the main bank monitors the firm on behalf of all other banks. And he certainly does not mean the bank will rescue his firm should it fall into trouble. He means only that his company borrows more from that bank than from others, or perhaps that his firm uses that bank for its payment functions. Sure the firm has a main bank. So does every firm on the New York Stock Exchange.

The academic "main bank system" has always been an elaborate theoretical construct with the scantiest of empirical foundations. It cohered within itself but bore no relation to the real world. The dozens of academic articles and game-theoretic models to the contrary notwithstanding, Japanese banks do not dominate corporate governance, do not delegate their monitoring, and do not agree to rescue distressed borrowers. They do not now—and never did.

Corporate Governance

Couple accounts of economic malaise (Japan) with tales of greed (Enron), and one can all too easily blame the former on the latter: the economy fell into recession because managers stole. Only when Japanese firms learn to cabin managerial greed (or indolence, or Confucian loyalty to nonshareholder goals) will they rebound. Only when Japanese firms install better governance systems will the economy recover. Or so one hears.

Basic economic theory should make one wonder. Japanese firms buy their inputs and sell their outputs on competitive markets. Necessarily, those that offer their shareholders a lower return should find it costlier to raise the funds they need. Those with higher capital costs should find it harder to undersell their rivals. Because only firms that sell good products cheap will survive, ultimately badly governed firms should not be among them. In equilibrium, firms with inappropriate governance schemes should go out of business or change. And in equilibrium, the firms that survive should maintain governance regimes reasonably suited to their needs.

If instead (as current reformers argue) Japanese firms suffer because insiders dominate management, then firms with more outsiders should outcompete those with fewer. They do not. Instead, exactly as basic economic theory suggests, Japanese firms apparently maintain governance structures reasonably close to what they need.

Government Leadership

Over the postwar decades, bureaucrats never had the power they would have needed to guide (much less control) the Japanese economy. They could not rely on the courts to defer to their discretion; instead, regulated parties occasionally challenged them in court, and when they did judges held bureaucrats to the statute. They could not use (indeed, did not even try to use) foreign exchange controls to force firms to comply with their unrelated dictates; instead, already by the 1960s most firms could freely obtain whatever foreign exchange they wanted. And they could not use any control over credit to force firms to comply with their wishes; instead, the credit market cleared at market rates.

Bureaucrats did not have the power to guide the economy because voters did not want to give them the power. Japanese voters had lived with controls before. The government had tried to control the economy during the war and the early Occupation, and they knew how disastrous such controls could be. They threw the postwar Socialists out of office in short order. Over the ensuing decades Socialists and Communists regularly offered them the option of a controlled economy. Regularly, they rejected it.

In Japan as in most modern democracies, bureaucrats answer to politicians. If voters do not want their bureaucrats to control the economy, politicians will not give bureaucrats the power to control it. Japanese voters did not want control bureaucrats. And Japanese politicians did not give their bureaucrats control.

Yet in bull markets politicians do like to take credit. For most of the 1960s and 1980s, the Japanese lived in a spectacular bull market (largely because the government did *not* try to control matters). When sitting politicians decided to take credit for the booms, they turned to their faithful agents in the bureaucracy. Those bureaucrats then wrote them the white papers they wanted.

One would not expect most ordinary voters to pay much attention to such credit-claiming, but academics are not ordinary voters. Until recently, most Japanese economists were Marxist. As such, they were hardly inclined to treat tales of government planning skeptically. Many Western scholars in Japanese studies were critics of what they called the "hegemony" of "imperialist economics" within their own universities. They were hardly inclined to be skeptical either.

And the legend of government planning ensued.

Other Fables

We could make this a much longer book, for these are not the only fables about the Japanese economy. Many readers will recall accounts of "lifetime employment." Large Japanese firms, they will have read, implicitly promise to keep their employees employed until they reach retirement age.

To be sure, large Japanese firms do not often lay off workers, but that they do not lay off *ex post* does not mean they implicitly promised to keep workers *ex ante*. During the 1960s very few large firms laid off their workers, but with double-digit annual growth few wanted to retrench. When the recession hit in the 1970s, many tried. The discharged workers sued, and the courts held for the workers. Unless the firm could show that it would fold unless it retrenched, the courts would not allow it to lay off its employees. Never mind that it had hired its workers on an "at-will" contract. In enforcing its contractual right to lay off, it "abused" that right. Large Japanese firms keep their workers on the payroll, but only because workers sue them if they try anything else.

Many readers will also recall stories of Japanese employees at the big firms working long hours. If a firm cannot lay off its employees, what else would one expect to happen? If it cannot fire redundant workers during bad times, it will not hire extra workers during good. Instead, it will just make its existing workers put in longer hours.

Readers will also recall from chapter 3 the way many Japanese firms contract on the market for components (such as automobile parts) that American firms produce in-house. Yet consider once again the implications of the firm's inability to lay off. A large firm like Toyota will seldom be able to show a court that it will fail unless it discharges its redundant workers. By contrast, in times of slack demand a small supplier can readily make that showing. By buying components on the market rather than making them internally, big firms can skirt the inefficiency courts create by refusing to let them lay off workers they cannot use.

But we have no interest in writing an encyclopedia of Japanese fables. Do Japanese firms avoid detailed contracts? In fact, they frequently attach to a short basic document extra sheets with detailed specifications. Do Japanese avoid litigation? In fact, they avoid it only because, with no juries, both parties more frequently agree on what the expected outcome would be if they did litigate, and then settle out of court by reference to that expected outcome. Do Japanese firms pay workers by age-based pay scales? Sure, but they add large biannual performance-based bonuses.

WHAT NOW?

Enough already. The point is simple: our collective vision of Japan is a mirage. It is not biased or exaggerated or misleading. It is fictitious. To understand the Japanese economy properly, one cannot build on secondary sources. One must start from the beginning.

And in starting from the beginning, one will need to couple theory with data. To study the economy, one will need to start with basic microeconomic foundations: rational self-interested people, profit-maximizing firms, and competitive markets. With that theory, one will then need to learn about the institutional structure and study the market response. Those microeconomic principles will not explain everything one sees in Japan, but they will explain most. In particular, they will explain most phenomena that involve nontrivial amounts of wealth.

In Japan (as, we suspect, most everywhere else), the East *is* the West, and the twain meet every day. The economy in postwar Japan has been a competitive market economy rather than a controlled one, and it grew rapidly for just that reason. The government did not heavily regulate markets, large groups of firms did not stifle competition, and banks did not control firms. Instead, firms bought and sold, borrowed and lent, and thrived or failed—in highly competitive markets.

It is one thing (and apparently a popular thing in the academy) to speculate about the effect of institutional change on market behavior. It is another thing entirely (and in the Japanese context apparently an abandoned art) to study the institutional arrangements and market behavior actually in place. "Know thy data," Zvi Grilliches told generations of budding Harvard econometricians. They already knew the economic theory, but most area specialists outside of economics do not. They would do well to learn some basic economic theory, but then learn some real data too.

Notes

CHAPTER TWO

1. By *keiretsu*, writers on the economy refer to these putative corporate groups. The use of the term for this purpose seems to date from the late 1950s or early 1960s. As the standard dictionary *Kojien* explains, the term refers more generally to the sequence of phenomena.

2. Because many observers claim that keiretsu ties weakened during the capital market liberalization of the 1980s and the recession of the 1990s, we focus on the supposed heyday of the keiretsu, the mid-1960s. Things were not much different in the 1970s, however, as we show in Miwa and Ramseyer 2001b.

3. We omit shareholdings among the Sanwa, Fuji, and Daiichi groups because we obtain our shareholding data from the *ROK*, but not all lunch club members (six members each for Fuji and Sanwa, one for Daiichi) were on the *ROK* rosters. We also omit Hitachi from our data more generally because it was in both the Fuji and the Sanwa clubs (indeed, it would later join the Daiichi Kangyo club as well).

4. E.g., Nakatani 1984; Khanna and Yafeh 2000; Weinstein and Yafeh 1998.

5. Nihon denso 1974, 243-44; Koito 1985, 42; Akebono bureeki 1979, 347; Kayaba 1986, 284-86.

6. In this section we rely heavily on Nihon rodo kenkyu kiko 1992 and secondarily on Rodo sho 1998; Miwa 1996, sec. 4.2 and 64-68; and conversations with the original investigators. Where appropriate we update the data through Miyoshi 1999; Nihon keizai shimbun sha, *Nikkei kaisha joho*, relevant years; and Shukan toyo keizai, *Shikiho*, various years. The observations apply to firms such as Nissan and Toyota as well. To preserve confidentiality, we do not identify the firms.

CHAPTER THREE

1. The figures for Japan include "prime movers" only; the figures for the United States include all machinery. For Japan, see Minami 1965, table 27; for the United States, see U.S. Bureau of the Census 1997, tables P68-73 and S32-43).

2. In the 1940s U.S. counterintelligence agents successfully decoded many cables sent by Soviet offices back to Moscow. These cables were released to the public in the late 1990s. Bisson figures prominently in several of them as someone passing military information to an agent of Soviet military intelligence. See Venona cable of June 16, 1943, available at www.nsa.gov; see also June 17 and June 24, 1943. Bisson wrote his 1945 volume for the

Institute of Pacific Relations, which itself operated as a front for Soviet and communist Chinese spies. See generally Miwa and Ramseyer 2005b.

CHAPTER FOUR

1. In the parentheses, we give the number of firms in the cell. We exclude firms that switch their main bank affiliation.

2. Exactly how it paid it is another matter. No rational firm (whether bank or no) would offer another firm an insurance policy without charging for it. To date, however, even main bank partisans have no consensus on how the main banks charge their borrowers for this purported insurance.

CHAPTER FIVE

1. We follow the literature on Japan in defining these directors as outsiders. Obviously, one could—and some do—argue that persons from affiliated institutions such as banks are not true outsiders.

2. *Japan v. [No name given]*, 1199 Hanrei jiho 157 (S. Ct. June 27, 1987).

3. *Matsumaru v. Otsuru*, 1518 Hanrei jiho 4 (Tokyo D. Ct. Dec. 22, 1994).

4. *Japan v. Kono*, 1611 Hanrei jiho 36 (Tokyo D. Ct. March 21, 1997).

5. Sociologists and business consultants sometimes argue that this also lets Japanese firms make longer-term investments. Given that investors price stock by discounting future (whether near-term or distant-term) revenues to the present, the claim is simply nonsensical.

CHAPTER SIX

1. *Kuni v. Goto*, 1114 Hanrei jiho 10, 13 (Tokyo D. Ct. Feb. 24, 1984).

2. *Yamaki kensetsu, K.K. v. Suzuki*, 1151 Hanrei jiho 12 (Tokyo High Ct. Mar. 26, 1980).

3. *Yamaki kensetsu, K.K. v. Musashino*, 803 Hanrei jiho 18 (Tokyo High Ct. Dec. 8, 1975).

4. *Kuni v. Goto*, 1323 Hanrei jiho 16 (S. Ct. Nov. 7, 1989), *aff'g* 1166 Hanrei jiho 41 (Tokyo High Ct. Aug. 30, 1985), *aff'g* 1114 Hanrei jiho 10 (Tokyo D. Ct. Feb. 24, 1984).

5. *Yamada v. Goto*, 1354 Hanrei jiho 62 (S. Ct. Mar. 23, 1990), *aff'g* 1186 Hanrei jiho 46 (Tokyo High Ct. Mar. 26, 1986), *aff'g* 1080 Hanrei jiho 40 (Tokyo D. Ct. May 27, 1983).

6. *Yamaki kensetsu, K.K. v. Musashino*, 1465 Hanrei jiho 106 (Tokyo D. Ct. Dec. 9, 1992).

7. *Nollan v. California Coastal Commission*, 483 U.S. 825, 837 (1987); see *Dolan v. City of Tigard*, 114 S. Ct. 2309 (1994).

8. So constrained were interest rates, argue some scholars, that banks sometimes circumvented them by requiring borrowers to take more than they needed and deposit the "compensating balance" in a low-interest-bearing account at the bank. Through the ploy, they raised the effective interest rate on the loan. In fact, this largely did not happen—for the simple reason that banks lent at market-clearing rates (as we explain later). See Miwa and Ramseyer 2004b, 182–85.

9. Textual references here are to contemporary newspapers.

10. Presumably MITI caved because it would have lost the suit—for reasons we detail in connection with the Chinese trade fair.

11. Lockwood (1965, 501) asserted that in the 1950s MITI "allocat[ed] foreign exchange for raw cotton imports only to cooperating spinners." A decade later, Caves and Uekusa (1976b, 55) repeated the claim: in cotton spinning, "MITI allocated foreign exchange for raw-cotton imports only to cooperating firms." Taken at face value, the claims seem to imply that MITI used foreign exchange in the textile industry to take Edo's revenge in Nagasaki. Even for the 1950s, the implication was untrue. MITI did not have the power to allocate foreign exchange among cotton-spinning firms in a discretionary fashion. Rather, the law simply prohibited firms from spinning cotton thread unless they registered their spindles with the government.

12. Sekiyu gyo ho [Petroleum Industry Act], Law. No. 128 of 1962.

13. The high government-win rates in court are a separate matter that reflects the nonrandom selection of disputes for litigation. See generally Ramseyer and Rasmusen 2003, chap. 5.

14. *Fujisawa kensetsu, K.K. v. Tokyo*, 1074 Hanrei jiho 80 (Tokyo D. Ct. Nov. 12, 1982).

15. *Sankei kanko, Y.G. v. Kyoto*, 1116 Hanrei jiho 56 (Kyoto D. Ct. Jan. 19, 1984).

16. *Tokyo v. G.G. Nakaya honten*, 1168 Hanrei jiho 45 (S. Ct. July 16, 1985).

17. *Shiroyama kankyo joka, Y.G. v. Tochigi*, 1385 Hanrei jiho 42 (Utsunomiya D. Ct. Feb. 28, 1991).

18. *Arakawa kensetsu kogyo, K.K. v. Yamanashi*, 1457 Hanrei jiho 85 (Kofu D. Ct. Feb. 24, 1992).

19. *Toho jutaku sangyo, K.K. v. Shime*, 1438 Hanrei jiho 118 (Fukuoka D. Ct Feb. 13, 1992).

20. *K.K. Yasu koporeeshon v. Ego*, 1634 Hanrei jiho 84 (Osaka High Ct. May 27, 1997) (golf course); *Odaka v. Funabashi*, 1513 Hanrei jiho 145 (Chiba D. Ct. Nov. 19, 1993) (pachinko parlor).

21. *Daisei kikaku v. Gunma*, 1757 Hanrei jiho 81 (Tokyo High Ct. July 16, 2001).

22. *Y. G. Seron nyusu sha v. Tanashi*, 504 Hanrei taimuzu 128 (Tokyo D. Ct. May 11, 1983).

23. *Takahashi v. Musashino*, 1506 Hanrei jiho 106 (S. Ct. Feb. 18, 1993). The courts did not award refunds in those cases where they found the earlier compliance truly voluntary.

24. *1969 nen Hokkyo Jokai Nihon kogyo tenran kai v. Japan*, 560 Hanrei jiho 6 (Tokyo D. Ct. July 8, 1969). The court denied the plaintiffs damages, however.

25. *1969 nen*, 560 Hanrei jiho at 21–22.

26. *Japan v. Idemitsu kosan*, 985 Hanrei jiho 3 (Tokyo High Ct. Sept. 26, 1980), aff'd in part and rev'd in part, 1108 Hanrei jiho 3 (S. Ct. Feb. 24, 1984) (two of the firms and one of the executives were acquitted on appeal); *Japan v. Sekiyu renmei*, 983 Hanrei jiho 22 (Tokyo High Ct. Sept. 26, 1980) (acquitting the Petroleum Federation).

27. *Japan v. Idemitsu kosan*, 1108 Hanrei jiho 3 (S. Ct. Feb. 24, 1984) (other than the convictions of two of the firms and one of the executives).

28. Because banks could freely avoid the cap by adjusting the size or term of a loan, they seldom demanded deposits to adjust the effective interest charge. Because the larger

firms were so safe, banks never had demanded deposits from most of them. With the small firms, they largely stopped demanding offsetting deposits by the mid-1960s.

29. Komiya 1972, 71, table 2. Thus, claims that liberalization essentially began in the 1980s (e.g., Schaede 2000, 2) are simply wrong. The details of industry-specific practice are crucial—as much as Western scholars routinely miss the point. For example, statements like those by Kaplan (1972, 145) that "until 1965 MITI directly controlled the importation and allocation of . . . [steel] ore . . . through the mechanism of foreign exchange import quotas" are flatly untrue. Instead, by 1965 steel had already been freely importable for several years.

CHAPTER SEVEN

1. We take the profitability figures from the *Hojin kigyo tokei nempo* [Corporate firm statistics annual]. We take the interest rate from Bank of Japan sources and use the rate for loans of one year or less because the longer-term rates are unavailable for years before 1977.

2. To similar effect, e.g., Gao 2001, 184; Gilson 1998, 216–17; Kester 1992, 39; Miyajima 1998.

References

Agrawal, A., and C. R. Knoeber. 2001. "Do Some Outside Directors Play a Political Role?" *Journal of Law and Economics* 44:179.

Ahmadjian, Christina L. 2001. "Changing Japanese Corporate Governance." Unpublished.

Akebono bureeki. 1979. *Hanseiki no ayumi* [A half century of progress]. Tokyo.

Alchian, Armen A., and Harold Demsetz. 1972. "Production, Information Costs, and Economic Organization." *American Economic Review*, 777–95.

Allinson, Gary D. 1997. *Japan's Postwar History*. Ithaca: Cornell University Press.

Anderson, Andy. 2001. *The Compleat Dr. Rowing*. Groton: Bend the Timber Press.

Anderson, Erin. 1988. "Transaction Costs as Determinants of Opportunism in Integrated and Independent Sales Forces." *Journal of Economic Behavior and Organization* 9:247.

Aoki, Masahiko. 1988. *Information, Incentives, and Bargaining in the Japanese Economy*. New York: Cambridge University Press.

———. 1990. "Toward an Economic Model of the Japanese Firm." *Journal of Economic Literature* 28:1.

———. 1994. "Monitoring Characteristics of the Main Bank System: An Analytical and Developmental View." In Aoki and Patrick 1994, 109–41.

———. 2000. *Information, Corporate Governance, and Institutional Diversity: Competitiveness in Japan, the USA, and the Transitional Economies*. Trans. Stacey Jehlik. New York: Oxford University Press.

Aoki, Masahiko, and Serdar Dinc. 2000. "Relational Financing as an Institution and Its Viability under Competition." In Aoki and Saxonhouse 2000, 19–42.

Aoki, Masahiko, and Hugh Patrick, eds. 1994. *The Japanese Main Bank System: Its Relevance for Developing and Transforming Economies*. Oxford: Oxford University Press.

Aoki, Masahiko, Hugh Patrick, and Paul Sheard. 1994. "The Japanese Main Bank System: An Introductory Overview." In Aoki and Patrick 1994, 3.

Aoki, Masahiko, and Gary R. Saxonhouse, eds. 2000. *Finance, Governance, and Competitiveness in Japan*. Oxford: Oxford University Press.

"Apareru sangyo 'shissoku'" [Apparel industry nose dives]. 1978. *Shukan toyo keizai*, May 13, 80.

Asai, Yoshio. 1977. "1920 nendai ni okeru Mitsui ginko to Mitsui zaibatsu" [The Mitsui Bank and the Mitsui zaibatsu in the 1920s]. *Mitsui bunko ronso* 11:251.

Asajima, Shoichi. 1987. "Mitsubishi zaibatsu" [The Mitsubishi zaibatsu]. In *Zaibatsu kin'yu kozo on hikaku kenkyu* [A comparative study of zaibatsu financial structure], ed. Shoichi Asajima, 219–71. Tokyo: Ochanomizu shobo.

———. 1995. "Daikigyo no shikin chotatsu" [Capital raising among large firms]. In *Nihon keiei shi 3: Dai kigyo jidai no torai* [History of Japanese management, 3: The advent of the age of the large firm], ed. Tsunehiko Yui and Eisuke Daito, 219–69. Tokyo: Iwanami shoten.

Asanuma, Banri. 1989. "Manufacturer–Supplier Relationships in Japan and the Concept of Relation-Specific Skill." *Journal of the Japanese and International Economies* 3:1.

———. 1998. "Nihon ni okeru meekaa to sapuraiyaa to no kankei" [The manufacturer–supplier relationship in Japan]. In *Sapuraiyaa shisutemu* [Supplier system], ed. Takahiro Fujimoto, Toshihiro Nishiguchi, and Hideshi Ito, 1. Tokyo: Yuhikaku.

Beason, David. 1998. "*Keiretsu* Affiliation and Share Price Volatility in Japan." *Pacific-Basin Finance Journal* 6:27–43.

Bergloef, Erik, and Enrico Perotti. 1994. "The Governance Structure of the Japanese Financial Keiretsu." *Journal of Financial Economics* 36:259–84.

Bisson, T. A. 1945. *Japan's War Economy.* New York: Institute of Pacific Relations.

———. 1954. *Zaibatsu Dissolution in Japan.* Berkeley: University of California Press.

Business Roundtable. 1999. Statement on corporate governance.

Cable, J. 1985. "Capital Market Information and Industrial Performance: The Role of West German Banks." *Economic Journal* 95:118.

Calder, Kent E. 1989. "Elites in an Equalizing Role: Ex-Bureaucrats as Coordinators and Intermediaries in the Japanese Government–Business Relationship." *Comparative Politics* 21:379.

———. 1993. *Strategic Capitalism: Private Business and Public Purpose in Japanese Industrial Finance.* Princeton: Princeton University Press.

CalPERS. 1998. "Corporate Governance Core Principles and Guidelines: The United States." www.calpers-governance.org.

Casadesus-Masanell, Ramon, and Daniel F. Spulber. 2000. "The Fable of Fisher Body." *Journal of Law and Economics* 43:67.

Caves, Richard E., and Masu Uekusa. 1976a. "Industrial Organization." In Patrick and Rosovsky 1976, 459.

———. 1976b. *Industrial Organization in Japan.* Washington, DC: Brookings Institution.

Clark, Rodney. 1979. *The Japanese Company.* New Haven: Yale University Press.

Crawford, Robert J. 1998. "Reinterpreting the Japanese Economic Miracle." *Harvard Business Review,* Jan.–Feb., 179–84.

Crocker, Keith J., and Kenneth J. Reynolds. 1993. "The Efficiency of Incomplete Contracts: An Analysis of Air Force Engine Procurement." *Rand Journal of Economics* 24:126.

Cutts, Robert L. 1992. "Capitalism in Japan: Cartels and Keiretsu." *Harvard Business Review.*

Daiwa shoken keizai kenkyujo, ed. Various years. *Anarisuto gaido* [Analyst guide]. Tokyo.

Dalton, Dan R., Catherine M. Daily, Alan E. Ellstrand, and Jonathan L. Johnson. 1998. "Meta-Analytic Reviews of Board Composition, Leadership Structure, and Financial Performance." *Strategic Management Journal* 19:269.

Demsetz, Harold, and Kenneth Lehn. 1985. "The Structure of Corporate Ownership." *Journal of Political Economy* 93:1155–77.

Dodwell Marketing Consultants. Various years. *Industrial Groupings in Japan*. Tokyo.

Dore, Ronald P. 1986. *Flexible Rigidities: Industrial Policy and Structural Adjustment in the Japanese Economy, 1970–80*. Stanford: Stanford University Press.

———. 1987. *Taking Japan Seriously: A Confucian Perspective on Leading Economic Issues*. London: Athlone Press.

———. 2000. *Stock Market Capitalism: Welfare Capitalism—Japan and Germany versus the Anglo-Saxons*. Oxford: Oxford University Press.

———. 2002. "Setting Agendas." In *Anglo-Japanese Academy Proceedings*, 19. Publication no. 7. International Center for Comparative Law and Politics, University of Tokyo.

Dower, John W. 1993. "Peace and Democracy in Two Systems: External Policy and Internal Conflict." In *Postwar Japan as History*, ed. Andrew Gordon, 3. Berkeley: University of California Press.

Dyer, Jeffrey H. 1994. "Dedicated Assets: Japan's Manufacturing Edge." *Harvard Business Review*, Nov.–Dec., 174.

Eads, George C., and Kozo Yamamura. 1987. "The Future of Industrial Policy." In *The Political Economy of Japan*: vol. 1, *The Domestic Transformation*, ed. Kozo Yamamura and Yasukichi Yasuba, 423. Stanford: Stanford University Press.

[Edwards, Corwin D.] 1946. *Report of the Mission on Japanese Combines*. Pt. 1. Department of State Publication 2628. Far Eastern Series 14. March.

———. 1956. *Big Business and the Policy of Competition*. Cleveland: Press of Case Western Reserve University.

Flath, David. 1996. "The Keiretsu Puzzle." *Journal of the Japanese and International Economies* 10:101–21.

———. 2000. *The Japanese Economy*. Oxford: Oxford University Press.

Francks, Penelope. 1999. *Japanese Economic Development: Theory and Practice*. 2nd ed. London: Routledge.

Fujino, Shozaburo, Shiro Fujino, and Akira Ono. 1979. *Choki keizai tokei: Sen'i kogyo* [Long-term economic statistics: Textiles]. Tokyo: Toyo keizai shimpo sha.

Gao, Bai. 2001. *Japan's Economic Dilemma: The Institutional Origins of Prosperity and Stagnation*. Cambridge: Cambridge University Press.

Garon, Sheldon. 1997. *Molding Japanese Minds: The State in Everyday Life*. Princeton: Princeton University Press.

Gerlach, Michael L. 1992. *Alliance Capitalism: The Social Organization of Japanese Business*. Berkeley: University of California Press.

Gilson, Ronald J. 1998. "Reflections in a Distant Mirror: Japanese Corporate Governance through American Eyes." *Columbia Business Law Review*: 203.

Gilson, Ronald, and Mark Roe. 1993. "Understanding the Japanese Keiretsu: Overlaps between Corporate Governance and Industrial Organization." *Yale Law Journal* 102:871–920.

Ginko kanri. 1978. *Shukan toyo keizai*. March 18, 80–87.

Ginko kyokai, ed. 1965. *Ginko kyokai 20-nen shi* [A 20-year history of the Banking Association]. Tokyo.

Hadley, Eleanor M. 1970. *Antitrust in Japan*. Princeton: Princeton University Press.

———. 2003. *Memoir of a Trustbuster: A Lifelong Adventure with Japan*. Honolulu: University of Hawaii Press.

Hall, Brian J., and David E. Weinstein. 2000. "Main Banks, Creditor Concentration, and the Resolution of Financial Distress in Japan." In Aoki and Saxonhouse 2000, 64–80.

Hanazaki, Masaharu, and Akiyoshi Horiuchi. 1998. "A Vacuum of Governance in the Japanese Bank Management." University of Tokyo Faculty of Economics Discussion Paper CIRJE-F-29 Dec.

Hashimoto, Juro. 1992. "Zaibatsu no kontsuerunka" [Making conglomerates of the zaibatsu]. In *Nihon keizai no hatten to kigyo shudan* [Corporate groups and the development of the Japanese economy], ed. Juro Hashimoto and Haruhito Takeda. Tokyo: University of Tokyo Press.

Hayashi, Fumio. 2000. "The Main Bank System and Corporate Investment: An Empirical Reassessment," In Aoki and Saxonhouse 2000, 81–97.

Hayashi, Fumio, and Edward C. Prescott. 2001. "The 1990s in Japan: A Lost Decade." Unpublished.

Hellmann, Thomas F., Kevin C. Murdock, and Joseph E. Stiglitz. 2000. "Liberalization, Moral Hazard in Banking, and Prudential Regulation: Are Capital Requirements Enough." *American Economic Review* 90:147–65.

Henderson, Dan F. 1986. "Access to the Japanese Market: Some Aspects of Foreign Exchange Controls and Banking Law." In Saxonhouse and Yamamura 1986, 131–56.

Hermalin, Benjamin E., and Michael S. Weisbach. 1998. "Endogenously Chosen Boards of Directors and Their Monitoring of the CEO." *American Economic Review* 88:96–118.

Herman, E. S. 1981. *Corporate Control, Corporate Power*. Cambridge: Cambridge University Press.

Horiuchi, Akiyoshi, and Katsutoshi Shimizu. 2001. "Did Amakudari Undermine the Effectiveness of Regulator Monitoring in Japan?" *Journal of Banking and Finance* 25:573.

Hoshi, Takeo. 1995. "Evolution of the Main Bank System in Japan." In *The Structure of the Japanese Economy*, ed. Mitsuaki Okabe. Oxford: Oxford University Press.

———. 1998. "Japanese Corporate Governance as a System." In *Comparative Corporate Governance: The State of the Art and Emerging Research*, ed. Klaus J. Hopt et al., 847–75. Oxford: Clarendon Press.

Hoshi, Takeo, and Anil Kashyap. 1999. "The Japanese Banking Crisis: Where Did It Come from and How Will It End?" *NBER Macroeconomics Annual*, 129.

———. 2001. *Corporate Financing and Governance in Japan: The Road to the Future*. Cambridge: MIT Press.

Hoshi, Takeo, Anil Kashyap, and David Scharfstein. 1990a. "Bank Monitoring and Investment: Evidence from the Changing Structure of Japanese Corporate Banking Relationships." In *Asymmetric Information, Corporate Finance, and Investment*, ed. R. Glenn Hubbard. Chicago: University of Chicago Press.

———. 1990b. "The Role of Banks in Reducing the Costs of Financial Distress in Japan." *Journal of Financial Economics* 27:67–88.

———. 1991. "Corporate Structure, Liquidity, and Investment: Evidence from Japanese Industrial Groups." *Quarterly Journal of Economics* 106:33–60.

Hoshi, Takeo, and Hugh Patrick, eds. 2000. *Crisis and Change in the Japanese Financial System*. Boston: Kluwer Academic.

Imuta, Toshimitsu. 1976. *Meiji ki kabushiki kaisha bunseki josetsu* [Introduction to the analysis of Meiji era corporations]. Tokyo: Hosei University Press.

Ito, Takatoshi. 1992. *The Japanese Economy*. Cambridge: MIT Press.

———. 2000. "The Stagnant Japanese Economy in the 1990s: The Need for Financial Supervision to Restore Sustained Growth." In Hoshi and Patrick 2000, 85–107.

Japan Corporate Governance Forum. 1998. *Koporeeto gabanansu gensoku* [Principles of corporate governance]. www.jcgf.org/jp.

———. 2003. Interview. In *Japan Corporate Governance Report*, 2. Michael Solomon Associates. January.

JAPIA. See Nihon jidosha buhin kogyo kai.

Johnson, Chalmers. 1974. "The Reemployment of Retired Government Bureaucrats in Japanese Big Business." *Asian Survey* 14:953.

———. 1982. *MITI and the Japanese Miracle: The Growth of Industrial Policy, 1925–1975*. Stanford: Stanford University Press.

———. 1995. *Japan: Who Governs? The Rise of the Developmental State*. New York: W. W. Norton.

Joskow, Paul L. 1985. "Vertical Integration and Long-Term Contracts: The Case of Coal-Burning Electric Generating Plants." *Journal of Law, Economics and Organization* 1 (1985): 33.

———. 1987. "Contract Duration and Relationship-Specific Investments: Empirical Evidence from Coal Markets." *American Economic Review* 77 (1987): 168.

———. 1988. "Price Adjustment in Long-Term Contracts: The Case of Coal." *Journal of Law and Economics* 31 (1988): 47.

Kaminsky, Graciela L., and Carmen M. Reinhart. 1999. "The Twin Crises: The Causes of Banking and Balance-of-Payments Problems." *American Economic Review* 89:473–92.

Kanto jidosha kogyo, ed. 1986. *Kanto jidosha kogyo 40 nen shi* [A 40-year history of Kanto jidosha kogyo]. Yokosuka.

Kaplan, Eugene J. 1972. *Japan: The Government–Business Relationship*. Washington, DC: U.S. Bureau of International Commerce.

Kaplan, Steven N., and Bernadette A. Minton. 1994. "Appointments of Outsiders to Japanese Boards: Determinants and Implications for Managers." *Journal of Financial Economics* 35:225–58.

Kasuga, Yutaka. 1987. "Mitsui zaibatsu" [The Mitsui zaibatsu]. In *Zaibatsu kin'yu kozo no hikaku kenkyu* [A comparative study of zaibatsu financial structure], ed. Shoichi Asajima. Tokyo: Ochanomizu shobo.

Kayaba kogyo. 1986. *Kayaba kogyo 50 nen shi* [A 50-year history of Kayaba kogyo].

Keizai chosa kai, ed. Various years. *Keiretsu no kenkyu* [Research on the keiretsu]. Tokyo. [Cited as *ROK*.]

Keizai kikaku cho, ed. 1974. *Sekai keizai hakusho* [World economy white paper]. Tokyo: Okura sho.

Kelly, Kevin, and Otis Port. 1992. "Learning from Japan." *Business Week*, January 27.

Kensy, Rainer. 2001. *Keiretsu Economy—New Economy? Japan's Multinational Enterprises from a Postmodern Perspective*. Houndmills: Palgrave.

Kester, W. Carl. 1991. *Japanese Takeovers: The Global Contest for Corporate Control*. Boston: Harvard Business School Press.

———. 1992. "Industrial Groups as Systems of Contractual Governance." *Oxford Review of Economic Policy* 8:24–44.

———. 1993. "Banks in the Board Room: Japan, Germany, and the United States." In *Financial Services: Perspectives and Challenges*, ed. S. L. Hayes III, 65. Boston: Harvard Business School Press.

Khanna, Tarun, and Yishay Yafeh. 2000. "Business Groups and Risk Sharing around the World." Unpublished.

Kigyo keiretsu soran. See Shukan toyo keizai.

Kikkawa, Takeo. 1995. *Nihon denryoku gyo no hatten to Matsunaga Yasuzaemon* [Yasuzaemon Matsunaga and the development of the Japanese electrical power industry]. Nagoya: Nagoya daigaku shuppan kai.

Kin'yu bijinesu. 1996. "96 nen 3 gatsu kessan, ginko sogo rankingu" [Consolidated Bank rankings, March 1996]. *Kin'yu bijinesu,* September, 48.

Klein, Benjamin, Robert G. Crawford, and Armen A. Alchian. 1978. "Vertical Integration, Appropriable Rents, and the Competitive Contracting Process." *Journal of Law and Economics* 21:297.

Koito seisakusho. 1985. *Koito seisakusho 70 nen shi* [A 70-year history of Koito seisakusho].

Komiya, Ryutaro. 1972. "Kogyohin ni kansuru NTB" [NTBs relating to industrial products]. In *Nihon no hikansei shoheki* [Japan's nontariff barriers], ed. Kiyoshi Kojima and Ryutaro Koniya.

Kosei torihiki iinkai, ed. 1979. *Kosei yokin no jittai* [The reality of compulsory deposits]. Tokyo.

———, ed. 1994a. *Kosei torihiki iinkai nenji hokoku* [Fair Trade Commission annual report]. Tokyo.

———, ed. 1994b. *Saishin: Nihon no rokudai kigyo shudan no jittai* [New: The reality of Japan's six large enterprise groups]. Tokyo: Toyo keizai shimpo sha.

Krugman, Paul. 1990. *The Age of Diminished Expectations: U.S. Economic Policy in the 1990s.* Cambridge: MIT Press.

Kuroda, Iwao, and Yoshiharu Oritani. 1979. "Waga kuni no 'kin'yu kozo tokucho' no saikento" [A reexamination of "the peculiarity of financial structure" in our country]. [*Nichigin*] *Kin'yu kenkyu shiryo* 2:1–22.

Kyoiku sha, ed. 1980. *Kaiun gyokai: Joi 10sha no keiei hikaku* [The ocean shipping industry: The comparative management of the top 10 firms]. Tokyo.

Lawrence, Robert Z. 1991. "Efficient or Exclusionist? The Import Behavior of Japanese Corporate Groups." *Brookings Papers on Economic Activity* 1.

———. 1993. "Japan's Different Trade Regime: An Analysis with Particular Reference to Keiretsu." *Journal of Economic Perspectives* 7(3): 3–19.

Lincoln, James R., Michael Gerlach, and Christina Ahmadjian. 1998. "Evolving Patterns of *Keiretsu* Organization and Action in Japan." *Research in Organizational Behavior* 20:203–345.

Lincoln, James R., Michael Gerlach, and P. Takahashi. 1992. "Keiretsu Networks in the Japanese Economy: A Dyad Analysis of Intercorporate Ties." *American Sociological Review* 57:561–85.

Litt, David G., Jonathan R. Macey, Geoffrey P. Miller, and Edward L. Rubin. 1990. "Politics, Bureaucracies, and Financial Markets: Bank Entry into Commercial Paper

Underwriting in the United States and Japan." *University of Pennsylvania Law Review* 139:369.

Lockwood, William W. 1954. *The Economic Development of Japan: Growth and Structural Change, 1868–1938*. Princeton: Princeton University Press.

———. 1965. "Japan's 'New Capitalism.'" In *The State and Economic Enterprise in Japan*, ed. W. W. Lockwood, 447. Princeton: Princeton University Press.

Macey, Jonathan R., and Geoffrey P. Miller. 1995. "Corporate Governance and Commercial Banking: A Comparative Examination of Germany, Japan, and the United States." *Stanford Law Review* 48:73–112.

Magaziner, Ira C., and Thomas M. Hout. 1981. *Japanese Industrial Policy*. Berkeley: Institute of International Studies, University of California.

Magaziner, Ira C., and Robert B. Reich. 1982. *Minding America's Business: The Decline and Rise of the American Economy*. New York: Harcourt Brace Jovanovich.

Markoff, John, and Jennifer L. Schenker. 2003. "Europe Exceeds U.S. in Refining Grid Computing." *New York Times*, November 10.

Masten, Scott E. 1984. "The Organization of Production: Evidence from the Aerospace Industry." *Journal of Law and Economics* 27:403.

Masten, Scott E., James W. Meehan, Jr., and Edward A. Snyder. 1991. "The Costs of Organization." *Journal of Law, Economics, and Organization* 7:1.

Matsuo, Shoichi. 1973. "Buhin seisaku wa ikkan shita 'kyozon kyoei'" [Consistency turns parts policy into one of "co-existence and co-prosperity"]. In *Nihon jidosha* 1998: 138–39.

McLaughlin, Kenneth J. 2002. Review. *Journal of Economic Literature* 40:943–44.

Milgrom, Paul, and John Roberts. 1994. "Complementarities and Systems: Understanding Japanese Economic Organization." *Estudios Economicos* 9:3–42.

Milhaupt, Curtis J. 2001. "Creative Norm Destruction: The Evolution of Nonlegal Rules in Japanese Corporate Governance." *University of Pennsylvania Law Review* 149: 2083–2129.

Milhaupt, Curtis J., and Geoffrey P. Miller. 1997. "Cooperation, Conflict and Convergence in Japanese Finance: Evidence from the 'Jusen' Problem." *Law and Policy in International Business* 29:1.

Milhaupt, Curtis J., and Mark D. West. 2002. "Law's Dominion and the Market for Legal Elites in Japan." University of Michigan, Olin Center for Law and Economic Studies, no. 02-006, and Columbia Law School Center for Law and Economic Studies, no. 206. June 14.

Minami, Ryoshin. 1965. *Choki keizai tokei: Tetsudo to denryku* [Long-term economic statistics: Railroads and electric utilities]. Tokyo: Toyo keizai shinpo sha.

Minda, Gary. 1999. *Boycott in America: How Imagination and Ideology Shape the Legal Mind*. Carbondale: Southern Illinois University Press.

Mitsubishi keizai kenkyu jo, ed. Various years. *Honpo jigyo seisaku bunseki* [Analysis of Japanese firm performance]. Tokyo.

Mitsui ginko, ed. 1957. *Mitsui ginko 80 nen shi* [An 80-year history of the Mitsui Bank]. Tokyo.

Miwa, Yoshiro. 1996. *Firms and Industrial Organization in Japan*. Houndmills: Macmillan.

———. 1998. "Torishimari yaku kai to torishimari yaku" [Boards of directors and directors]. In *Kaisha ho no keizaigaku* [The economics of corporate law], ed. Yoshiro Miwa, Hideki Kanda, and Noriyuki Yanagawa, 89–115. Tokyo: University of Tokyo Press.

———. 1999. "Corporate Social Responsibility: Dangerous and Harmful, though Maybe Not Irrelevant." *Cornell Law Review* 84:1227.

Miwa, Yoshiro, and J. Mark Ramseyer. 2000. "Corporate Governance in Transitional Economies: Lessons from the Prewar Japanese Cotton Textile Industry." *Journal of Legal Studies* 29:171–203.

———. 2001a. *Nihon keizai ron no gokai: "Keiretsu" no jubaku kara no kaiho* [Misunderstandings in the theory of the Japanese economy: Liberation from the spell of the "keiretsu"]. Tokyo: Toyo keizai shimpo sha.

———. 2001b. "Nihon no keizai seisaku to seisaku kenkyu" [Japanese economic policy and policy research]. *Keizai kenkyu* 52:193–204.

———. 2002a. "Banks and Economic Growth: Implications from Japanese History." *Journal of Law and Economics* 45:127–64.

———. 2002b. "The Fable of the Keiretsu." *Journal of Economics and Management Strategy* 11:169–224.

———. 2002c. "The Myth of the Main Bank: Japan and Comparative Corporate Governance." *Law and Social Inquiry* 27:401–24.

———. 2002d. "The Value of Prominent Directors: Corporate Governance and Bank Access in Transitional Japan." *Journal of Legal Studies* 31:273–301.

———. 2003a. "Capitalist Politicians, Socialist Bureaucrats? Legends of Government Planning from Japan." *Antitrust Bulletin* 48:595–627.

———. 2003b. "Does Ownership Matter? Evidence from the Zaibatsu Dissolution Program." *Journal of Economics and Management Strategy* 12:67–89.

———. 2003c. "Does Relationship Banking Matter? Japanese Bank–Borrower Ties in Good Times and Bad." Harvard Law School John M. Olin Program in Law, Economics and Business, Discussion Paper No. 433.

———. 2003d. "Financial Malaise and the Myth of the Misgoverned Bank." In *Global Markets, Domestic Institutions: Corporate Law and Governance in a New Era of Cross-Border Deals*, ed. Curtis J. Milhaupt, 339–72. New York: Columbia University Press.

———. 2004a. "Conflicts of Interest in Japanese Insolvencies: The Problem of Bank Rescues." *Theoretical Inquiries in Law* 6:301.

———. 2004b. "Directed Credit? The Loan Market in High-Growth Japan." *Journal of Economics and Management Strategy* 13:171–205.

———. 2005a. "Does Relationship Banking Matter? The Myth of the Japanese Main Bank." *Journal of Empirical Legal Studies* 2:261.

———. 2005b. "The Good Occupation." Working Paper No. 514. Harvard Law School John M. Olin Center for Law, Economics and Business.

———. 2005c. "Who Appoints Them, What Do They Do? Evidence on Outside Directors from Japan." *Journal of Economics and Management Strategy* 14:299–337.

Miyajima, Hideaki. 1998. "The Impact of Deregulation on Corporate Governance and Finance." In *Is Japan Really Changing its Ways? Regulatory Reform and the Japanese Economy*, ed. Lonny E. Carlile and Mark C. Tilton, 33. Washington, DC: Brookings Institution.

Miyashita, Kenichi, and David W. Russell. 1994. *Keiretsu: Inside the Hidden Japanese Conglomerates.* New York: McGraw-Hill.

Miyoshi, Fuyumi. 1999. *Jidosha gyokai hayawakari mappu* [Easy-to-read map of the automobile industry].

Mochikabu gaisha seiri iinkai. 1951. *Nihon zaibatsu to sono kaitai* [The Japanese zaibatsu and their dissolution]. Tokyo.

Monks, R. A. G., and N. Minow. 1995. *Corporate Governance.* Oxford: Blackwell.

Morck, Randall, and Masao Nakamura. 1999a. "Banks and Corporate Control in Japan." *Journal of Finance* 54:319–39.

———. 1999b. "Japanese Corporate Governance and Macroeconomic Problems." Harvard Institute of Economic Research Discussion Paper 1893. February.

———. 2003. "Been There, Done That: The History of Corporate Ownership in Japan." European Corporate Governance Institute Finance Working Paper 20/2003.

Morck, Randall, Masao Nakamura, and Anil Shivdasani. 2000. "Banks, Ownership Structure, and Firm Value in Japan." *Journal of Business* 73:539–67.

Myers, Stewart C. 2001. "Capital Structure." *Journal of Economic Perspectives* 15(2): 81–102.

Nakamura, Takafusa. 1983. *Economic Growth in Prewar Japan.* Trans. Robert A. Feldman. New Haven: Yale University Press.

Nakatani, Iwao. 1984. "The Economic Role of Financial Corporate Grouping." In *The Economic Analysis of the Japanese Firm,* ed. Masahiko Aoki, 227–58. Elsevier Science.

Nihon denso, ed. 1974. *Nihon denso 25 nen shi* [A 25-year history of Nihon denso]. Kariya.

Nihon fudosan kenkyu jo, ed. 1998. *Shigai chikakaku shisu* [Price indexes for metropolitan real estate]. Tokyo.

Nihon ginko, ed. 1960. *Honpo keizai tokei (Showa 35 nenban)* [Economic statistics of Japan (1960)]. Tokyo: Okura sho insatsu kyoku.

———, ed. 1971. *Nihon kin'yu shi shiryo, Showa hen* [Materials on Japanese financial history, Showa period]. Tokyo: Okura sho insatsu kyoku.

———, ed. 1977. *Waga kuni no kin'yu seido, dai 8 ban* [The financial system in our country, 8th ed.]. Tokyo.

———, ed. 1995. *Shimpan: Waga kuni no kin'yu seido* [New edition: Our country's financial system]. Tokyo.

———, ed. Various years. *Keizai tokei nempo* [Economic statistics annual]. Tokyo.

Nihon jidosha buhin kogyo kai and Oto toreedo jaaneru, eds. 1998. *Nihon no jidosha buhin kogyo (1998 nen ban)* [Japanese automotive parts industry, 1998]. Tokyo: Oto toreedo jaaneru. [Cited as *JAPIA.*]

Nihon keizai shimbun sha, ed. Various years. *Kaisha soran* [Annual corporation reports]. Tokyo.

———, ed. Various years. *Nikkei kaisha joho* [Nikkei company information]. Tokyo.

Nihon rodo kenkyu kiko, ed. 1992. *Sangyo bungyo kozo to rodo shijo no kaiso sei* [The structure of the division of labor in production, and the class structure of the labor market]. Tokyo.

Nihon sekiyu seisei, ed. 1982. *Nihon sekiyu seisei 30 nen shi* [A 30-year history of Nisseki]. Tokyo.

Nihon senshu kyokai, ed. Various years. *Kaiun tokei yoran* [Survey of ocean shipping statistics]. Tokyo.

Nihon shoken keizai kenkyu jo, ed. Various years. *Kabushiki toshi shueki ritsu* [Rates of return on common stock]. Tokyo: Nihon shoken keizai kenkyu jo.

Nihon tankaa kyokai, ed. 1980. *Nihon tankaa 50-nen no ayumi* [The 50-year history of the Japan Tanker Association]. Tokyo.

Nihon tokei kyoku, ed. 1988. *Nihon choki tokei soran* [Historical statistics of Japan]. Tokyo.

Nihon zosen kogyo kai, ed. 1980. *Nihon zosen kogyo kai 30 nen shi* [A 30-year history of the Japan Shipbuilding Industry Association]. Tokyo.

Nikkei QUICK joho, K.K. As updated. NEEDS. Tokyo: Nikkei QUICK joho.

———. As updated. QUICK, Tokyo, Nikkei QUICK joho.

Nisshin boseki. 1969. *Nisshin boseki rokuju nen shi* [A 60-year history of Nisshin boseki].

NYSE Corporate Accountability and Listing Standards Committee. 2002. Report. June 6.

Okaniwa, Hiroshi. 1981. *Shintei: Kaiun no gaiyo* [Revised edition: An outline of ocean shipping]. Tokyo: Seisan do.

Okimoto, Daniel I. 1989. *Between MITI and the Market: Japanese Industrial Policy for High Technology.* Stanford: Stanford University Press.

Okura sho, ed. Various years. *Ginko kyoku nempo* [Annual report of the Banking Bureau]. Tokyo.

———, ed. Various years. *Hojin kigyo tokei nempo* [Corporate firm statistics annual]. Tokyo.

Osaka kabushiki torihiki jo, ed. 1928. *Daikabu 50 nen shi* [A 50-year history of the Osaka Stock Exchange]. Osaka.

Osakaya shoten, ed. Various years. *Kabushiki nenkan* [Stock annual]. Osaka.

Pascale, Richard, and Thomas P. Rohlen. 1983. "The Mazda Turnaround." *Journal of Japanese Studies* 9:219–63.

Patrick, Hugh T. 1972. "Finance, Capital Markets and Economic Growth in Japan." In *Financial Development and Economic Growth: The Economic Consequences of Underdeveloped Capital Markets*, ed. Arnold W. Sametz, 109–39. New York: New York University Press.

———. 1994. "The Relevance of Japanese Finance and Its Main Bank System." In Aoki and Patrick 1994, 353–408.

Patrick, Hugh T., and Henry Rosovsky, eds. 1976. *Asia's New Giant: How the Japanese Economy Works.* Washington, DC: Brookings Institution.

Pekkanen, Saadia. 2003. *Picking Winners? From Technology Catch-up to the Space Race in Japan.* Stanford: Stanford University Press.

Prestowitz, Clyde. 1988. *Trading Places: How We Allowed Japan to Take the Lead.* New York: Basic Books.

Rajan, Raghuram G. 1996. Review of *The Japanese Main Bank System*, by Masahiko Aoki and Hugh Patrick. *Journal of Economic Literature* 34:1363–65.

Rajan, Raghuram G., and Luigi Zingales. 1995. "What Do We Know about Capital Structure? Some Evidence from International Data." *Journal of Finance* 50:1421–60.

———. 1999. "Which Capitalism? Lessons from the East Asian Crisis." *Journal of Applied Corporate Finance* 11(4):40–48.

Ramseyer, J. Mark, and Eric B. Rasmusen. 2003. *Measuring Judicial Independence: The Political Economy of Judging in Japan*. Chicago: University of Chicago Press.

Ramseyer, J. Mark, and Frances M. Rosenbluth. 1995. *The Politics of Oligarchy: Institutional Choice in Imperial Japan*. New York: Cambridge University Press.

Reischauer, Edwin O. 1978. *The Japanese*. Cambridge: Harvard University Press.

Richter, Frank-Juergen. 2000. *Strategic Networks: The Art of Japanese Interfirm Cooperation*. New York: International Business Press.

Rodo sho, ed. 1998. *Chingin sensasu, Heisei 9 nen chingin kozo kihon tokei chosa* [Basic survey on wage structure, 1997]. Tokyo.

ROK. See Keizai chosa kai.

Romano, Roberta. 1991. "The Shareholder Suit: Litigation without Foundation?" *Journal of Law, Economics, and Organization* 7:55.

———. 1996. "Corporate Law and Corporate Governance." *Industrial and Corporate Change* 5:277.

Rosovsky, Henry. 1972. "What Are the Lessons of Japanese Economic History?" In *Economic Development in the Long-Run*, ed. A. J. Youngson, 229. London: Allen and Unwin.

Samuelson, Paul A. 2000. "Japan's Future Financial Structure." *Japan and the World Economy* 12:185–87.

Sangyo keikaku kaigi, ed. 1965. *Kokusai sekiyu josei to Nihon no sekiyu seisaku* [The international petroleum state of affairs and Japanese petroleum policy]. Tokyo: Heibon sha.

Sanko kisen, K. K., ed. 1968. *Shagyo kaiko roku* [Records of the company business]. Tokyo.

Sawai, Minoru. 1992. "Senji keizai to zaibatsu" [The zaibatsu and the wartime economy]. In *Nihon keizai no hatten to kigyo shudan* [Corporate groups and the development of the Japanese economy], ed. Juro Hashimoto and Haruhito Takeda. Tokyo: University of Tokyo Press.

Saxonhouse, Gary R. 1991. "Comments and Discussion." *Brookings Papers on Economic Activity* 1:331–36.

———. 1993. "What Does Japanese Trade Structure Tell Us about Japanese Trade Policy." *Journal of Economic Perspectives* 7:399.

Saxonhouse, Gary R., and Kozo Yamamura, eds. 1986. *Law and Trade Issues of the Japanese Economy: American and Japanese Perspectives*. Seattle: University of Washington Press.

Schaede, Ulrike. 1994. "Understanding Corporate Governance in Japan: Do Classical Concepts Apply?" *Industrial and Corporate Change* 3:285.

———. 1995. "The 'Old Boy' Network and Government–Business Relationship in Japan." *Journal of Japanese Studies* 21:293.

———. 2000. "The Japanese Financial System: From Postwar to the New Millennium." Harvard Business School Case 9-700-049.

Sheard, Paul. 1989. "The Main Bank System and Corporate Monitoring and Control in Japan." *Journal of Economic Behavior and Organization* 11:399–422.

———. 1994a. "Main Banks and the Governance of Financial Distress." In Aoki and Patrick 1994, 188–230.

———. 1994b. "Reciprocal Delegated Monitoring in the Japanese Main Bank System." *Journal of the Japanese and International Economies* 8:1–21.

———. 1996. "Banks, Blockholders and Corporate Governance: The Role of External Appointees to the Board." In *Japanese Firms, Finance and Markets*, ed. Paul Sheard, 181. Melbourne: Addison-Wesley.

Shimura, Kaichi. 1969. *Nihon shihon shijo bunseki* [An analysis of Japanese capital markets]. Tokyo: University of Tokyo Press.

Shukan toyo keizai, ed. Various years. *Kigyo keiretsu soran* [Overview of firm keiretsus]. Tokyo: Toyo keizai shimpo sha. [Cited as *Kigyo keiretsu soran.*]

Spulber, Daniel F. 2002. *Famous Fables of Economics: Myths of Market Failure*. Malden: Blackwell.

Stiglitz, Joseph E. 2001. "From Miracle to Crisis to Recovery: Lessons from Four Decades of East Asian Experience." In Stiglitz and Yusuf 2001, 509–26.

Stiglitz, Joseph E., and Shahid Yusuf, eds. 2001. *Rethinking the East Asia Miracle*. New York: Oxford University Press.

Sumitomo ginko, ed. 1979. *Sumitomo ginko 80 nen shi* [An 80-year history of the Sumitomo Bank]. Osaka.

Takahashi, Kamekichi. 1930. *Nippon zaibatsu no kaibo* [An anatomy of Japanese zaibatsu]. Tokyo: Chuo koron sha.

Takeda, Haruhito. 1992. *Teikoku shugi to minpon shugi* [Imperialism and democracy]. Tokyo: Shuei sha.

———. 1995. *Zaibatsu no jidai* [The age of zaibatsu]. Tokyo: Shin'yo sha.

Takeda, Mansaku. 1978. "Ginko keiei no 'genten' in kaeru toki" [Returning to the fundamentals of bank management]. *Shukan toyo keizai*, March 11, 40–43.

Tetsudo kyoku, ed. 1900. *Meiji 32 nendo Tetsudo kyoku nempo* [1899 Railway Bureau annual report]. Tokyo.

TIAA-CREF. 2000. Policy Statement on Corporate Governance. www.tiaa-cref.org/libra/ governance.

Tokyo kabushiki torihiki jo, ed. 1928. *Tokyo kabushiki torihiki jo 50 nen shi* [A 50-year history of the Tokyo Stock Exchange]. Tokyo.

Tokyo shoken torihiki jo, ed. Various years. *Shoken tokei nempo* [Securities statistics annual]. Tokyo.

———, ed. Various years. *Tosho tokei nempo* [TSE statistical annual]. Tokyo.

Tonen tankaa, ed. 1979. *Tonen tankaa 20-yen shi* [A 20-year history of Tonen Tanker]. Tokyo.

Toyo keizai shimpo sha, ed. Various years. *Keizai hendo shuhyo soran* [Overview of principal economic indicators]. Tokyo.

———, ed. Various years. *Kigyo keiretsu soran* [Firm keiretsu overview]. Tokyo.

———, ed. Various years. *Shikiho: Mijojo gaisha ban* [Seasonal reports: Unlisted companies]. Tokyo.

Treece, James B., and Karen Lowry Miller. 1992. "If the Japanese Were Running GM." *Business Week*, January 27.

Trezise, Philip H., and Yukio Suzuki. 1976. "Social and Cultural Factors in Japanese Economic Growth." In Patrick and Rosovsky 1976, 753.

Tsusho sangyo sho, ed. 1966a. *Nihon boseki geppo* [Japanese spinning monthly]. May.

———, ed. 1966b. *Tsusansho nempo* [MITI annual]. Tokyo: Okura sho insatsu kyoku.

————, ed. 1967. *Tsusansho nempo* [MITI annual]. Tokyo: Okura sho insatsu kyoku.

————, ed. 1975. *Sekai no kigyo no keiei bunseki* [Management analysis of international firms]. Tokyo: Okurasho insatsu kyoku.

————, ed. 1990. *Tsusho sangyo seisaku shi, dai 6 kan* [A history of trade and industry policy, vol. 6]. Tokyo: Tsusho sangyo chosa kai.

Tyson, Laura D'Andrea, and John Zysman. 1989. "Preface: The Argument Outlined." In *Politics and Productivity: The Real Story of Why Japan Works*, ed. Chalmers Johnson, Laura D'Andrea Tyson, and John Zysman, xiii. New York: Ballinger.

Udagawa, Masaru. 1979. "Nissan kontsuerun no tenkai" [The evolution of the Nissan combine]." In *Kindai Nihon keiei shi* [Early modern Japanese management history], rev. ed., ed. Keiichiro Nakagawa, Hidemasa Morikawa, and Tsunehiko Yui, 204. Tokyo: Yuhikaku.

Uekusa, Masu. 1974a. "Fusai rishi ritsu kettei no shoyoin" [Factors in the determination of interest rates on debt]. *Keizai hyoron*, August, 66–78.

————. 1974b. "Kigyo rijun ritsu no kettei yoin" [Factors in the determination of firm profitability]. *Mita gakkai zasshi* 67(10): 984–1001.

————. 1982. *Sangyo soshiki ron* [The theory of industrial structure]. Tokyo: Chikuma shobo.

Un'yu sho, ed. 1980. *Nihon kaiun no genkyo* [The current status of Japanese ocean shipping]. Tokyo: Nihon kaiji koho kyokai.

————, ed. 1986. *Gaiko kaiun no genkyo* [The current status of overseas ocean shipping]. Tokyo: Nihon kaiji koho kyokai.

Upham, Frank K. 1987. *Law and Social Change in Postwar Japan*. Cambridge: Harvard University Press.

U.S. Bureau of the Census. Various years. *Statistical Abstract of the United States*. Washington, DC: Bureau of the Census.

van Rixtel, Adrian A. R. J. M., and Wolter H. J. Hassink. 2002. "Monitoring the Monitors: Are Old Boys Networks Being Used to Monitor Japanese Private Banks?" *Journal of Japanese and International Economies* 16:1–30.

van Wolferen, Karel. 1989. *The Enigma of Japanese Power*. New York: Vantage.

Vogel, Ezra. 1979. *Japan as Number One: Lessons for America*. Cambridge: Harvard University Press.

Wallich, Henry C., and Mable I. Wallich. 1976. *Banking and Finance*. In Patrick and Rosovsky 1976, 249–315.

Weinstein, David E., and Yishay Yafeh. 1995. "Japan's Corporate Groups: Collusive or Competitive? An Empirical Investigation of *Keiretsu* Behavior." *Journal of Industrial Economics* 43:359–76.

————. 1998. "On the Costs of a Bank-Centered Financial System: Evidence from the Changing Main Bank Relations in Japan." *Journal of Finance* 53:635–72.

West, Mark D. 1994. "The Pricing of Shareholder Derivative Actions in Japan and the United States." *Northwestern University Law Review* 88:1436.

————. 1999. "Information, Institutions, and Extortion in Japan and the United States: Making Sense of *Sokaiya* Racketeers." *Northwestern University Law Review* 93: 767.

————. 2001. "Why Shareholders Sue: The Evidence from Japan." *Journal of Legal Studies* 30:351–82.

Williamson, Oliver E. 1979. "Transaction-Cost Economics: The Governance of Contractual Relations." *Journal of Law and Economics* 22:233.

Williamson, Stephen D. 1986. "Costly Monitoring, Financial Intermediation, and Equilibrium Credit Rationing." *Journal of Monetary Economics* 18:159–79.

Womack, James P., Daniel T. Jones, and Daniel Roos. 1990. *The Machine That Changed the World*. New York: Rawson Associates.

Woodall, Brian. 1996. *Japan under Construction: Corruption, Politics, and Public Works.* Berkeley: University of California Press.

World Bank. 2000. *World Development Indicators*. Washington, DC.

Yafeh, Yishay. 2000. "Corporate Governance in Japan: Past Performance and Future Prospects." *Oxford Review of Economic Policy* 16(2): 74–84.

Yamaguchi, Kazuo. 1968. "Meiji 31 nen zengo boseki gaisha no kabunushi ni tsuite" [Regarding spinning firm shareholders at around 1898]. [*Meiji daigaku*] *Keiei ronshu* 15(2): 1.

Yamamura, Kozo. 1972. "Japan 1868–1930: A Revised View." In *Banking and Economic Development: Some Lessons of History*, ed. Rondo Cameron, 168–98. New York: Oxford University Press.

Yasuoka, Shigeaki. 1998. *Zaibatsu keiseishi no kenkyu* [A study in the formation of the zaibatsu]. Tokyo: Mineruba shobo.

Zenkoku chiho ginko kyokai, ed. Various years. *Kin'yu ginko shotokei* [Statistics for finance and banking]. Tokyo.

Index